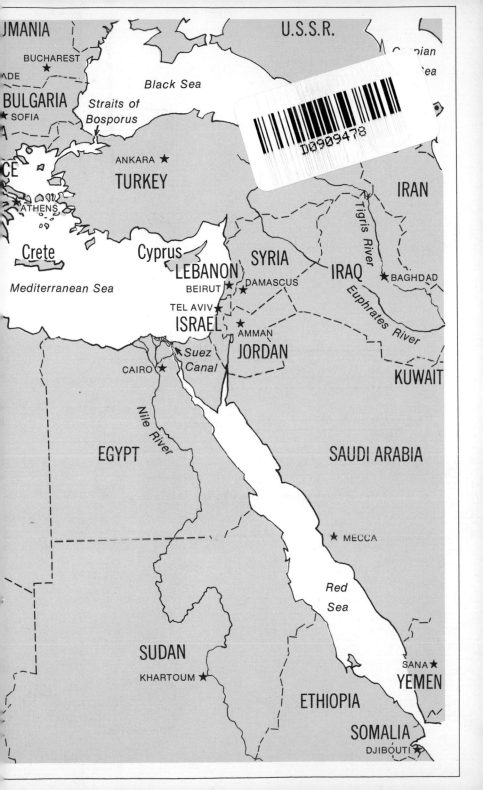

COUNTDOWN IN THE HOLY LAND

Lester Velie **COUNTDOWN**

IN THE HOLY LAND

FUNK & WAGNALLS, NEW YORK

*To Frances, who helps brighten and tighten
the words—and lighten the drudgery*

PREFACE

I first visited Israel in April, 1967, and like others before me, was caught up with the Israelis and their land. When war came two months later, I returned to piece together a story within a story: the Soviet's use of proxies to carve a Communist empire in the Arab world; and the collision with that effort by a brave and resourceful people who harness an ancient tradition and inspiration to the job of surviving. To tell this double story was the task I set myself in this book.

Along the way I discovered that during two fateful days of the Six-Day War, the U.S. and the U.S.S.R. had squared off in a Hot Line confrontation that brought nuclear war perilously near. Eighteen months later the Soviets had escalated their drive in the Middle East. An atomic clock was ticking in the Holy Land. It was ticking not only for Arabs and Jews, but for all of us.

LESTER VELIE
February, 1969

CONTENTS

PRELUDE

Late in August, 1968, Gamal Abdel Nasser settled back contentedly in the Soviet jet airliner that was flying him home from a three weeks' stay in the Soviet Union. Nasser was in a state of euphoria. For the first time since the Israelis had humiliated him and smashed his Soviet-supported dream of a Nasserite empire from the Atlantic to the Persian Gulf, Nasser could now look forward to the restoration of all his hopes.

Nasser had come to the Soviet Union on July 28, so it was announced, for medical treatment of the diabetes that had plagued him for years. But the Soviets had treated Nasser with something stronger than medicine. Nasser was going home with a secret deal, both military and diplomatic.

Communist Party Boss Leonid Brezhnev and Premier Alexei Kosygin had agreed to send new, lavish shipments of tanks and planes during 1969 and so prepare Nasser for the fulfillment of two aims: eliminate Israel as a military power in the Middle East and resume his pre-June, 1967, efforts to topple pro-Western Arab regimes—those in Jordan, Lybia, Saudi Arabia, and Lebanon. For his part of the deal, Nasser agreed to follow the Kremlin's lead in a diplomatic offensive, which, it was hoped, would gull the United States into a Middle East Munich in which Israel would be forced back behind the fragile borders of May, 1947, without Arab recognition or contractual arrangements that established permanent borders.

Here, as several Intelligence services pieced it together, was the military part of the Kremlin-Nasser deal:

As of late 1968, the Soviets had helped Nasser equip, train, and deploy seven divisions of infantry and armor along the Suez Canal. In addition, the Soviets were training two Egyptian

xi

infantry divisions for crossing water obstacles. The Egyptians, then, had nine divisions already deployed or in training. Now, it was planned to create a new Egyptian army corps of three armored and mechanized divisions—to serve as a "mailed fist" to smash the Israelis. For this "mailed fist," the Russians promised to deliver, during 1969, five hundred T-54 and T-55 tanks, their newest and heaviest. They also promised Nasser one to two hundred additional Mig-21s.

What this meant to the balance of Arab-Israeli power could be seen by comparing the present situation with that of June, 1967.

Then, Nasser could put only seven divisions into the Sinai. For the next round, he could muster twelve! In June, 1967, Nasser could deploy a thousand tanks—many of them medium-sized Soviet 34s. Now, he could look forward to putting thirteen hundred in the field—virtually all of them T-54s and T-55s, which mount a 100 mm. cannon, and bear infrared equipment that permits driving and firing by night. In the last war the Egyptians had some three hundred and fifty strike aircraft. Now, with new Soviet deliveries, they would have at least five hundred, including the supersonic Mig-21s, which fly at twice the speed of sound, and Sukhoi-7s.

In the June, 1967, war the Arabs had enjoyed a three-to-one superiority over the Israelis in armor and in planes. Now, unless the Israelis kept pace, the Arab superiority would rise to four to one in armor and a frightening six to one in planes.

As the UN Ambassadors of the United States, the Soviet Union, France, and England began to discuss an Arab-Israeli peace settlement in February, 1969, the stage was already being set for the next war. It could be avoided only by a peace settlement that called for recognition and conciliation between the Arabs and Israelis. War could be avoided, too, by giving Israel the borders and the arms that would convince the Arabs that Israel could defend herself.

If the United States settled for anything short of these two requirements for peace—the way would be open for the truncation or destruction of Israel, and for the Sovietization of the Middle East.

COUNTDOWN IN THE HOLY LAND

1

THE WEEK
THE HOT LINE
BURNED

For President Lyndon B. Johnson, June 6, 1967, the second day of the Arab-Israeli Six-Day War, was "the most awesomely difficult day of my life." This was the day the Russians first used the Hot Line from Moscow in anger.

While the world was engrossed with the drama of Israel's lightning victory over its Arab enemies, a more momentous struggle unfolded in secret between the two world superpowers.

Over the Hot Line on Tuesday and again on Saturday, President Johnson and Premier Alexei Kosygin waged a war of nerves and of wills. In it, as one Presidential advisor later related, "the confrontation we had tried to avoid threatened to get out of hand. And we moved very close to the precipice." So close, that on the final day of the Six-Day War, as Israel was crushing the Syrian Army and Kosygin heated-up the Hot Line with threats of intervention, President Johnson ordered the Sixth Fleet to move east in the Mediterranean toward the theatre of war for possible action against the Russians.

President Johnson's "most difficult day," Tuesday, June 6th, began at 5:50 a.m. The white telephone at his bedside jangled him awake. It was Walt Rostow, the President's special assistant for national security. On the previous day, Monday, Rostow had awakened President Johnson at 4:30 a.m. to inform him that Israel and Egypt were at war. Now, the news was just as grave. Over the Hot Line from Moscow, the Kremlin had signalled that Premier Alexei Kosygin was sending a message to the President of the United States. It would arrive within fifteen or twenty minutes. The President dressed hurriedly and gulped some coffee. His press secretary, George Christian—big, always unruffled, and always at the President's side in times of crisis—had already arrived. Together, the two men descended to the White House basement in the President's small elevator and began the 100-yard walk to the Situation Room. This is a suite of rooms embracing a conference area the size of an ordinary living-room, with an adjoining small communications center crowded with teleprinters and with "security telephones" that link the White House with the intelligence community and with the Pentagon.

The Situation Room is a by-product of the Cold War with the Soviet Union. Here, every morning, Walt Rostow, Henry F. Kissinger's predecessor, met with his staff to sort out and appraise reports from Vietnam, the Middle East, and other troubled areas—for presentation to the President. In the wake of President John F. Kennedy's Cuban missile confrontation with Nikita Khrushchev, the Situation Room had also become a crisis room.

After that brush with nuclear disaster, President Kennedy and Khrushchev agreed that ordinary channels of communications were too cumbersome to deal with crises in an age of intercontinental nuclear missiles. A direct wire—the Hot Line—with teleprinters in the Kremlin and in the National Military Command Center in the Pentagon was set up as a result. The Russians transmitted in Russian, the Americans in English. A translator stood by at all times at the Pentagon Hot Line teleprinter, ready to relay a Kremlin message by "secure telephone" to the communications center in the White House Situation Room. To be near that telephone, President Johnson and his advisors met, during times of crisis, in the Situation Room.

For three years and nine months the Hot Line had remained

blessedly quiescent. There had been no impending collision requiring its use. The only messages the Hot Line carried were exchanges of greetings on New Year's Day and on the anniversary of the line's installation, August 30, 1963. Sometimes, to check the condition of the Hot Line, the Russians transmitted long spates of poetry. American teletype operators used the more prosaic testing message: "The quick brown fox jumped over the lazy dog's back 1234567890."

Then, on Monday morning, June 5, the first day of the Six-Day War, the President got the electrifying news that the Hot Line was being activated from Moscow for the first time. The President had hurried to the Situation Room, just as he was striding there now, with great trepidation.

But the Monday message, to everyone's relief, was a reassuring one. The Soviet Union would keep hands off the Middle East War, if the United States did. In a cautiously worded message, Johnson agreed. The Hot Line had played its appointed role of keeping the two nuclear giants at peace.

Now, on Tuesday morning, as President Johnson entered the Situation Room to hear the new Hot Line message, the place was crowded with men whose appearance, together, at 8:15 a.m., could only spell "hot crisis."

Vice President Hubert H. Humphrey, usually ebullient, but now long-faced, was there. So was Secretary of State Dean Rusk and Defense Secretary Robert S. McNamara. The President had also called in additional intellectual muscle, men who had been tested in other crises with other presidents and whose cool heads and experience were good to have around in a confrontation with the Russians. Dean Acheson, Harry Truman's Secretary of State, and Clark Clifford, Truman's legal advisor, and later, Johnson's Secretary of Defense, had been intercepted on their way to their law offices. McGeorge Bundy, who had coordinated security information for John F. Kennedy as well as for Johnson, had flown down from New York. Llewellyn Thompson, Ambassador to the Soviet Union, had been called in for insights into Russian behavior.

Six of the men in the room, including the President, had participated in John F. Kennedy's "eyeball-to-eyeball" encounter with Khrushchev. Walt Rostow, heavy-lidded from two sleepless nights, handed the President a rough translation of the Hot Line message from Alexei Kosygin.

The message was ominous.

Kosygin had dropped the "let's-both-keep-hands-off" line of the previous message. Now, he wanted the U.S. to get into the act, to use its influence with the Israelis to halt their advance in the Sinai and to withdraw to their borders. With this demand came a thinly veiled threat—the suggestion that the Russians might have to intervene. In effect, Kosygin was saying: Get them out of there, or *we* will!

The President and his advisors were dealing with shocked and angry men. As the President later said, the Russians had made a vast miscalculation. They had overestimated their protégé, Gamal Abdel Nasser, and they had underestimated the Israelis. The Russians believed Nasser would triumph. So, for three weeks, while Nasser moved eighty thousand troops and nine hundred tanks to Israel's southern borders and boasted publicly "our basic aim is the destruction of Israel," the Russians had blocked every move inside the United Nations to de-fuse the crisis and prevent war. When war came, the Russians, still secure in the calculation that Nasser would win, had stalled the UN efforts to achieve a swift ceasefire. The Soviet ambassador, Nikolai Fedorenko, on orders from his government, played 'possum. It was virtually impossible for other delegates to talk privately with him about a ceasefire resolution. That is why on Monday Kosygin had suggested to President Johnson over the Hot Line that both powers stand aside. President Johnson had readily agreed because he, in turn, believed the Israelis would win. The CIA, the Pentagon, and the State Department, in separate appraisals, had told him so.

But in the twenty-four hours that intervened between Kosygin's first friendly message and the one President Johnson now read and re-read, the Russians had learned the full measure of their miscalculation. They were "in shock," as a participant later said, over Nasser's swift collapse. Nasser's vaunted air force of Russian Migs was a charred ruin, destroyed in the first one hundred seventy minutes of the war. Nasser's Russian-equipped armies were turning into a fleeing rabble in the Sinai. The Russians had invested $2 billion in arms for Nasser in the dream that Nasser would one day head a pro-Soviet Arab empire. Both dreams and arms were going up in fire and smoke.

At the mahogany conference table, the President read Kosygin's message to the somber-faced men around him and plunged into a discussion of the choices open to him—and of the consequences.

Should the U.S. pressure the Israelis to withdraw to their borders as the Soviet Union demanded?

If Johnson took this course, he would be doing what another president before him, Dwight D. Eisenhower, had done in roughly similar circumstances. That was in 1956, when Nasser also massed troops and armor on Israel's southern borders, and the Israelis chased them from the Sinai in less than 100 hours. At that time, Nikita Khrushchev rattled his nuclear rockets and demanded, just as Kosygin was now doing, that the Israelis withdraw—or else. The United States joined hands with the Soviet Union then to insist in the UN that the Israelis pull out forthwith. The U.S. also acted alone. Privately, the then Secretary of State, John Foster Dulles, told Israel's Foreign Minister, Mrs. Golda Meir, and Israel's ambassador, Abba Eban, that Israel must withdraw or face American reprisals. These would have included an embargo on the $200 million of money gifts that flow from Jewish Americans to Israel yearly. In vain, Golda Meir and Abba Eban had pleaded tearfully with Dulles. They argued that such a withdrawal, without a prior lasting settlement with Egypt, would only set the stage for another Arab attempt to destroy Israel. Dulles was firm. A decade later, on the eve of the June War, Dwight D. Eisenhower confessed a doubt that his action had been correct.

President Johnson was determined not to repeat this mistake. He would not knuckle under to Kosygin's demand for an Israeli pull-back. Negotiations and a settlement must come first.

But, what if the Soviets intervened on the side of the Arabs? Could the U.S. stand aside while the Soviets helped the Arabs add

2 million more victims to the 6 million Hitler had slaughtered? Morally, it was inconceivable. Practically, in the context of the Cold War with the Soviet Union, it was inconceivable, too. For one thing, Israel is one of the few democracies in all Asia. Its destruction with Soviet help, while the U.S. stood idly by, would send tremors of fear throughout the non-Communist world. Since the world regards the United States as Israel's protector, whether or not the U.S. wishes to be, the destruction of Israel would raise serious questions as to American ability or will to come to the aid of an ally. Furthermore, if Israel went down, no other pro-Western nation in the Middle East would be safe from Nasser and the Russians.

If Johnson said "no" to Kosygin and Kosygin intervened, it could mean war between the two superpowers.

Two hours sped by in searching and anxious discussion. If the confrontation with the Russians was to be kept secret, the President had to keep as many of his day's regular appointments as possible. The President was already late for his weekly Tuesday breakfast with Congressional leaders, scheduled for 8:30 a.m. in the family dining room upstairs. With Dean Rusk, Robert McNamara, and Walt Rostow, the President framed a reply to Kosygin.

The import of the President's message to Kosygin was this: the United States would not act unilaterally. The place to seek an end to the Arab-Israeli War was at the United Nations. The method was a UN ceasefire resolution. The note referred Kosygin to New York.

There, the President had already ordered UN Ambassador Arthur J. Goldberg not to knuckle under to Russian demands either: he was to stand firm against any Russian pressure inside the UN Security Council for a forced Israeli withdrawal.

President Johnson's reply on the Hot Line, coupled with the American stand at the UN, crowded Kosygin and company into an uncomfortable corner. The United States had the votes at the UN to block the Soviet Union. This political impotence would not be lost on the Russians' Arab protégés. If the Russians didn't intercede to save Nasser's armies, Russian military impotence would be exposed, too. Would the Russians come out of their corner fighting?

As the President's reply to Kosygin was telephoned from the Situation Room to the Pentagon Command Center for transmission over the Hot Line, the President acted.

He ordered Admiral William I. Martin, Commander of the Sixth Fleet in the Mediterranean, to dispatch an aircraft carrier east toward the theatre of war. At the outbreak of war on Monday, the Sixth Fleet's two aircraft attack carriers, the USS *America* and the USS *Saratoga*, had ostentatiously abandoned all jet fighter exercises to assure the watchful Russians that the U.S. was sitting out the Arab-Israeli War, in line with the Monday Hot Line agreement. Now, just as ostentatiously, the aircraft carrier *America* steamed east from Crete at twenty knots under a state of alert—known as readiness condition three—two steps away from the call to battle stations. On her flight decks were 100 aircraft, including F-4 Phantom Jet fighter bombers and A-4 Skyhawk attack jets. A Soviet destroyer that had been shadowing the *America* for days would undoubtedly inform Moscow at once of the carrier's movements. The Russians would know the Americans meant business.

As the President plodded through his day—the breakfast meeting with Congressional leaders (billed as a discussion of rail strike legislation), the regular weekly luncheon with Secretaries Rusk and McNamara, and the perusal of news bulletins in the Oval Room—the hours dragged by in mounting suspense. Most of the President's advisors had remained in the Situation Room to await Russian reaction to the President's reply.

What would that reaction be?

Would the Russians send bombers to the Sinai? Would their Mediterranean rocketships bombard Israel's coastal cities? The Israelis themselves had made last-minute preparations for such a contingency. In Tel Aviv, the Defense Ministry preempted hospitals and set aside land in public parks to accommodate some 20,000 graves. The Rabbinate had consecrated them according to custom.

Toward evening, the Hot Line signalled the second message

that day from Kosygin. At 6:20 p.m. the President, who had tried vainly to take a nap, hurried once more to the Situation Room.

Between his two messages, Kosygin had learned that the Soviets faced defeat in the UN. The Security Council, supporting the U.S., would not force the Israelis to pull back. Again Kosygin insisted that Johnson leash the Israelis. If the U.S. didn't act, if the Israelis didn't halt, the Soviets would have to make perilous decisions. The Kremlin was assessing steps with dire consequences.

"We didn't know what those dangerous decisions might be," a participant in the confrontation said. But it was clear the Russians were coming as close as they could to saying that they were prepared to risk nuclear war.

As the President studied the Kosygin message, news came that the UN had adopted the expected simple ceasefire resolution. The UN asked the belligerents to hold their fire, but made no demands on Israel to quit the Sinai—a giant, political victory for the U.S., a humiliating defeat for the Russians.

Television cameras waited in the White House theatre to broadcast a Presidential statement to the country. Actually, the ceasefire resolution meant nothing unless the Israelis and Egyptians accepted it. Since Nasser, inexplicably, would refuse for two days to accept the ceasefire that might have saved some of his forces, the war in the Sinai would continue until Thursday night. But the President couldn't know this, and his 107-word statement, which took less than two minutes of air time, was optimistic.

"The ceasefire vote of the Security Council," the President said, "opens a very hopeful path away from danger in the Middle East."

None of the millions who listened to the President could suspect from his words or from the set, benign smile that he assumed on television, that the U.S. and the Soviet Union were at that moment on a collision course that could lead to war. Nor could they know that the President would hurry from the microphones to the Situation Room to deal, for the second time that day, with a sizzling Hot Line message from Kosygin.

In the Situation Room at 8:30 p.m., the President found a cluster of haggard men. It wasn't easy to get through a Tuesday that might turn into a Doomsday. Humphrey, Rusk, McNamara, and the other advisors had been in and out of the Situation Room during the long fourteen hours since morning. All were bone weary. All felt older. As Humphrey said later:

"You can't sit in the Situation Room with the Middle East crisis boiling up and wonder whether you're going to have trouble with the Soviet Union without something happening to you. You grow up."

There would be considerably more "growing up" before the week was over. But now, the President, Rusk, McNamara, and Walt Rostow bent to the immediate task of framing their second reply of the day to Kosygin's Hot Line demand. In this reply, the U.S. yielded no more ground than in the first.

It was now 9 p.m. in Washington, 4 a.m. in Moscow. The reply would not be in Kosygin's hands for some twenty minutes. Kosygin and his colleagues, just as weary as their American counterparts, probably would want to sleep on their next move.

The President left the Situation Room, and in his living quarters in the Mansion slumped heavily before a television set to watch Israel's Foreign Minister, Abba Eban, state Israel's case before the United Nations and the American people. As the South African-born and Cambridge-educated Eban's Churchillian sentences rolled out in eloquent appeal, the President could recall Eban's visit in these White House living quarters only little more than a week before, on May 26. Over drinks, Eban had asked the President, Secretary McNamara, and other officials: would the United States honor its commitment, first given by President Eisenhower, to keep the Straits of Aqaba open. (Nasser had closed them on May 22.)

President Johnson had assured Eban that the commitment would be honored. But he said he needed time to rally Congress and the American people.

"Israel will not stand alone, if she doesn't choose to stand alone," the President had said.

But Israel no longer had any choice, Eban had replied. That very day Nasser had announced: "We intend to open a general assault. This will be total war." In his pocket Eban had an urgent cable from his Prime Minister, Levi Eshkol. It was no longer a case of the right to use a waterway, the cable said. It was a case of survival. Eban had intimated Israel couldn't afford to wait.

"There is no difference between being strangled to death [by blockade] or being shot to death," Eban had said. "You're dead just the same."

Eban left the White House empty-handed and depressed. How could he know that Johnson would risk war to keep the Soviet superpower off the tiny nation's back?

It was after 10 p.m. when Eban finished his UN oration, and it suddenly occurred to the President that he had had no dinner. Lunch with Rusk, McNamara, and Press Secretary Christian had been a skimpy affair. In the middle of it came news that Egypt, Algeria, and Syria had broken relations with the United States, killing what little appetites the four men had. The President, ravenous, ordered up the kind of dinner he sometimes enjoyed at his Texas ranch, but seldom had at the White House: pot roast, black-eyed peas, and greens.

At 1:30 a.m., the President went to bed. Thus ended a day of which an aide later said:

"Had we waffled on that Tuesday, there is no doubt the Russians would have moved—and we could have been at war."

It was now 7:30 a.m. Wednesday in the Sinai. The war was roaring into its third day. As the President dozed off, a debate was raging among top Israeli policy-makers in the Government compound at Tel Aviv. Its outcome was to set the U.S. on a new collision course with the Soviet Union, and bring three near-ultimatums from the Kremlin over the Hot Line in as many hours.

With the outbreak of the war, Prime Minister Levi Eshkol had formed a five-man "advisory cabinet" composed of the new Defense Minister, General Moshe Dayan; the archaeologist and ex-Chief of Staff, Professor Yigael Yadin; the Labor Minister and 1948 war hero, Yigal Allon, and Foreign Minister Abba Eban. As the third day's fighting revealed that the war against Egypt was already won, Eshkol and his advisors turned their thoughts to Syria.

The Syrians were the most implacable of Israel's Arab foes. For years, from their Golan Heights, they had raked Jewish settlements in the Jordan Valley with artillery fire, and had sent down terrorists to mine the public roads and to waylay farm workers. It was Syria that provided the spark that set off the war. This was the fabrication, supported by the Russians, that the Israelis were massing troops on Syria's borders.

As war broke out, Radio Damascus clamored for Israeli blood.

"This campaign is a campaign of annihilation. Strike at the nests of aggression! Crush the Zionist gang!" screamed Radio Damascus. "Strike with all your strength so that there will not remain any remembrance of the rabble on the Holy Soil!" On the second day of the war, the Syrians sent tanks down to attack border settlements. Radio Damascus proclaimed that Syrian troops were already in possession of the Israeli port of Acre—a premature announcement.

All but one of Eshkol's advisors supported a full-dress assault on Syria. But the dissenting voice was a formidable one. It was that of General Moshe Dayan.

It was Dayan's entry into the Israeli Cabinet on June 2 that stiffened everyone's backbone and cast the die for war. Yet, now, Dayan advised prudence. Dayan argued that Syria was the Soviet Union's most cherished protégé, the one it hoped would soon turn into a Soviet satellite. An attack on Syria would surely bring Soviet troops or missiles to the Syrians' rescue. Israel had already achieved its war aims—the destruction of the Egyptian army and the reopening of the Strait of Tiran. The Russians already had much to swallow in Nasser's defeat, Dayan argued. Why bait the Russian Bear beyond endurance? Dayan convinced his colleagues. The decision on Syria was put aside.

But as the war in the Sinai and in Jordan entered its fourth day, the pressure to do something about the shelling from the Syrian (Golan) Heights—and about the Syrians—became overwhelming. The politically powerful association of Israeli kibbutzim, some of whose member settlements were literally under the Syrian gun, demanded surcease from the plague of shellings. The Israeli army insisted it would be a wanton waste to pass up the opportunity to silence the Syrian positions.

By Thursday, Dayan had bowed to the pressure. He gave orders to attack the Syrian Heights as soon as troops arrived from the Sinai and Jordanian fronts.

At 5:30 a.m. Friday, June 9, New York time (11:30 a.m. Israel time) Israeli tanks and infantry crossed the border into Syria. This set the stage for the second agonizing Hot Line cliff hanger of the week. Again, nuclear war hung in the balance. This time, as one participant put it, "it could have gone either way."

As the Israelis started their mad dash up the Syrian ramparts, concern rolled like a temblor through the White House, the State Department, and the Pentagon.

What would the Russians do?

If the Israelis got up those cliffs in a hurry, silenced the Syrian guns, and went no farther, the Russians probably would accept this *fait accompli*, as they had accepted Nasser's defeat. But, if the Israelis pushed beyond the Golan Heights and threatened the Russians' protégé regime in Damascus, the Soviets could intervene.

With one eye on the war bulletins and another on the Hot Line from the Kremlin, an anxious President and his senior advisors waited for what the long Friday would bring.

By 3 p.m. Washington time (9 p.m. Israel time) the Israelis had somehow scrambled up the Golan Heights, then had punched a hole through one sector of the forty-mile-long line of bunkers and trenches. Gen. Moshe Dayan had telephoned Chief of Staff Rabin to say that the UN Security Council had been meeting in New York for the past two hours. A ceasefire was coming, Rabin could have another three hours at most. He'd better finish up.

Rabin changed his original battle plan. Instead of pushing on to the Syrian town of Kuneitra as originally planned, to slice off a twelve-mile belt along the Golan Heights, Rabin ordered his forces to fan out north and south immediately behind the Syrian positions.

Tension grew in Washington. Now, at 3 p.m. Washington time, Secretary Rusk called Israel's Ambassador Avraham Harman.

What were the Israelis' intentions, Rusk inquired. Did the Israelis intend to take Damascus?

No, the Israeli ambassador assured Rusk.

Rusk observed that the situation was fraught with great danger. Both men knew what that danger was: Soviet intervention.

This danger weighed heavily on official minds and spirits in Washington as the afternoon passed into evening and evening passed into night.

At 10 p.m., another senior advisor to the President called the Israeli embassy. It was Walt Rostow. To First Minister Ephraim Evron, Rostow, usually cheerful, but now deeply troubled, put the same question Rusk had asked earlier in the day. What were the Israelis' intentions?

The situation was more critical. At the UN the Syrians charged that the Israelis were bombing Damascus with the intention of marching on it. Actually, the Israelis were neither bombing Damascus nor marching on the city. Dayan had given Rabin another time extension—until dawn Saturday. So, Rabin had changed his plans again. Now the Israelis moved toward Kuneitra on the road to Damascus, but thirty-five miles short of the capital. But the Syrians took a leaf from the book of the Egyptians. Earlier in the week, to draw the Russians into the war, Nasser had fabricated the big lie that American planes were bombing Cairo. Now, with the same object of involving the Russians, the Syrians proclaimed the bombing and imminent seizure of Damascus.

This was the meaning of Damascus: If the Israelis took it, the Russians could move in. Damascus, the oldest city in the world, had become a threat to every modern city in the world.

Throughout early Saturday, as the UN Security Council met in pre-dawn emergency session, the Syrians kept up their accusation that the Israelis were marching on Damascus.

Now, at 8 a.m. Washington time, the Russians took alarm. In the Pentagon military control center, a signal flashed that a Kremlin message was on its way over the Hot Line.

Bromley Smith, who monitered the Hot Line from the White

House Situation Room, called Walt Rostow at his home. Rostow, who starts every other day with an hour on the tennis courts, changed into his business clothes and hurried to the Situation Room.

The President was already there. It was clear from the Hot Line message that the new crisis was more serious than the first. This time Kosygin's demands were tougher than either of his two messages of Tuesday. The United States, he demanded, must forthwith halt the Israelis.

Discussion boiled up in the Situation Room. The Russians were in an embarrassing spot and might take desperate measures to get out of it. They had stood by ignominiously as the Israelis crushed Nasser's armies. Now the stunned Arab world was clamoring to know where the Russians were when the Arabs needed them. The Soviets couldn't remain idle while the Israelis inflicted the ultimate insult and toppled the Damascus regime.

Those in the Situation Room who had participated with President Kennedy in his confrontation with Khrushchev over the Cuban missiles, knew that the present confrontation with Kosygin held more danger. Then, John F. Kennedy dealt only with Nikita Khrushchev. What Fidel Castro did or said was irrelevant. But in the Six-Day War, Johnson and Kosygin were not the masters of events. Johnson had to deal with Israel, while Kosygin and Brezhnev had to deal with six Arab countries.

The Israelis had assured Secretary Rusk that they would not attack Damascus. But they had not accepted a ceasefire either. Even now they were plunging eastward into Syria.

Nevertheless, the United States had to keep the Russians from intervening. Over the Hot Line the President told Kosygin the United States could no more control the Israelis than Kosygin could control the Egyptians or Syrians. Johnson also reminded the Russians: if they had cooperated with the United States in mid-May there would have been no war in June.

Two more Hot Line messages whipped in from Kosygin. The Russians talked tougher and tougher. Some in the Situation Room began to fear that the Soviets might intervene not only to halt the Israelis in Syria, but to recoup all of the Arabs' shattered fortunes in the war.

The President made a fateful decision. To the Sixth Fleet, cruising in the western Mediterranean some 400 miles from the Syrian battlefield, went the order to send three task groups east toward the Syrian coast. The aircraft carriers *Saratoga* and *America* with their 200 fighter-bomber aircraft and destroyer escorts, and a 2000-man Marine battalion landing team from the Second Marine Division at Camp Lejeune, N. C., steamed east. "They had war paint on their cheeks, packs on their backs, ready to go," a navy man said.

As the President served this notice on the Russians to keep hands off, he also took steps to end the fighting in Syria.

In the absence of Dean Rusk, Under Secretary of State Nicholas deB. Katzenbach, acting on the President's orders, called Israel's Ambassador Harman to the State Department.

Harman and his First Minister, Ephraim Evron, had been up all night relaying urgent messages of American concern and UN activity to Eshkol's advisory cabinet. Eshkol, in turn, had used these to gauge the time left to Israeli forces in Syria. The Israeli ambassador and his minister were red-eyed and grim.

Surrounded by State Department aides, Katzenbach asked the Israeli ambassador "in the strongest possible terms" to accept a ceasefire. He pointed to the grave possibility that the Soviets might intervene to dislodge Israel from all Arab territory.

The Israeli ambassador assured Katzenbach a mutual ceasefire was near. Dayan, at this moment, was working out a ceasefire deal with the Syrians through General Odd Bull, commander of the United Nations Truce Supervisory Organization forces in Jerusalem.

As the United States and the Soviet Union stood toe-to-toe and traded "thought for thought" over the Hot Line, both were saved by the bell. A UN ceasefire, accepted by Israel and Syria, went into effect. Israeli tanks and troops had reached Kuneitra, their goal, with only ten minutes to spare.

In the Situation Room, the President and his advisors knew the worst was over. They expected no fourth Hot Line message from Kosygin, and none came.

Like John F. Kennedy, Lyndon B. Johnson learned the hard way that the Soviet's assertion of "peaceful co-existence" had not ended the Cold War. Kosygin and Brezhnev were pursuing Communist expansion aims as vigorously as Khrushchev and Stalin did. The Arab-Israeli conflict was a crucial battle in the Cold War. More depended on it than the fate of a small, democratic nation alone. This war held the fate of a strategic area stretching from the Atlantic on the West to the Persian Gulf on the East. On it, too, as West Germany's Foreign Office—and NATO officials in Paris—told this writer, depended the fate of Europe itself.

2

MOTHER
RUSSIA

"That Bear is Capable of Anything"—KARL MARX

In the spring of 1853, the London correspondent for the *New York Tribune* tried to wake up the Western world to an imminent danger. Czarist Russia, he warned, meant to seize the Middle East. It was then controlled by the decaying Ottoman (Turkish) Empire.

The correspondent was Karl Marx, the father of Communism. Marx had published his *Communist Manifesto* five years before. He little dreamed that the country that would embrace communism first would be Russia. Nor could he have dreamed that when Communists seized Russia, they would continue to expand the Russian empire just as the Czars did. As a correspondent, Karl Marx thundered:

"Let Russia get possession of [the Mid-East] and her strength is increased nearly half. She becomes superior to all the rest of Europe put together. Such an event would be an unspeakable calamity to . . . democratic ideas and man's native thirst for freedom."[1]

As Karl Marx warmed up to his job, he sounded more and more like the editorial page in your daily newspaper.

[1] I am indebted for these researches to Jay Lovestone, Director of the AFL-CIO Department of International Affairs.

"In all essential points, Russia has steadily, one after another, gained her ends, thanks to the ignorance, dullness, and consequent inconsistency and cowardice of Western Governments," Karl Marx wrote.

The Czars never did get possession of the Middle East, as Karl Marx had warned. But monuments to their efforts abound in the area in the form of Russian orthodox churches. These testify to the Czarist effort to seek a foothold in the Holy Land by trying to subordinate Middle Eastern Orthodox Church hierarchies to Moscow. The visitor to Jerusalem can see one such Czarist monument in the Russian Compound in the city's western section. This block-square inclosure houses a Russian orthodox church, dormitory and school staffed today by monks, priests and such Soviet citizens who—until the June 4 war at least—held diplomatic passports. These, it is generally suspected, doubled as espionage agents.

The Communists picked up where the Czars left off. When Joseph Stalin divided up the world with Adolf Hitler in the Nazi-Soviet pact of 1939, the Soviet Union—as a secret clause revealed later—staked out the mid-East as its preserve. Stalin tried again in 1945 with occupation troops which carved out a Soviet Socialist Republic from the northern half of today's Iran. The United Nations, in one of its rare achievements of this sort, forced the Communists out.

The Russian Bear put his paw into the area, soon after. And here, let's listen to a story by Karl Marx of two naturalists who examined a bear.

"One naturalist who had never seen such an animal before inquired whether the bear dropped its cubs alive or laid eggs," Marx related. "To which the other, who was better informed, replied: that animal is capable of anything."

Marx went on: "The Russian bear is certainly capable of anything, so long as he knows the other animals he has to deal with to be capable of nothing."

One thing of which the Russian Bear was capable was to help give birth to the State of Israel. Russian and Arab schoolboys read in their histories that "Western Imperialists" are responsible for Israel. But non-doctored history tells another story. Ironically, the United States and Great Britain did their best to prevent birth. The Soviet Union fought for it. Had it not been for the Soviet Union, there might not have been an Israel today.

The Soviet Union and satellites intervened in three crucial stages of Israel's birth and survival.

First, the Soviet bloc helped Jewish underground fighters engineer the 1946 Jewish exodus to Palestine which dealt the death blow to British rule there. Next, the Soviet Union battled for and won the United Nations partition plan that divided Palestine into independent Jewish and Arab states. Then, when six invading Arab nations threatened to strangle the infant state at birth, the Soviet Union helped rush the weapons that saved Israel's life. The Communists were as indignant then over "Arab aggression," as they were to be later over "Israeli aggression."

The Soviet Union's all-out pro-Jewish and anti-Arab role marks one of the most amazing and cynical flip-flops in Soviet foreign relations and in the Communist line. Pieced together from the archives of the United Nations and from the testimony of Israeli leaders who lived through it and from American and British intelligence officers who observed it, the story makes believe-it-or-not reading.

"As far as the Soviet Union is concerned," Russia's Foreign Minister, Andrei Gromyko, once said, "there is only one kind of logic in foreign affairs: the logic of what is best for the Soviet Union."

What "was best for the Soviet Union" after World War II, was to get Great Britain, then the dominant power in the Middle East, out of the area.

"That's what we're here to do," a Soviet delegate to the UN told a Jewish spokesman from Palestine. Left unsaid was the Soviet assumption that a new Jewish state, smarting from British repression, could be turned into a Russian proxy in the Cold War. It could serve as an anti-Western base for Soviet penetration of the Middle East—and beyond. The Russians never did understand the Jews.

The Bear Plays Samaritan

Let's pick up the narrative at Vienna in 1946, then occupied by the Americans, British, French, and Russians.

Here, in the gloomy prison-like mass of institutional buildings known as the Rothschild Hospital, American counterintelligence observed a curious periodic inflow and outflow. An American officer, stationed in Vienna at the time, recalls that the Rothschild Hospital normally housed some one thousand persons. But now, in 1946, it was usually crammed with some ten thousand human beings. And every fortnight or so these would pour out, and in their place other thousands would pour in.

American occupation officials—interested to see who, in postwar Europe, was going where—took a periodic census at the Rothschild Hospital and puzzled over their discovery. One fortnight, the buildings would bulge with Jewish Rumanians. Next, the guests would all be Jewish Poles, or Jewish Hungarians, or Jewish Germans.

Further investigation showed that, on evacuating the Rothschild Hospital, these temporary residents made their way by truck or train to Mediterranean or Adriatic ports where they embarked on ships—usually bearing no flag—bound for Palestine.

The Rothschild Hospital, American occupation officials concluded, was the staging center for a mass Jewish exodus to Palestine. It was clear that the migration was meticulously organized. Somebody in eastern Europe was directing the flow of Jewish refugees, turning the tap on or off as the Rothschild Hospital filled up or emptied. Something else was clear, too. Since Soviet Union troops controlled every road, every railroad junction, every border in eastern Europe, the packed refugee trains could roll through Poland, Czechoslovakia, and into Austria only with the approval or actual assistance of the Soviet military and the Kremlin.

In the light of its later behavior, the Soviet Union would just as soon forget the secret role of Good Samaritan it played in a migration that was to bring a hundred thousand-odd Jewish refugees to Palestine. But evidence of that role, as the author discovered from conversations in Israel, London, and Washington, is conclusive.

In 1946, Europe's Jews badly needed a Good Samaritan, secret or not.

Some million survivors of Hitler's "final solution" wandered homeless or remained caged in German or Polish concentration camps. They couldn't go where they wanted. The United States virtually shut them out with stringent immigration quotas. Poland was no more hospitable. Christian Poles, reluctant to yield Jewish property seized during the war, met returning Jewish Poles with murderous pogroms. As for Germany, few Jewish Germans wanted to set foot in the land of the horror camps again. Only burning rage against a callous and indifferent world sustained the homeless Jews in their isolation. That, and the hope for many that they could somehow reach Palestine.

Into this sorry chapter of man's inhumanity to man, now entered a small army of energetic and resourceful young men from the Haganah, the Jewish underground fighting force in Palestine. They mounted a rescue operation which was, at the same time, a vast recruitment drive to bring Europe's Jews to Palestine, preferably young Jews who could help build a country and fight for it.

Only one thing stood in the way: the diplomatic and military might of Great Britain. The British, governing Palestine under a 1922 League of Nations mandate, barred all but a trickle of Jewish immigration—fifteen hundred a year. This was an illegal repudiation of the terms of the mandate which bound the British to "facilitate Jewish immigration and encourage close settlement by the Jews on the land." The immigration bar, instigated by Arab pressure, had come at a cruel time, 1939, when the Hitler night was closing down on the Jews. Its rigid enforcement slammed shut a chief escape hatch and condemned hundreds of thousands to death.

Now, in 1946, the best brains in the British military intelligence were deployed in Mediterranean ports to ferret out news of refugee ships bound for Palestine. Royal Air Force planes hunted these ships at sea. And the Royal British Navy blockaded the

Palestine coast, intercepted the ships, and dragged their wretched human cargoes to concentration camps on Cyprus.

The Haganah had a simple and bold plan: ship so many immigrants to Palestine that their interception by the British would flood the Cyprus camps. This would become so embarrassing morally, and so expensive militarily, that the British would tire of their mandate in Palestine and get out.

The Haganah's men needed ships, and these could be obtained with money from co-religionists in the United States. But first, the Haganah needed governmental support in Eastern Europe where the Hitler tide had washed up most of Europe's surviving Jews. This is where the Soviet Union and the Communist bloc came in. Polish officials agreed to release Poland's Jews and permit them to cross the country into Czechoslovakia which gave transit rights across its territory.

The Soviet Union did more. It provided scarce trains and, as ex-Haganah leaders in Israel told this writer, the Russians turned their backs as the trains crossed the borders their forces controlled. Soviet officials also supplied collective passports to expedite refugee sailings from Black Sea ports.

An ex-Haganah operative, now an Israeli Army colonel, recalled this story:

The British complained to the Soviet commanding general in Vienna. The general promised to stop the Jewish refugee trains at the Austrian border. But to Haganah men who came to protest, the Soviet general said:

"I only promised to prevent the trains from crossing the border, not the passengers."

Soviet border patrols stopped refugee trains, but looked the other way as the passengers crossed over on foot, mounted waiting trucks, and continued their journey.

Further evidence of the Soviet Union's aid to the Jewish exodus came from the head of the United Nations Relief and Rehabilitation Administration (UNRRA) in Berlin, the British Lt. General Sir Frederick E. Morgan, a wartime deputy chief of staff to General Dwight D. Eisenhower.

General Morgan told a press conference on January 2, 1946, that he had seen an "exodus of Jews from Poland on Russian trains over a regular route from Lodz to Berlin." The general added that the "refugees were well dressed and had pockets bulging with Russian printed occupation marks."

Since the British general couched his findings in somewhat less than compassionate terms, he raised an uproar and was temporarily suspended. But the U.S. Third Army confirmed the truth of his statement soon after.

In his memoirs, General Morgan gave details.

"We were witnessing an admirably organized second exodus," he wrote, "with Russian connivance."

"My information told me that . . . there were two collecting centers in Poland for Jewish refugees from Eastern Europe, at Lodz and Katowice. The refugees were transported to Berlin by rail or road. Truck convoys arrived during darkness [with] the passengers mainly vanishing into the night. . . . In the case of rail movement, in many instances the passengers would dismount at wayside halts and disappear into the countryside."

The general wrote, "One [had to] admire . . . the whole organization of the ceaseless movement of great numbers of these poor people across wartorn Germany—wherein legitimate movement was a highly problematical business—down into Austria, into Italy, and Yugoslavia for shipment, often in circumstances of terrifying danger, to Palestine."

With the support, then, of the Soviet Union and of the Communist bloc, the Haganah plan succeeded. As the Cyprus camps overflowed with intercepted Jewish immigrants to Palestine and dramatized Britain's undeclared war against a tortured people, the British foreign office lost its head altogether. In desperation, British destroyers fired on the Jewish refugee ships, many of them overloaded with children orphaned by Hitler.

Britain's Foreign Minister, Ernest Bevin, emerged as a Pharoah who would not let the Jewish people go. The Palestine mandate became a plague.

The British Colonial Office, which knew how to deal with native colonial peoples, did not know how to deal with the Jew. Freed from the cribbed and insecure life of the ghetto, the Jew reverted to Biblical type. He became a tiller of the soil and a resourceful warrior who fought for it. Confident that he would one day be part of a sovereign nation, the Palestine Jew organized an underground army, accumulated caches of weapons, and even set up underground munitions plants. In vain the British arrested Jews without warrant, jailed them without trial, deported and shot them. In retaliation, Jewish underground fighters turned British administration into a nightmare, bombed military headquarters and on one occasion—in retaliation for the death of two Jews—hanged two British soldiers.

It took an army of one hundred twenty thousand to guard the beaches against the Jewish immigrants and to cope with open Jewish insurrection. Some fifteen thousand police and prison personnel supplemented the military and this took up most of the administration budget—$18 million a year for "law and order," for instance, as against $2 million yearly for education.

Virtual civil war between Arabs and Jews added to British troubles. They announced they wanted out, and on April 2, 1947, asked the United Nations to decide what to do about Palestine.

The Soviets now took the lead in the UN to create a Jewish state.

Andrei Gromyko—Zionist

The man to whom the Kremlin entrusted the Jewish cause was Andrei Andreievich Gromyko, then thirty-seven, already a deputy foreign minister of the Soviet Union and soon to be its foreign minister.

Gromyko is a heavyset man with outsized hands and feet whose features hint his peasant origins but are handsome enough to have won from office secretaries the accolade: Krasavets Diplomat— "diplomat beauty." To journalists, however, Gromyko is so dour a figure and so devoid of human warmth that *their* phrase for him is "Grim Grom." An extremely taciturn man—even for a Soviet diplomat—Gromyko for years seldom achieved more than a grunt when reporters sought his comments.

While all delegates to the UN take their line from their governments, the Soviet delegate is held on a tighter leash than most.

"If I tell him to sit on a block of ice and stay there for months,"

Nikita Khrushchev once said of Gromyko, "he'll do it without backtalk."

Gromyko's "cake of ice" prior to the 1947 Palestine debate was to snarl the UN's work with twenty-three vetoes in the Security Council and with numerous sullen walkouts from UN deliberations. To the world, then, he was a gloomy "nyetnik."

"He dresses in dull brown," said a *New York Times* reporter, "and he talks in dull brown."

But for nine months in 1947 and in 1948, Gromyko's voice became an angry growl, charged—as one observer put it—with "smoldering emotion and deep complaint."

Put side by side with Communist tirades against Israel after the 1967 June war, Gromyko's words—as spread over the day-to-day record of the UN's proceedings—make strange reading.

"It would be unjust if we do not take into account the aspirations of the Jews to a state of their own, and if we deny the Jews the right to realize this aspiration," Gromyko hammered at the UN.

To the Communists, Zionism—Jewish nationhood—had always been the most wicked kind of bourgeois nationalism. For years, the Communists castigated Zionism as a "tool of British imperialism." But no Zionist ever made more fiery speeches for a Jewish state than Gromyko did, nor appealed more passionately to the conscience of mankind.

"During the last war, the Jewish people underwent indescribable sorrow and suffering," Gromyko reminded UN delegates. "No western Europe state was able [to help] the Jewish people defend its rights and its very existence. Now thousands are still behind barbed wire . . . The time has come to help these people not by words but by deeds!"

Gromyko had a wealth of negotiating experience learned at Stalin's side at Yalta and Potsdam and at the founding of the United Nations at San Francisco. He was tough and knew every nook and cranny of UN procedure. He worked so hard at his UN job that he was known as a one-man delegation.

All these Gromyko put to work in a dogged step-by-step fight against an equally dogged American, British, and Arab opposition. Gromyko's first task was to win the Jews a voice in the debate over their fate in Palestine.

All five Arab states—Egypt, Syria, Saudi Arabia, Lebanon, and Iraq—had representatives at the UN. But, since no Jewish state existed, there was no spokesman for the six hundred thousand Jewish colonists in Palestine, nor for the Jewish refugees in Europe, nor for the Jews throughout the world, who had labored and sacrificed for a Jewish homeland.

"We are playing Hamlet without the Prince of Denmark," an Indian delegate said. "Where are the Jews?"

The Jews were offstage. They sat silent in the audience—while the Arabs castigated them—or wandered frustrated in the corridors.

Gromyko demanded that the Jewish Agency in Palestine and other Jewish spokesmen be permitted to appear before the UN General Assembly. The United States led the opposition. Only sovereign states had a right to be heard, the American delegates argued. To do otherwise would violate the Charter of the United Nations and lower the UN's prestige. If the Jews had anything to say, they could submit documents to one of the subcommittees of the Assembly.

Gromyko chided the American delegation:

"It is incomprehensible how an invitation to Jewish representatives to [discuss] the Palestine question with which the Jews are vitally interested can [hurt] the authority of the United Nations. Rather the reverse." And Gromyko's Polish colleague became eloquent.

"The darkness which has engulfed the Jews for so long can only be dispelled by a ray of light kindled here for them," the Polish delegate pleaded. "If we refuse to give them a hearing, we shall extinguish that light before it has had a chance to become a steady glow."

It was the U.S. that succeeded in keeping the Jewish spokesmen from the assembly. Only Gromyko's persistence won them the right to appear at all: before the UN's First Committee, also known as the political committee. This opened the door to men of giant oratorical stature. Moshe Shertok (who changed his name to Sharett in 1948), later Israel's foreign minister and prime minister, pleaded the Jewish cause brilliantly and extemporaneously in eight languages. The leonine Dr. Abba Hillel Silver, president of the Zionist Organization of America, could now inject his powerful personality into the struggle.

Fighting side by side with the Jewish spokesmen, Gromyko could now win the next phase: instructions to a special UN committee on how to investigate the Palestine problem.

Gromyko and the Communist bloc argued that the special UN committee not only visit Palestine but the Jewish refugee camps in Europe as well. Gromyko won. The committee spent three months in Palestine and Europe and recommended that Palestine be partitioned into two independent states, one Jewish, the other Arab, with an economic union.

The preliminaries were over, and the stage was now set for the main bout—the fight over partition.

In November, 1946, President Harry Truman made public a straightforward letter to King Ibn Saud of Saudi Arabia.

"The Government and people of the United States have supported the concept of a Jewish National Home in Palestine since the [end] of the first World War," Truman wrote. "It still adheres to this position."

Since the Soviet Union also favored the concept of a Jewish state, speedy approval was expected for the partition plan. But, as the UN proceedings reveal, the American delegation to the UN threw so many roadblocks in the path of the deliberations that weeks dragged by without action.

Since the President initiates foreign policy, how could the American delegation to the UN work at cross-purposes with him? The answer is that the President proposes, but the State Department—which handles day-to-day foreign affairs—often disposes. And it was the State Department that gave orders to the U.S. delegation at the UN.

The State Department's record with regard to "Jewish questions," during and immediately after the war, was unmarred by any consideration of moral issues or American humane traditions. In 1942, the State Department suppressed evidence that Hitler had ordered the extermination of Europe's Jews and a then Assistant Secretary of State, Breckinridge Long, fought against the lowering of immigration bars that would have saved even a desperate handful. In 1946, an Anglo-American committee, named by the American and British Governments, urged that a hundred thousand European Jews, then rotting in concentration camps, be admitted to Palestine. The State Department and the British Colonial Office conspired to bury the report.

Now, in 1947, specialists in the State Department's Office of Near Eastern and African Affairs—many of them sons of missionaries who had grown up in Arab lands—said openly: "There is no point risking our friendship with 80 million Arabs for the sake of a few thousand Jews." Their superior, Loy Henderson, a career official, made no secret of his belief that support of a Jewish state would "wreck our Arab policy." He and fellow experts argued that the security of the United States "requires that we play ball with Arab military power."—a curious judgment, in the light of later events. Two future secretaries of state shared this view. One was John Foster Dulles, then an American delegate to the UN. The other was Dean Rusk who had come to the State Department in March, 1947, to handle problems that would arise from the creation of a Jewish state. In January, 1948, while the Palestine debate was boiling, Rusk took charge of the State Department's Office of UN Affairs.

The State Department's pro-Arab bias not only defied President Truman but repudiated promises made by every President since Woodrow Wilson. It also meant taking a long-shot gamble on the loyalty of Arab leaders who had already betrayed the Western democracies, and would betray them again.

Five Arab states owed their independence to British troops that had freed them from the Turks in the first world war. Arab leaders repaid this debt by siding with the Nazis during the Second World War. Their chief spokesman, The Grand Mufti of Jerusalem, spent the war in Berlin working for the Hitler war effort. Furthermore, the area that a Jewish state would occupy would be no bigger than ½ of 1 percent of the Arab land the British had liberated in 1918—a small price with which to repay the West.

Nevertheless, the State Department bet on the Arabs.

First, American delegate John Foster Dulles argued at the United Nations that it had no legal right to deal with the Palestine problem at all. The Arab delegates immediately put this proposition forward in a motion. It was defeated by only one vote—twenty-one to twenty. Only the votes of Gromyko's bloc prevented the sudden death of the Jewish state then and there.

When persistent prodding from the White House forced the American delegation to announce, finally, that it would vote for partition, State Department experts tried still another maneuver. Although the boundaries of the new Jewish and Arab states were already agreed on, the American delegation proposed to give about half of the Negev Desert—including access to the all-important Gulf of Aqaba—to the Arabs.

Here Dr. Chaim Weizmann, the Russian-born English Zionist leader who, like Moses, had led the Jews within sight of the Promised Land, went to Washington to plead with President Truman.

That afternoon, back at the United Nations, an old-fashioned melodrama unfolded.

As Dr. Weizmann told the story: the head of the American delegation called the Palestine Jewish Agency's spokesman, Moshe Shertok, to his office. As Shertok entered, his face tense with anxiety, he could read on the faces of the American delegates that the die had been cast for an amputated Jewish state. But before Herschel V. Johnson, the chief U.S. delegate, could speak, he was called to the telephone. It was President Truman. The delegation was ordered to keep its hands off the Negev and Aqaba. Even so, the American delegation succeeded in trimming 2 million *dunams* (five hundred thousand acres) from the area allotted to the Jewish state. But the baby was saved.

As the crucial partition vote approached and the American delegation made no effort to round up votes for it—even among dependent states like the Philippines which announced it would vote *against*—the *Washington Post* observed:

"An ancient and fishlike smell comes out of Lake Success (then the home of the UN). It is the smell of chicanery."

The vote on November 29, 1947, showed thirty-three in favor, thirteen against, and ten abstentions. Partition had squeaked through, obtaining the required two-thirds majority with not a vote to spare. The Communist Bloc's support had been decisive. Had the USSR, Czechoslovakia, Poland, the Ukraine, and Bye-lorussia voted against partition—or even abstained—the partition resolution would have failed.

But the Western democracies weren't finished yet. When the UN named a Palestine Commission to implement partition, the British refused to cooperate with it in Palestine. Encouraged, the Arab states sent armed bands to burn and pillage Jewish vil-lages and plunged the area into a civil war. American spokesmen at the UN promptly declared that partition, already voted, wouldn't work. They urged it be scrapped and that a UN trusteeship—in effect, a rejection of a Jewish state—be set up instead.

This turnabout brought Gromyko running.

"Full responsibility for blocking the partition of Palestine must fall on the United States," he told the UN. "Not only has it refused to support a decision, already adopted, but has introduced proposals to revoke it. The United States is not concerned with the just settlement of the future of Palestine, but with its own military strategic interests in the Mid-East."

As the West and East continued locked in oratorical combat, the Jewish colonists took matters into their own hands. With the UN partition vote as authority, they declared the birth of the State of Israel on May 14, 1948.

The Soviet Union promptly provided all important diplomatic support. It became the first Government in the world to give full official (*de jure*) recognition to Israel. The Communist Bloc followed suit. (President Truman had extended *de facto* recogni-tion to Israel a day before the Soviet Union, but withheld full recognition for eight months.)

The Israelis say:

"In Israel, if you don't believe in miracles, you're not a realist."

In 1948, what newly-born Israel needed was a miracle. The British had barred the accumulation of weapons by the Jews. Al-though the Jewish colonists had smuggled in rifles and machine guns they had no tanks, artillery, or planes with which to meet those of six invading Arab states. The Jewish fighters didn't even have enough rifles to go around. Sometimes, two fighters were assigned to one rifle, and when one fell, the other picked up the rifle.

The early fighting went badly for the Israelis.

The Jordanian Legion, armed, trained, and led by the British, cut off the Jewish section of Jerusalem. The Egyptian Air Force, flying American Dakota bombers, ranged over Tel Aviv at will. An attack on the central bus depot killed forty civilians.

To make matters more desperate for the Israelis, the West would not sell it arms because the UN, with equal impartiality, had decreed an embargo against both sides.

Here, the Soviet Union provided the miracle that saved Israel.

Gromyko fought for a series of UN ceasefires, and during the truce periods the Soviet Bloc defied the UN embargo to rush weapons to the reeling Israelis. The American embassy in Prague tried to stop the shipments. But the weapons kept flowing, and with each truce the Israelis became stronger.

Czech machine guns and rifles, arriving by plane during one touch-and-go moment in the battle for Jerusalem, helped the Israelis hold their section of the city. Seventy-five Messerschmidts and Spitfires, purchased from the Czechs, drove Arab planes from the skies. With the planes went training. One Israeli who got his pilot training from the Communists was Mordecai Hod, who— as General Mordecai Hod, twenty years later—commanded the Israeli Air Force that destroyed Egypt's air power, a Soviet gift, within one hundred seventy minutes.

The world little noted nor long remembered the Soviet Union's gift of life to the Jewish state in 1947-48. As for the Soviet Union, it began almost at once to wipe from its memory and its history books the lone moral and constructive act it had brought off after the war. The Soviet Union had found it couldn't manage the Jews.

Here was a people whose leaders—David Ben-Gurion, Moshe Sharett, and others—had been born in Russia, were Socialists, and had a lingering admiration for the Communist Revolution. They had created the only working communal settlements in the world, the kibbutzim. Yet they wanted no part of state communism and set up a parliamentary government in the Middle East, a democratic oasis in a desert of feudal sheikdoms and military dictatorships. Nor had they restored the Jewish Commonwealth after a lapse of 20 centuries in order to turn it into a Soviet pawn.

Israel's foreign affairs minister, Moshe Sharett, put it this way:

"Why are we pro-West? Is there any choice between the open world and the closed world?"

To make matters worse, this perky little country had the chutzpah (gall) to start a war of religious liberation *inside Russia.* No sooner had Israel's first Minister to the Soviet Union, Mrs. Golda Meir, arrived with her staff in Moscow, than they began to distribute proscribed religious manuals, Hebrew texts—and booster literature on Israel—to Jews in the Soviet Union. In their war against religion, the Soviets had discouraged church attendance, but thousands of Soviet Jews flocked to Moscow's lone synagogue to see and talk to Golda Meir and her fellow Israelis. Behind the Israeli's undiplomatic activities was the old dream of someday tapping the 3-million-man reservoir of Russian Jews to swell the population of Israel.

Before long, the Soviet Union had second thoughts about the little nation it had helped create.

3

BEAR IN A
CHINA
SHOP

When Nikita Khrushchev was rising to power in the USSR, those who knew him best called him "the football." It wasn't because the round Mr. K. resembled an outsized soccer ball. It was because of the elastic and slippery quality of his maneuvers and intrigues. This enabled him to carry out purge orders for Stalin, yet pop up later as the exposer of Stalin's crimes. This permitted him, too, to start out as one of four collective leader-successors to Stalin, then bounce up, soon after, as the sole leader.

Khrushchev was just as resourceful in his dealings with the outside world.

"How is it," Khrushchev once asked some diplomats, "that I, who couldn't read or write until I was 19, can run rings around you educated Western gentlemen?"

One of the rings Khrushchev "ran around you gentlemen" was to break into the Middle East. He did it moreover under the nose of the watchdog Sixth Fleet and in the face of proclaimed Moslem antipathy toward Communism.

How Khrushchev did it provides a portentous case history of new tactics in the global conflict between the U.S. and the Soviet

Union—for which the United States, seemingly, has as yet found no answer.

To understand Khrushchev's tactics, it is necessary to examine briefly the Kremlin's undeclared war, as old as the Bolshevik Revolution itself, to organize the world along Communist lines. This undeclared war has occupied the energies and thoughts of every Communist leader since Lenin. Conversely, every American president since Harry Truman has had to devise strategies— sometimes peaceful (The Marshall Plan, The Berlin Airlift); sometimes violent (Korea)—to cope with it. Since World War II, the Communist probing of Western will has plunged the world into a rising crescendo of violence. There have been so many Communist-inspired insurrections—(Greece and Indonesia); crises (Berlin, Cuba, the Congo, Lebanon, Jordan); limited wars (Korea, Malaya, French Indonesia); big wars (Vietnam, Israel-Arab)— that historians despair of peace in our time, and, indeed, in the time of our grandchildren.

Prof. Robert Strausz-Hupé, director of the Foreign Policy Research Institute of the University of Pennsylvania, has described the unending Communist war as "The Protracted Conflict" and compares it to a global guerrilla war that employs political and propaganda means—as well as violence—to achieve victory.[1]

Chief Soviet tactic in the protracted conflict is deception, or —more specifically—action through indirection. Don't intervene directly with your own forces (except, of course, to quell "counter revolution" within your own Communist empire). Avoid open challenge to the more powerful West. Operate through proxies, such as other Communist Parties in other countries (as in the unsuccessful post-war Communist riots in France and Japan) or Communist puppet regimes (as in Korea).

Khrushchev, being Khrushchev, added two layers of deception. He proclaimed the new Soviet line: "Peaceful Co-existence," "Détente," "Relaxation of Tensions." War is unthinkable in the age of the hydrogen bomb, he told President Eisenhower and

[1] "The Protracted Conflict," *Harper's*, 1959.

other Western leaders at Geneva in 1955. These words, hailed as the "Geneva Spirit," fell like balm on the ears of the conflict-weary West.

But before Communist Party congresses, the author of "Peaceful Co-existence" piped a different tune. As Khrushchev spelled it out in his historic lecture of January 6, 1961, to the Soviet Communist Party apparatus, he barred only one kind of war— nuclear war. It was always open season for "wars of liberation" against the West. "[We] fully and unreservedly support such wars," he said, "and march in the van of peoples fighting wars of liberation." The author of "Détente" and "Relaxation of Tensions," precipitated the Sinai War of 1956, the attempted Communist overthrow in Jordan and Lebanon in 1957 and 1958, and the Cuban missile crisis of 1962. These adventures far exceeded the "cold war" Stalin had waged. Yet so beguiling was Khrushchev's "Peaceful Co-existence" line that he is remembered today as the father of a thaw between East and West.

Khrushchev's second piece of deception involved the use of a new kind of Soviet proxy. This was the nationalist leader, say like Gamal Abdel Nasser, who pursued his own country's interests in seeming independence of Kremlin dictates, but waged war against the West's interest and friends just the same. Such a proxy could even be anti-Communist and purge the Communists in his own country. This only increased the deception. The U.S. State Department's Arabists— experts on the Middle East—saw Nasser's war against his own Communists and set him down as "anti-Communist." But Khrushchev had a shrewder insight into Nasser's role. At a secret meeting at the 23rd Congress of the Soviet Communist Party in Moscow in 1961, Khrushchev told dumbfounded Arab Communists who had been fighting Nasser as a "Fascist dictator" to disband the Communist Party in Egypt. Khrushchev told the Communists that Nasser, not they, was now the instrument of Soviet policy in the Middle East!

The combined deception of the "Peaceful Co-existence" line and of the use of Nasser as a proxy so bemused Washington for years before the Arab-Israeli war, that it paralyzed any meaningful response to Soviet moves even after imperilled pro-Western nations there raised urgent alarms.

But we are running somewhat ahead of the story. Let's begin at the beginning.

Bear Trap

When Stalin died, Khrushchev and his colleagues inherited a nation that was a vast armed camp, cowed by purges, grinding to a halt economically, and with its agriculture a shambles. The Soviet Union had also withdrawn into itself. Soviet delegates had walked out of the United Nations Security Council, thus reducing communications with the outside world. Stalin had even quarreled with a fellow Communist state, Yugoslavia, and had severed relations with it. Adventures in Communist expansion abroad had ground to a halt, too. Stalin had been checkmated in Europe, in Indonesia, Malaya, the Philippines, and Korea.

First, Khrushchev consolidated his power, cleared out the worst of Stalin's slave labor camps, and released Russian energies for the job of moving their stagnating economy at home and repairing their relations abroad. Then he turned toward the Messianic task that began with Stalin: to undermine the West and to hasten, in his words, "the victory of socialism throughout the world which is inevitable by virtue of the laws of historical development."

Blocked in Europe, Khrushchev, being Khrushchev, decided on an end run, a flanking movement against the West, through the Arab World. The region had obvious allure for Khrushchev. If he looked at it through the eyes of the Czars, the area was, after all, to Mother Russia, what Latin America is to the United States. If he looked at it through the eyes of a Communist protagonist in the global conflict, the Arab World beckoned on two accounts.

For one thing, it was a rich prize. Here, in an area that linked the continents of Europe, Asia, and Africa, was the chance to hit the West where it hurt: in its investments (the Middle East contains 60 percent of the world's oil reserves, mostly worked by

Western capital); in the West's oil supplies (Western Europe depends on the area for half its oil needs); and in its air and water routes (through the Middle East go the shortest air and water routes from Europe to Southern Asia). And, of course, there was the chance to hit the West in its bases, to squeeze concessions from Europe by turning off the oil taps, and to seize a staging area for a Communist push south into Africa, and east into India.

On top of all this, the Arab World was ripe for Khrushchevian seduction. It simmered with anger and frustrated dreams.

No less an authority on the Arab character than Nasser has written:

"It sometimes appears to me that we content ourselves overmuch by wishful thinking. In flights of fancy, we fulfill our desires and enjoy in imagination things which we never bestir ourselves to realize." (*Egypt's Liberation: The Philosophy of the Revolution.*)

The most persistent "flight of fancy" in which Arabs indulge themselves is that the state of Israel can and must be destroyed.

This fantasy has been nourished by profound feelings of injustice.

The United Nations decision to set aside a portion of Palestine for a Jewish homeland in 1947 collided head-on with rising Arab nationalism, pride, and quest for independence. To Arab nationalists, it was outrageous that outside powers could preempt a piece of the "Arab nation" and turn it over to other outsiders to build an alien enclave in the Arabs' midst.

Given this profound conviction, a dialogue between a Western visitor and an Arab nationalist was likely to be a futile exercise:

Western Visitor: "But the land that the UN gave to the Jews constituted only one half of one percent of all the land in the Arab World. Surely, the Arabs could live happily in the remaining ninety-nine and a half percent."

Arab Nationalist: "But Arabs were living on that land and their ancestors had lived there seven hundred years before them."

Western Visitor: "But Jews were there first. They have roots and traditions there that go back to Biblical times."

Arab Nationalist: "But the Jews didn't stay there. We did."

If one invoked compassion, as Andrei Gromyko did at the UN, and argued that the world owes Jews a place to call their own after the Hitler slaughter, the reply was:

"Anti-semitism is a Western disease. We never suffered from it. You created the problem of the persecuted Jew. Why solve it at our expense?"

Because of these feelings, the continued existence of Israel brings other Arab traits into play:

The Lebanese scholar, Cecil Hourani, who for ten years was a close advisor to President Bourguiba of Tunisia, put it this way:

"That which we do not like we pretend does not exist. Because we refused to recognize a situation which was distasteful to us (the existence of Israel), we were unable to define our own relationship to that situation, or to distinguish between what we would have liked ideally, and what we were able to achieve in practice." [2]

Had the Arab World accepted the reality of Israel as created by the UN, there would be no Israeli-Arab problem today, Dr. Hourani argues. For, had it remained within its UN partition borders, says Dr. Hourani, Israel would have been "confined to a tiny territory which was strategically weak and scarcely viable economically." In time, "Israel would have become just another Levantine state, part Jewish, part Arab, but overwhelmingly Oriental."

But by nurturing fantasies of conquest, the Arabs precipitated wars from which Israel emerged bigger and bigger.

The war of 1948, for instance, virtually doubled Israel's original territory. To feelings of injustice the defeat now added the more corrosive emotions of outraged pride and a living reminder of Arab shame: the homeless Palestinian war refugees. New fears and fantasies arose.

One was that the million-odd Jews already in Israel in 1948 were only a beginning. There were 13 million Jewish Americans, Englishmen, Frenchmen, and Russians out there in the Western world, and they all meant someday to come and live in Israel.

It was futile to point out the reality to an Arab—that Jewish

2 Cecil Hourani, "The Moment of Truth," *Encounter*, Nov., 1967.

Americans and Europeans like it so well where they are, that few have immigrated to Israel. As for the 3 million Jewish citizens of Russia, they were barred from leaving, even if they wanted to.

To this an Arab would reply:

"Yes, but the Bible predicts that the Jews will one day hold dominion over land from the Nile to the Euphrates. In fact, this prediction is inscribed on the walls of the Knesset (Israeli Parliament) in Jerusalem."

Of course, there is no such inscription. Nor does *Genesis* mention the Nile. "Unto thy seed," the Lord tells Abraham, "have I given this land from the river of Egypt unto the great river, the river Euphrates." Biblical scholars believe the "river of Egypt" may refer to a *wadi* (dry lake) in today's Sinai.

Along with this fear of a Jewish super-State goes another: Israel is a bridgehead for the expansion of Western imperialist interests in the Arab World. It is an article of Arab faith that the Western powers foisted the state of Israel on the Arabs. It is futile to point out the reality: that it was the Soviet bloc that led the fight for a Jewish state, and that the Soviet Union was the first to grant formal recognition to Israel.

Looking southward in 1955, Khrushchev was eager to play friend to the aggrieved Arab World. The needs and drives of that world's chief leader, President Nasser, provided the opportunity.

As one of a band of "Young Officers" who overthrew King Farouk, Nasser like Khrushchev—came to power via collective leadership. Like Khrushchev, Nasser had the gift of elastic maneuver that soon levitated him to the top. By 1955 he was both "El Rayis," the president, and "El Rayiis," the boss.

The handsome, six-foot Nasser resembled the strikingly plain five-foot, five-inch Khrushchev in yet another way. He, too, was able to convince the West he was a moderate man. Nasser could tell the editor of a neo-Nazi West German weekly that he meant to crush Israel and add for good measure: "Our sympathies were with the Germans in the second world war. Nobody seriously believes the lie that six million Jews were murdered." Then, Nasser could talk so reasonably to the editor of the pro-Israel *Manchester Guardian* that the editor would go away convinced that Nasser was an enlightened socialist who didn't intend his threats against Israel's Jews to be taken seriously.

A British correspondent, James Morris, described how Nasser projected the image of the moderate man.

"Sensible liberalism oozes from his manner," the correspondent wrote. "Nasser will be in his shirtsleeves, his shirt showing between his vest buttons, and he will talk pleasantly and intelligently for as long as you like.

"And what will he tell you? That all he wants for Egypt is peace and prosperity. The West has constantly thwarted him—he will say with an air of letting bygones be bygones—by supporting the intruder state of Israel, by refusing him arms to defend Egypt against Israeli attacks.

"The hours will slip by easily as he expounds these persuasive theories, compounded of understandable patriotism and kindly reproach. The coffee cups will come and go, and when the President rises from his table to see you to the door, his sandals flip-flopping across the linoleum, you may well walk out into the night a warm believer in the liberalism of Col. Nasser."

Nasser's needs and drives inevitably propelled him toward Khrushchev and entrapment into the role of Soviet proxy.

Nasser spelled out these drives in his own "Mein Kampf," *The Philosophy of the Revolution.* Three heroic roles beckoned to him, Nasser wrote, in three separate geographical spheres he described as "circles."

First, there was the "Arab Circle"—the Arab World which cried out for a hero to unite and lead it. Second was the "African Circle"—the African continent. The "Third Circle" was nothing less than all Islam, i.e., everybody who believed in Muhammed. Nasser reckoned this involved some 460 million souls in lands stretching from Indonesia and Malaya in Southeast Asia to the Arab nations and Iran in the Middle East.

Nasser had little with which to turn his three-ring dream into reality.

Although Egypt is almost as large as France and Spain combined, 96 percent of it is unused desert. It's as if, in the United States, only an area the size of Montana was available to feed and provide raw materials for all of the country. Worse, the limited land—some 5 million acres—had to feed a population that grows at the rate of seven hundred thousand a year. Egypt had no oil at the time of Nasser's rise, and had developed but little of its mineral resources.

The picture of human resources was just as bleak. Even today, there are really two Egypts: one, of 8 million city dwellers who are the nucleus of a modern society, another of 22 million fellaheen (peasants or agricultural laborers). These still ply the primitive agricultural tools of Pharaonic times. They see virtually no money the year-round, subsist on an inadequate three pounds of corn bread and some onions a day, and suffer ancient afflictions, such as bilharziasis (a parasitic disease that attacks the bladder and rectum) whose ravages can be seen in the listless aspect of two-thirds of the fellaheen. To this, in dust-blown villages and bustling Alexandria and Cairo alike, add the incredibly widespread use of narcotics. Some 30 percent of Egyptians, so a member of the National Assembly found, smoke hashish. In Cairo a psychiatrist found that 70 percent of the city's bus drivers were addicted to hashish or opium. (Along with the military booty the Israelis took in the Sinai Desert after the Six-Day War, was a ton of hashish. The Israelis destroyed it.)

If Nasser had military power, (he felt in 1955) he could build economic power as well. For with military power, he could achieve his "first-circle" goal, that of uniting and leading the Arab World. By uniting with—and leading—other Arab states, he could share in their oil riches. "Nasser's eternal target," as Jordan's King Hussein has declared, "is the oil-rich Persian Gulf." [3]

The shortest road to Arab leadership, Nasser knew, was to make the dream of conquering Israel come true. But this brought Nasser back to where he started, his need for military power.

For Nasser, this need—in 1955—was urgent. He had trained a corps of fedayeen (self-sacrificers) who crossed over from the Gaza Strip and from Jordan and Syria to attack settlements and mine roads and to blow up installations inside Israel. Nasser declared over Cairo Radio that this undeclared war would bring

[3] King Hussein, *Uneasy Lies the Head*, Bernard Geis Associates, 1962.

Israel to its knees. Instead, the Israelis demonstrated in February of that year that they could march into Cairo if they wished. In retaliation for the fedayeen raids, the Israelis easily destroyed the Taggert Fort inside Egypt's Gaza Strip, killing thirty-eight Egyptians and wounding thirty. The Egyptians were no match for the Israelis.

Nasser launched an anxious search for modern arms, first in the West which turned him down (Britain and the U.S. wanted to know what Nasser would use them for; Nasser refused to say); then in the Soviet Union, which was eager to comply—no questions asked.

The wily Khrushchev now had his foot in the door—and a trap in his hand.

Nasser was delighted to find that he could get Soviet Migs and tanks and submarines at bargain prices: 40 percent off the "diplomatic price," the price at which one country usually sells arms to another. And he could pay for them on an easy payment plan, by mortgaging his cotton and rice crops far into the future.

Nasser was delighted to find, too, that Khrushchev seemingly attached no strings to the deal. But the strings were there—to ensnarl even so wary a customer as Nasser.

Khrushchev flooded Nasser with so many arms—$80 million worth in the first year, $170 million worth in the next two— that there was no room for purchases from the West. Even if he wanted, Nasser could not balance his Soviet arms with purchases from other sources, and so reduce his reliance on one supplier. Nasser also relied on the Soviet Union completely for spare parts—and these could be turned on and off, to squeeze Nasser.

To reassure the West that he remained a neutral, Nasser declared:

"We are importing arms, not political ideas." But "importing ideas" was one of the hidden strings of Khrushchev's "no strings" deal, too. Since Nasser depended on the Russians for training in the use of the new weapons, Egyptian officers went to the Soviet Union, and Russian military advisors came to Egypt.

Some five thousand Egyptian officers destined for middle or

senior grade leadership came to Moscow over the next decade. They spent from two months to a year at Soviet military and technical schools that taught them how to handle and maintain the Russian equipment, how to command brigades and divisions, how to plan a campaign. (The instruction, seemingly, was specific. When Israeli troops overran Egyptian command posts in Gaza and in the Sinai, they found exercise maps, made in the Soviet Union, telling Egyptians how to take and occupy Jerusalem, Haifa, Tel Aviv. Place names were in Cyrillic characters, written over with Arabic.)

After school hours, the Egyptian officers were fair game for the ideas that Nasser said he was not importing. The officers were taken on excursions to industrial showplaces to marvel at the "socialist achievements" of Soviet technology. They visited Soviet arsenals to view and be impressed with Soviet military might. Some participated in study groups of the Soviet system. At night there was good fellowship and entertainment for all who sought it. Where especially close Russian-Egyptian friendships blossomed, Soviet military intelligence recruited Egyptian officers as agents and informers.

Meanwhile, back at the Cairo Airport, twenty-one gun salutes, honor guards, and welcoming bands became an almost daily occurrence as Soviet dignitaries, their uniformed breasts blazing with emblems of their high rank, journeyed down to Egypt.

The first deputy defense minister came, and so did the chief of staff of the Soviet navy. The chief of Soviet military intelligence came to consult and instruct, and so did the deputy commander of the Soviet air force. Paraded through shouting Cairo crowds, the Soviet bigwigs were visible proof that the Arab world had a new, powerful friend. All was for the best in the poorest of all worlds. There would be more jobs and food for everybody. Israel would be wiped off the map.

Five hundred Soviet and Czechoslovak technicians and military advisors poured into Cairo. Their job, ostensibly, was to train Egyptian officers to operate tanks and fly Migs, and to show Egyptian mechanics how to maintain them. But the advisors and technicians had other duties. As agents in a Soviet intelligence network, centered in the Soviet Embassy, they soon knew every foot of every military and naval installation in Egypt. Seemingly, they had orders to act independently of their Egyptian pupils in time of crisis. When the British and French attacked the Suez area in 1956, the Soviet military advisors surprised—and outraged— the Egyptians by getting into their new, light Soviet bombers and flying them out, first to Damascus, then to the Soviet Union for safety.

With the invisible strings, there were visible ones. Along with the weapons, separate agreements called for the delivery of Soviet culture. A Soviet Cultural Center sprouted in Cairo. Russian ballet troupes and opera companies came. Egyptian schoolchildren and club members began to view documentaries and full-length films that glamorized Soviet life. Communist bookshops opened where none existed before. Egyptian journalists and doctors journeyed to Moscow.

Amidst all this good feeling, Egypt's illegal Communist Party, which had been fighting Nasser's "Fascist persecution of Egyptian progressive forces," now flip-flopped over and supported Nasser. Some Communists moved into key press and radio jobs and gave a new gloss to Egypt's anti-Western propaganda.

Cairo Radio broadcasters who had announced Communist purgings and jailings in early 1955, soon read from new scripts.

"American democracy leaves the capitalists free to rule the country," one commentator instructed his listeners. "But the Soviet Union is a true democracy, in which the rulers are chosen by the people through the Communist Party."

Nasser had let the Russian bear's muzzle into the Arab tent. More of the bear followed as Khrushchev widened the opening with other Khrushchevian maneuvers. One was "love through hate." If the way to Arab hearts was through hostility toward Israel, the Soviet Union would out-Arab the Arabs with campaigns of hatred.

The first step in the "love through hate" campaign was to rewrite history so as to make the Arabs love it. In 1948, when Soviet satellite arms helped Israel survive, the Communist press called the Arab invasion of the young state an "unjust war."

Israel's struggle for independence won official Communist approval as a "war of liberation."

But in 1957, Radio Moscow and the Soviet press discovered that "Israel was the aggressor in the war of 1948," after all. The Communist line, beamed in Arabic to Middle East listeners, now was that "Israel had taken advantage of the young Arab national movement."

With the Soviet discovery of Israeli perfidy in 1948 came other discoveries more sinister. Israel, it turned out, wasn't an independent country, after all. "It was a stooge of Western imperialism and the willing instrument of CIA plots against Arab independence."

The Kremlin's propaganda experts invented a technique for telling the Arabs what they wanted to hear and shutting Arab eyes to what the Russians, themselves, were up to in the area.

First, the Soviet press announced the discovery of an imminent Israeli attack on its neighbors. Press and radio repeated the discovery over and over until Arab radios and press picked up the accusation virtually word-for-word. Then, the Soviet press presented the Arab echoings as authentic news from the area, to support the Soviet allegation.

For instance, in July, 1957, a Soviet newspaper reported that "the aggressive circles of Israel are working out, with the support of the United States, plans for a military assault on Syria. With the knowledge of Washington, Israeli forces are being concentrated on the Syrian frontier. . . . By means of these provocations the American imperialists are aiming to draw Syria and Egypt into war with Israel, in order then to intervene by military force in their domestic affairs." (Please note that this fabrication, repeated ten years later, helped precipitate the June, 1967, war.)

Then, after Arab newspapers and radio had picked up this Moscow scare, Soviet journals quoted them as evidence.

"It is no secret to anyone that Israel is pursuing this policy (i.e., "provocations") at the dictation of Washington," a Russian paper wrote. "In connection with this, *the Egyptian newspaper Al-Sha'ab writes that the United States is inciting Israel to provocative actions against Egypt for the single purpose of 'causing a crisis' and creating complications in this part of the world.*"

To the campaign of "love through hate," was added "love through flattery."

When Nasser paid his first state visit to the Soviet Union on April 29, 1958, Khrushchev organized a welcome fit for the mighty of the earth. A Soviet jet transport brought Nasser to Moscow in style, and as it approached Moscow airport, nine Yak fighters provided an honor escort. A military band played a solemn march as the Nasser plane taxied to a halt on the runway. Waiting on a rolled-out red carpet was everybody who was anybody in the higher echelons of the Soviet Government and Communist Party. The smiling Khrushchev was there to embrace Nasser; so was the head of state, the grizzled Marshal Voroshilov.

On the wall of an airport building, facing Nasser as he alighted, was a huge portrait of Nasser side-by-side with that of Marshal Voroshilov, with the hammer and sickle blessing both. Nasser could see his own smiling face on portrait cards waving in the hands of several thousand schoolchildren. Nasser rode like a hero in an open car through the Moscow streets, while thousands of citizens, dutifully marshalled for the occasion, waved Egyptian and Soviet flags. Several days later, Nasser did what no other head of a non-Communist state had done before. Beside the Soviet Union's great, he reviewed the annual May Day parade in which the Soviets traditionally demonstrate their might.

Naturally, when Nasser needed loans to launch his first 5-year development plan—and to build the Aswan High Dam—he turned to his new friend, Khrushchev. This opened further vistas of opportunity for propaganda victories over the West and for further Russian ensnarement of Nasser.

Consider the Aswan High Dam.

An Egyptian could crane his neck at the mountain of concrete, one-third of a mile high and two miles across, and reflect ecstatically that thanks to the Russians, Egypt could boast undertakings such as it had not seen since the Pharaohs. Pharaohs? Why, the Aswan Dam was seventeen times the cubic size of the Pyramids!

Visiting Arab leaders from Syria, Lebanon, and Jordan could marvel at the economic and technological power of a Communist system that harnessed the Nile and provided the irrigation that would add one million two hundred thousand arable acres to Egypt's tillable land, a 25 percent boost. To the underdeveloped world, the Aswan Dam had the smashing psychological impact of a Sputnik.

And there was the delicious irony that the Americans, unwittingly, helped pay for the Soviet economic aid triumph. The $500 million of loans (about one-third of the total cost) that the Soviet Union advanced for construction and materials was to be repaid with Egyptian cotton and rice. In 1963 and 1964 the United States shipped some $400 million of wheat and rice under Public Law 480 provisions (payment in Egyptian currency on a long-term, deferred basis). The American rice permitted the Egyptians to ship their own rice to the Soviet Union in repayment for Aswan construction loans!

As for Soviet loans for Nasser's five-year plan, the Russians—so economists, who studied the deal, concluded—were out to overload Nasser with debt and turn Egypt into an economic fief.

One expert who spent five years in Egypt studying its economy reported: "They (the Russians) sought to provide Egypt with credits far in excess of the country's absorptive capacity . . . and to gain political advantage by over-extending the Egyptian economy." The authority, Keith Wheelock of the University of Pennsylvania, stated further: "For a country that wished to help Egypt," the Soviet Union imposed "some extraordinary conditions to the economic development loan" agreement. "The Egyptians had to pay separately for the expense of Soviet technicians in Egypt and for Egyptian trainees in the Soviet Union." They also had to borrow additional sums from the Russians to pay for ocean freight, most spare parts, raw materials—at terms that were higher than those in the economic assistance agreement.

Nasser found himself in a further bind. Most of Egypt's exports, consisting of cotton, soon were flowing to the Soviet Union and satellite countries to pay for the arms and other deals. But most of Egypt's buying continued from the West. As this caused Egypt to run out of foreign currency, the *London Times* observed:

"Behind that formula (selling too much to the East, and buying too much from the West) lies a Muscovite lesson in elementary political economy in which President Nasser's dream of independence from the West has been neatly concerted into the fact of strangulation by the East."

Economic aid "without strings" had deepened the Egyptian dependence on the Soviet Union that the arms aid, "without strings," had begun. More, the "no strings" economic aid was tying Egypt—the bellwether nation of the Arab World—economically into the Soviet bloc.

The Sixth Fleet and American bases in the Middle East had stood guard against the classic forms of Communist expansion: domestic insurrection or a putsch from outside. But Khrushchev had used a new tactic—"arms diplomacy." With it, he had leapfrogged the Sixth Fleet and American bases to wedge himself into the Middle East. More, he had a proxy behind whom he could widen the Soviet beachhead in the Arab world. Nasser, beefed up by Soviet arms—and pursuing his own, nationalist aims —proceeded to fulfill the role in which Khrushchev had cast him —"the instrument of Soviet policy in the Middle East."

4

ARABIAN
NIGHTMARE

On a May day in 1964, at the Aswan High Dam, Nikita Khrushchev addressed President Nasser as "Comrade." He pinned the gold star of the Order of Lenin on Nasser's chest and conferred on him the title "Hero of the Soviet Union." This is the highest honor bestowed in the USSR. The Presidium of the Supreme Soviet votes it for extraordinary services to the Soviet Union.

By using Nasser as a conduit for Soviet arms, or by employing Soviet-trained Egyptian soldiers and guerrillas, the Soviet Union had waged wars of liberation without deploying one Red Army soldier or without even showing its hand. Nasser had helped depose Yemen's king and drive the British from Aden. Nasser's agents helped topple the pro-Western Iraqi monarchy and came within a hair's breadth of turning Jordan and Lebanon into pro-Soviet-bloc Egyptian satellites. Egyptian agents smashed American attempts to build a collective anti-Communist effort by Arab states.

Meanwhile, thanks to Nasser, the Kremlin had built an old-fashioned military and political presence in the Middle East, including air and naval base facilities, yet avoiding the stigma of "imperialism." Soviet Antonov transports landed on Egyptian airstrips. Their crews changed the Russian markings on the planes to Egyptian markings, then went about their secret business of delivering intelligence agents, money, and weapons to subversion targets in Syria, and Aden or Somalia, across the Red Sea in Africa. Soviet naval vessels put in at Alexandria or Port Said and, calling it merely a "visit," enjoyed all the benefits of a naval base. They refueled, had access to drydocks for repairs, and didn't even have to send home for spare parts. The Egyptian Navy, composed mostly of Soviet-built vessels, conveniently stocked them. Sometimes, when the Russians sought the secrecy they enjoyed back home, the Egyptians gave up their sovereignty over substantial sections of their harbors. Soviet troops cordoned off and policed the repair area.

As a further service to his Soviet sponsors, Nasser turned the Arab World into an Arabian nightmare of suspicion, intrigue, and turbulent instability. This diverted Arab energies and resources from the urgent task of bringing into the twentieth century one of the poorest, sickest and least trained people on the face of the earth. It also created a climate in which the Soviets·could nurture further conquests and further penetration.

"Not one country is safe!"

No other country's diplomats, not even those of the Soviet Union, have been booted from so many countries so many times as those of Egypt. Caught red-handed in plot and skullduggery, Egyptian ambassadors, consuls, and military and cultural attachés have been shown the border by the Congo, Ethiopia, Guinea, Iran, Iraq, Italy, Jordan, Lebanon, Libya, Malawi, Saudi Arabia, Sierra Leone, The Sudan, Tunisia, Turkey, Tanganyika, and Upper Volta.

To get caught out so often involves a certain professional untidiness. At times this has had its comic as well as macabre side.

In 1964 three members of the Egyptian Embassy in Rome were interrupted in the act of shipping out to Cairo, as diplomatic baggage, a double agent trussed up in an oversized wooden box. The wretch, drugged and gagged as he was, managed to raise a ruckus that brought the startled airport police. (The trunk, devised in Cairo by an ex-German SS expert, was so well-worn, the police believed it had been used often for similar diplomatic shipments.)

Yet, the Egyptian operatives could be effective, too. None of Nasser's fellow Arab rulers could be sure when they went to bed at night, that cloaked Egyptian agents, hatching conspiracy on some backstairs nearby, would not have his head by morning.

Nasser's hatchet men engineered the demise of pro-Western King Faisal of Iraq and his prime minister—so King Hussein of Jordan has charged. They also did in one of Hussein's prime ministers, blowing up a government building in the process, and killing twelve others. And Nasser's men kept trying. Those who got away make up a distinguished club: the Shah of Iran, Kings Hussein, Idris of Libya, and Saud of Saudi Arabia; Presidents Bourguiba of Tunisia and Camille Chamoun of Lebanon.

"Not one [Arab] country is safe from his [Nasser's] plotting!" King Saud once cried.

Behind the plotting was a Nasserite cold war against his neighbors, set in the context of the larger East-West Cold War.

When Nasser came to power, he talked of conquering Egypt's poverty and of building a modern Egypt. But when he and his "Young Officers" took a startled look at Egypt's resources and multiplying population, and realized the job would take decades, they sought shortcuts to power and glory beyond their borders.

Nasser aimed at Egyptian dominion from the Atlantic to the Persian Gulf. Control of Libya to the west, and Sudan to the south, for example, would provide *Lebensraum* for Egypt's surplus millions. Control of the Persian Gulf area would yield oil riches and the sinews of power.

And what Nasser wanted in the way of empire, his sponsors— the Soviets—wanted, too. For, as in the Mother Goose rhyme, wherever Nasser went, Russian arms and influence were sure to go.

To Soviet arms, the Kremlin added other aid that gave Nasser's foreign adventures a larger and more ominous dimension.

First, there was the gift of Communist rhetoric. The Soviets hide their expansionist aims under slogans of "world revolution" and "the victory of socialism." Nasser aped the Communists and raised the banner of "The Arab Revolution" and "Arab Socialism."

The Soviets provided clandestine collaboration from their own intelligence network in the area. Fully 90 percent of the Soviet Embassy staff in Lebanon, for instance, are intelligence operatives. In Iran, it's 80 percent (for years, in Teheran, the Soviet Embassy hid itself conspiratorially behind a twelve-foot-high wall with all gates barred, until the Iranians requested that one gate be left open). In Kuwait, 70 percent of the Soviet Embassy staff consists of intelligence agents. An average 60 percent of Soviet Embassy staffs in the Middle East double as intelligence agents.

From these, Nasser's agents received guidance and operating money as well. In 1958 King Hussein's security police discovered that after every important cabinet meeting three key ministers, including the Army chief of staff, took off for Damascus to closet themselves with the Soviet military attaché there. They returned, so Hussein's agents learned, with money to buy up army officers and political figures.

The Soviets also supplied Nasser with a pattern for subversive operations. The Soviet Union has organized its foreign relations on two levels, one—the diplomatic corps—open, the other, underground. Nasser followed suit. His close friend and spokesman, Muhammed Hassanain Haikal, editor of *Al Ahram*, makes no bones about it.

"Egypt is both a state and a revolution," he has written. "As a state, Egypt deals with all Arab governments . . . but as a revolution, Egypt deals only with people, crossing borders to initiate [revolution]."

The secret or underground instrument of "Egypt as a revolution" is General Intelligence, known as the al-Mukhaberat al-Amma.

The key operative of the Mukhaberat is the military attaché.

Nasser regards the military man as the most reliable and loyal. He also knows how to use weapons and sabotage materials and how to organize quasi-military uprisings. Cultural attachés, consuls, and even ambassadors double as Mukhaberat operatives. Because they enjoy diplomatic immunity, they are merely ushered to the border when caught plotting.

Until Soviet intelligence lent a guiding hand in 1958, the Mukhaberat was not distinguished for James Bondian finesse. Its diplomat-agents organized subversive fronts and other conspiracies openly, as if they were in their own country. Mukhaberat agents also ran a kind of bargain basement operation. They hired small armies of sub-agents, recruited from among the host country's small merchants, gas station operators, and others of the lower middle class, paying them a modest forty to fifty dollars monthly. These, in turn, hired hangers-on from the underworld and the jobless to work at piece rates: so much for distributing leaflets, or inciting a riot, or lobbing a bomb at a head of state.

The Russians tried to teach the Egyptians to use greater care in disguising their embassies' links with local agents, and to hire more reliable agents. More important, the Russians induced the Mukhaberat to work with local Communist Parties. Most Arab communist leaders have learned the conspiratorial trade in Moscow and have the skill and zest for it of old Bolsheviks.

The Mukhaberat worked at two chief tasks: to prevent Arab leaders from joining Western-sponsored mutual assistance pacts. (Such arrangements obviously hampered Nasser's efforts to tie Arab nations to his own kite.) They also tried to prevent Arab nations from amalgamating. Such *anschlusse*, too, would frustrate Nasserite designs. As sidelines and labors of love, Mukhaberat agents blew up Western oil installations, or procured terrorist gangs for forays into Israel.

In its machinations against pro-Western Arab neighbors, the Mukhaberat had an important resource, the Arab character.

The Lebanese-born sociologist, Dr. Sania Hamady, in her book *Temperament and Character of the Arabs*, explains it this way:

"Rarely does the Arab set his goal in the interest of his nation. He aims primarily at the improvement of the fate and position of his family and religious group. . . . The allegiance toward the state is shaky, and identification with leaders is not strong. Furthermore, there prevails a general mistrust of those that govern and lack of faith in them."

Consequently, the Mukhaberat could suborn treason outside Egypt by bribery even among high Arab government officials. The lack of allegiance to one's country or monarch had its bizarre manifestations.

Once, when Jordan's King Hussein fired a traitorous prime minister, the king's agents intercepted a Cairo cable to the official. It read:

"Do not give in. Remain in your position. Nasser."

Hussein's—and Jordan's—ordeal at the hands of the Mukhaberat provides a short, short story—both comic and sinister—of its methods.

When King Hussein of Jordan was twenty-seven years old in 1962, he wrote his memoirs. Men usually don't write memoirs at so youthful an age. But, perhaps, the young king didn't think he had many more years left. For the name of his book was *Uneasy Lies the Head*. In it Hussein relates how he almost lost *his* thirteen times. Most of these near misses Hussein traced to plots by Egyptian agents enjoying diplomatic privilege in his country.

The attempts to do him in were as varied as they were frequent. First, the Mukhaberat ambushed and shot-up a royal car. Hussein wasn't in it; an uncle, who was, escaped with bruises when the car careened into a ditch. Somebody in the king's household then put acid in the nose drops Hussein used for his sinus trouble. The plot was discovered and the phial was emptied. "The drops poured out," Hussein recalls, "with a hiss, as if they were alive." Sometime later, a cook, planning to poison the King's dinner, tried the potion on a cat first. The cat, seemingly, had less lives than the king. Its carcass, discovered on the palace grounds, gave the game away.

To stay alive, Hussein needed special talents.

Only Hussein's skill as an air force pilot saved him in November, 1958. Two Soviet Mig 17s, bearing the markings of the U.A.R. Air Force, attacked Hussein's plane over Syria as he flew to Europe. Hussein ducked down to ground level zero and skittered along like a scared rabbit—with the two planes diving at him—until he reached the sanctuary of his own border.

Hussein's Jordan had even closer calls than he did. In 1955, the year of Egypt's arms deal with the Soviets, Nasser's Mukhaberat almost turned Jordan into an Egyptian satellite. The previous year, the United States had induced Great Britain, Turkey, Pakistan, Iran, and Iraq to form a defense alliance (The Baghdad Pact) against Soviet Union penetration. In December the British, who trained and officered Jordan's army, sent their chief of staff to Amman to urge Hussein to join the pact. Hussein, then twenty, asked for time to seek the advice and consent of President Nasser.

Nasser's answer came promptly—but indirectly—via his Mukhaberat operative in Jordan, the military attaché, Colonel Mahmud Salah A-Din Mustafa. He ambushed and shot-up a royal household car, but Hussein wasn't in it.

The Mukhaberat operative took other steps. First, he persuaded young Jordanian officers to agitate against British control of Jordan's army. Soon, the British—led by Lt.-General Sir John Bagot Glubb, who had been in Jordan twenty-six years and was called Glubb Pasha—packed their bags. Hussein had to fire Glubb or face an army revolt. Next, with the help of Jordanian communists, Mustafa organized street riots in Amman, bringing in pro-Nasser Palestinian refugees for the demonstrations. Confronted by turbulent mobs and threatened by his own army, young Hussein backed away from the Baghdad Pact. So did Saudi Arabia and Lebanon. This was a great victory for the Soviet Union and the first big dividend from its arms investment in Nasser. As a curious footnote to the Egyptian military attaché's activities, King Hussein didn't ask for his expulsion. He was afraid to offend Nasser! (Col. Mustafa died as he had lived. A package delivered to him through the Jordanian mails exploded in his face. Since Col. Mustafa had been organizing terrorist raids against Israel on the side, it was believed the package was a billet-doux from Israeli Counterintelligence—the redoubtable Shin Beth.)

Hussein could never know whether he was sitting on a throne or a volcano.

"I am not ashamed to say that at times I felt even death itself would be a welcome relief," Hussein has said. "But I had to put on a good face. And so each day I was up with the dawn, usually after a miserable, sleepless night. I would dress quickly . . . and would take care to include in my dress a smile of confidence in our future."

From time to time Hussein broke off relations with Nasser, but patched up matters to avoid being isolated from the Arab world. But even during the stretches of peace, Cairo Radio kept hammering at him as "the traitor King Hussein." Once, when Hussein asked Nasser to explain the broadcasts, Nasser replied:

"But this is the first I've heard of it."

But for the grace of Israel, Hussein would have lost his country in 1958.

Hussein had joined his Jordan to that of King Faisal's Iraq. One Hashemite kingdom, it was felt, had a better chance of surviving against Nasser than two. Soon after, King Faisal (then twenty-three years old, like Hussein) and his prime minister were murdered.

"Exterminate the criminal King of Jordan as well," Cairo Radio demanded.

In Cairo Radio broadcasts after dark, Hussein was reminded of young Faisal's dismal end. Unless he abdicated, Hussein, too, could expect "blood," "agony," "dangling corpses," "murder," "screams," "mutilated bodies dragged in the streets." Only the creaking doors and clanking chains were missing.

Syria, then a province of Egypt, closed its border to Jordan, cutting Jordan's fuel lifeline from Lebanon. Jordan faced an electric power blackout and a shutdown of pumps that supplied water to Amman and other cities.

In extremis, Hussein appealed to the United States to airlift oil from the Persian Gulf across Saudi Arabia. But to Hussein's amazement, his Arab brother, King Saud of Saudi Arabia, refused to let American planes overfly his territory. Jordan seemed doomed, and Saud didn't want trouble with Nasser. But help came from an unexpected quarter. Israel opened its airspace to permit fuel to be flown down from Lebanon. "Our Arab friends refused to let us fly over their country—the air of brother Arabs," Hussein commented bitterly. "Where an Arab nation refused, an enemy agreed." In Lebanon, incidentally, American marines from the Sixth Fleet had just landed to prevent a Nasser-supported Communist uprising from toppling the pro-Western President Camille Chamoun.

Hussein expected the Mukhaberat to unleash street mobs against him at any moment and asked the British and Americans to send troops. With the U.S. occupied in Lebanon, the British answered the call. Again, Israel was the rescue corridor.

Hussein never did learn that as long as Israel stands, Jordan stands, for Israel has always regarded a threat againt Jordan as a threat against itself.

Early in its career, the Mukhaberat took a leaf from the Communist book and experimented with "wars of liberation."

To Libya, in 1956, as military attaché, came Mukhaberat Col. Ismail Sadek. To liberate Libya's oil and living space, Sadek organized a "Libyan People's Front," armed it with Soviet rifles and machine guns, and—in open incendiary speeches—urged it to rise against King Idris. When the People's Front took to tossing hand grenades into government officials' homes in Tripoli, King Idris demanded that Col. Sadek leave the country. Outraged at this lack of diplomatic courtesy, Sadek refused. Libyan police escorted him to the border anyway. A subsequent search of the People's Front headquarters revealed that the Egyptian attaché had begun to build a secret arsenal of Soviet weapons with the aim of arming Bedouin tribesmen against Idris.

When the Libyans protested to Nasser, he sent a personal note to Libya's prime minister.

"I hope," Nasser wrote, "that Egyptian-Libyan relations will not suffer as a consequence of the activities of the Egyptian military attaché, Col. Sadek."

To which the Libyan prime minister replied with equal courtesy that "this affair would not damage the relations between the two countries."

While "this affair" didn't damage relations, it didn't stop the Mukhaberat either.

Between 1958 and 1966, four more Egyptian military attachés

were expelled for fomenting sedition and for sabotage. In 1966, a Mukhaberat operative confessed he had organized the destruction of $2 million worth of Esso Standard and British Petroleum Company oil stores. Czech explosives blew up the storage depots. Seventeen workmen lost their lives.

As new states south of the Sahara emerged into statehood and accepted diplomatic missions, new horizons of mischief opened up for Nasser's Mukhaberat. Here, Nasser served as a double front for the Soviet Union. His Mukhaberat labored to undermine young African regimes and to replace them with pro-Communist governments. Egypt also served as a staging area for Soviet weapons airlifted in Soviet transport planes to pro-Communist rebels.

In Africa, the Mukhaberat used a new weapon of subversion —religion. Many African countries have substantial Moslem populations. Wherever an Egyptian embassy was established, it became the headquarters for well-heeled efforts to organize Moslem minorities into dissident factions, to split the host country, and to prepare a pro-Communist takeover.

Along with the military attaché, a new Mukhaberat agent appeared, the cultural attaché. He contacted leaders of Moslem communities and sought, by bribery or intimidation, to turn them against their government.

Some curious purveyors of Moslem culture turned up in African capitals.

Consider Lt. Col. Ahmed Abdel Aziz Hilmi, military attaché to Ethiopia. Haile Selassie's country presented an attractive target to the Mukhaberat. It was and is staunchly pro-American and contains, at Asmara, the biggest American communications base in the Middle East. Ethiopia's 22,600,000 population is one-fourth Moslem. Col. Hilmi formed a Moslem League, and tried to stir up Ethiopia's Moslem tribes to rise against the Emperor.

Booted out of Ethiopia for "activities prejudicial to the state," Col. Hilmi moved on to Ghana. Here Col. Hilmi set up an Egyptian Cultural Center as a rallying ground for Ghana's Moslem minority. Ghana, too, sent Col. Hilmi packing and closed the Egyptian Cultural Center.

Another purveyor of Moslem culture to the Africans was a Major Hilal. Expelled from Jordan, then Lebanon, for plots against the lives of King Hussein and President Camille Chamoun, Hilal showed up in the new state of Malawi, when it was carved out of Nyasaland in 1964. He organized an airlift from Cairo to bring in pro-leftist enemies of the Malawi regime and tried to bribe leaders of the Moslem community and cabinet ministers to join in an uprising. Airlift and bribes were exposed, and Hilal found *himself* on an airlift back to Cairo.

Altogether, some thirty Egyptian diplomats were expelled from African countries between 1956 and 1966.

In his *The Philosophy of the Revolution*, Nasser wrote:

"The peoples of Africa will continue to look to us (Egypt) who guard their northern gate. We will never in any circumstances be able to relinquish our responsibility to support, with all our might, the spread of enlightenment . . . to the remotest depths of the jungle."

Africa's desperate need for teachers provided special opportunities for "enlightenment." An estimated five-thousand-odd Egyptian teachers were deployed on the Dark Continent during 1963, but the "enlightenment" they brought was not what the recipient countries had bargained for. It turned out that the teachers received careful espionage training before leaving Cairo, and worked closely with the Mukhaberat to foment sedition in the host country. As a major step in protecting itself against Egyptian intrigue Morocco fired all of its Egyptian teachers in 1963. Over Egyptian protests, Libya refused to rehire half of the eight hundred teachers it had imported from Egypt.

Distrust of communism below the Sahara and long memories of Arab slave traders (Saudi Arabia permitted slavery as late as 1965) create stumbling blocks for the Mukhaberat in Africa. Another stumbling block is Israel. Although virtually unnoticed at the time, an Israeli idea and training helped prevent Nasser and the Kremlin from turning the biggest and potentially richest new nation in Africa, the Congo, into Africa's first Communist state.

Israel's role centered about Lt. General Joseph Mobutu, now the Congo's President.

General Mobutu, a thin, nervous man who has been described as the "Hamlet of the Congo," is one of the few Congolese leaders who have studied in a European university. He seems to be the only leader capable of maintaining some semblance of internal peace and stability in the Congo.

By 1963, Mobutu—then thirty-two—had established himself both as the most powerful figure in the Congo and as chief enemy of Communist infiltration. In 1960, for instance, three months after independence, he had overthrown the pro-Soviet Patrice Lumumba and expelled the Soviet and Czech technicians that Lumumba had brought in. Mobutu described them as "Communist political agents," seeking to subvert his country.

Now, in 1963, Mobutu—as chief of staff—pondered a problem. United Nations peacekeeping forces were about to leave under Communist bloc pressure.

At Stanleyville, Antoine Gizenga, successor to the following of pro-Communist Patrice Lumumba, in contact with Nasser by wireless, prepared an uprising. At Brazzaville, the Egyptian Embassy distributed arms clandestinely to rebel forces. And at Cairo, followers of Gizenga proclaimed the creation of a "People's Republic of the Congo."

To cope with all this Mobutu had only his casually-trained and ill-equipped Congolese Army.

Mobutu took his problem to friendly embassies at Leopoldville (now Kinshasa). The Israeli Embassy called in a military team from Israel to study Mobutu's military problems. It came up with a suggestion.

"Form an elite corps of paratroopers with your best men. With them you have a mobile force that can defy jungles and appear wherever rebellion raises its head."

Mobutu picked two hundred fifty officers and men and flew with them to Israel for a cram course in paratroop jumping and tactics.

On the day that Lt. General Mobutu made his first parachute jump, Israel's top military men and government officials held their breaths. A mishap to the Congo's chief of staff could have been embarrassing to Israel as well as the Congo. He landed safely.

Later that day, with Mobutu's wife looking on—with a several-months-old baby in her arms—Israel's chief of staff pinned Israeli paratroop wings on Mobutu. He, in turn, pinned the paratroop wings on his men.

On his return to the Congo, Mobutu sent other contingents of trainees to Israel, and, by 1964, had a striking force of two thousand paratroops.

Paratroops, both Belgian and Congolese, played an important role when the UN forces pulled out. The Soviet Union mounted an arms airlift to Stanleyville, using Egypt as a staging area and Soviet-trained Egyptians as pilots. But Mobutu's army, spearheaded by his Israeli-trained paratroopers, and supplemented by white mercenaries, soon had the Gizenga rebels on the run. By 1965, Nasser announced he would ship no more weapons to the Congo. He feared they would fall into Government hands.

5

VOICE AGAINST
AMERICA

Radio listeners all over the Arab World know for sure that their armies were not defeated by those "outcasts and scum of the earth," the Jews. As everyone knows, Jews can't fight. A "triple aggression" by the United States, Britain, and Israel did the job. The Arab radio listener knows for sure, too, that President Johnson presided over a White House meeting that "drew up the aggression plan" a week before the war. And the Arab listener knows why: "to destroy Arab nationalism and Arab socialism." Above all, the Arab radio listener knows that the United States is "the main enemy"—a "pirate and a bloodsucker," intent on "tearing apart the Arab homeland, harming Arab dignity and exhausting Arab strengths."

The Arab radio listener knows all this because "The Voice of the Arabs," broadcast over Cairo Radio, keeps telling him so.

In its undeclared propaganda war against the West, then, the Kremlin didn't have to act directly in the Arab world and in Africa. Cairo Radio did the job.

Cairo Radio is second only to Moscow in the number of hours on the air, twelve hundred weekly. But neither Peking nor Moscow top the virulence and emotionalism of Cairo Radio's tirades against the "Number One Enemy," the United States. This main theme, intermingled with subsidiary themes of hatred against Israel and Arab countries friendly to the West, is beamed in thirty-two languages to the Arab World, to Africa, to Southeast Asia, to Europe, and to Latin America.

To Ethiopia and Somalia, for instance, Cairo Radio broadcasts in Amharic and Somali; to West Africa, in Hausa; to Southeast Asia in Malay, Pushtu, Thai, and Urdu; to the Congo, Rhodesia, and Zambia in Lingala, Ndebele, and Njanga; to Europe in English, French, Italian, German, and Arabic. And to Israel (described as "occupied Palestine") in Hebrew.

When Nasser came to power, Egypt boasted only two small radio transmitters that operated twenty-two hours daily. But, as a student of Hitler's *Mein Kampf* (Nasser had the volume translated for distribution in the Arab World), Nasser heeded what Hitler taught: great thinkers and writers don't activate revolutions —orators do. Nasser also had the Arab love of words and the shrewd knowledge that radio is the incomparable carrier of propaganda to the people of the underdeveloped world, most of whom are beyond the reach of the written word. Even in the dustiest and most impoverished of Arab villages, where the fellaheen bed down in their mud huts with their cattle and poultry, transistor radios abound. It is the first thing an Arab peasant buys. A Bedouin in the desert is just as likely to have a transistor dangling on his chest. "Of all the instruments of propaganda," *Middle Eastern Affairs* magazine has reported, "radio plays the most outstanding role in the political and social life of the Arab countries."

Why does a mini-nation like Egypt, whose national interests are by no means global, invest so much passion and gold in radio propaganda, including a campaign of hate against the United States?

For an answer, let's look briefly at the evolution of the Cairo Radio line.

From 1952—when Nasser came to power—through 1954, his horizons extended no farther than Egypt's borders, or at most to the sister Nile country, the Sudan. There were the remnants of the corrupt Farouk regime to be cleaned up, land to be divided among the fellaheen, schools to be built, births to be controlled. The accent on Cairo Radio was reform. A famous crooner, Muhammad Abdel Wahhab, composed a song called "Unity, Order, Work." It became the signature song before every news broadcast. In its study of Cairo Radio, The Council for Middle Eastern Affairs found that, during this time, Cairo Radio's interests were only in domestic affairs. "There was a complete absence of any talk whatsoever about 'Arab unity' or 'pan-Arabism.' " [1]

Then, beginning in 1954, Nasser and Cairo Radio raised their sights. Nasser had discovered that pulling Egypt up by its bootstraps was a task without promise and without end. If he could build one big Arab Union for all, he could solve Egypt's problems and win an instant place in the sun. To achieve the dream of a Nasserite Arab Empire, Nasser and Cairo Radio raised the slogans of "Arab Unity" and "Arab Nationalism."

To this, in late 1961, Nasser added the slogan of "Arab Socialism." Arab leaders had shown little enthusiasm for Nasser's Arab unity which meant, in effect, that they turn their countries into Egyptian provinces. Those who tried it, like the Syrians, quickly changed their minds. Nasser took a page from Communist imperialism and went after the minds of the people—80 million Arabs. Radio became the chief weapon of a psychological war which mixed equal parts of love and hate. It wooed the Arab common man with the Socialist panacea for his ailments and poisoned the air against all who stood in the way of Nasser's dream of empire. Chief of these was the United States, whose presence in the region built a wall against Nasser subversion.

To his own talents at waging psychological warfare, Nasser could call on the skills of some old hands at the game, men who had practiced the art under Hitler.

Cairo has been a haven for notorious Nazi war criminals, among them Friedrich Warzoch who is responsible for the death of sixty thousand Poles, Christians as well as Jews. The Nazi refugees include two collaborators of Adolph Eichmann: Alois

[1] "Radio Propaganda of the United Arab Republic—An Analysis" *Middle Eastern Affairs*, April, 1962.

Brunner and Franz Abromeit, who are wanted in Austria, Hungary, Czechoslovakia, and West Germany.

In Cairo, too, are former members of the Goebbels propaganda ministry who serve in Egypt's Ministry of Information. Students of Egyptian propaganda see in it the unmistakable Goebbels stamp.

Psychological warfare employs the tools of mass communication—radio, newspapers, books, popular songs—to sway an enemy peoples' minds and emotions in order to gain set objectives.

The "enemy" or target of Nasser's psychological warfare is the Arab people, including his own Egyptians. The objective is to convince Arabs everywhere, that Nasser is the infallible leader who is destined to weld a unified Arab nation. A parallel objective is to stir the Arab multitudes to rise against those who oppose this leadership: other Arab leaders who oppose Nasser's plans, or the United States and other Western powers who befriend threatened Middle Eastern nations.

In a military dictatorship like Egypt's, the image of unchallenged leadership is created by nurturing the "cult of personality" which saturates the public mind with the image of the sole leader.

A visitor to Egypt after the disastrous June war could see Nasser's confident face peering down from virtually every surface that could hold a poster: from newsstands in the heart of Cairo, from shop windows, from telegraph poles, fences, office walls. Nasser's face, the visitor could conclude, is the only image of leadership the Arab man-in-the-street can have in his head.

Outside of Egypt the image-building goes on with words and music over Cairo Radio.

Dozens of songs and ditties extolling Nasser are chanted over and over on Cairo Radio by Egypt's most popular singers. Disc jockeys play old Nasser speeches "on request." Some are six hours long.

In commentators' news analyses, and in speeches by Nasser's aides—and by himself—Nasser is always the peerless leader who makes no mistakes. Those who oppose him are doomed. The British prime minister, Anthony Eden, tried it in 1956, and fell from power. In a broadcast speech on May 3, 1967, Nasser put it this way: "We opposed Mr. Eden. Mr. Eden went away." The French premier, Guy Mollet, "went away" too. So did King Faisal and his prime minister. Nasser opposed the Baghdad Pact which they signed with the West, and look at what happened to them. The Iraqi people, Cairo likes to repeat, rose up and slaughtered them. Since you can't beat Nasser, Cairo Radio infers, you had better join him. Thanks to this canonization by Cairo Radio, Nasser has developed followings in some Arab nations which are more loyal to Nasser than to their own leaders. Despite two disastrous wars, he remains the incomparable god of the Nile, the all-powerful and all-wise Pharaoh.

Nasser's trumpet to the Arab World and Africa for years was a bald, portly little weaver of spells whose name, Ahmed Said, was a household word in millions of Arab apartments, mud huts, and tents. Many Arab mothers named their babies after him. At sundown, all over the Arab World, came a pause in the day's occupation as old and young tuned in on Ahmed Said's "Voice of the Arabs" broadcast and heard him—as one correspondent described it—"hiss and cry, shout and whisper," his daily burden of news and comment. There wasn't a slow pulse in the house.

The Arab language is musical and lends itself to poetry. It also abounds in devices for assertion and exaggeration and, as scholars tell us, has "great vituperative resources." A master of the language has an incomparable instrument for stirring the emotions of the multitudes. With Ahmed Said, the object—more often than not—was to arouse emotion rather than convey ideas.

"Here, United States," Ahmed Said screamed during the June War, "we shall bury the imperialist base Israel. Here, we shall bury the American international gangsterism. Here Arabs, dig graves everywhere; dig them [to bury] America; dig them, Arabs, dig all the homeland a grave for U.S. existence; dig it, Arabs; dig it, Arabs; dig it, Arabs; dig it, Arabs!"

Sometimes there was a direct call to action. To Libyans, during the June war, Said directed this appeal:

"Your brothers in the Saudi kingdom destroyed the buildings and installations of Aramco there. When will *you* proclaim to the world *your* wrath? When will you impose your Arabism on the

British-American oil companies in Libya? We are waiting, waiting for news agency dispatches to bring the good tidings about
your triumph."

To Arabs, words like these are as strong drink to Westerners.
Not a few riots and acts of sabotage have been traced to Said's
heady broadcasts.

For years, Said's invocations over "The Voice of the Arabs"
were directed against King Hussein of Jordan, whom Said called
the "Mickey Mouse King," or at King Feisal of Saudi Arabia,
known to Said's listeners as "the CIA-agent king," or at President
Bourguiba of Tunisia, whom Said dismissed as "the idiot Bourguiba."

As Nasser, prodded by the Russians, split the Arab World into
two hostile camps ("the progressive," i.e., socialist group, and the
"reactionary," i.e., pro-Western group), a new target emerged on
Cairo Radio—the United States.

Here, the big radio propaganda weapon was the "big lie."
Ahmed Said has been compared to Goebbels, but Said didn't have
much to learn from *that* master.

"Lying is a widespread habit among Arabs, and they have a
low idea of truth," the Lebanese-born sociologist, Sania Hamadi,
has written. "The Arab has no scruples about lying if by it he
achieves his objective. His conscience possesses an interesting
elasticity."

Miss Hamadi quotes a Muslim theologian:

"Know that a lie is not *haram* (wrong) in itself . . . If a lie is
the only way to reach a good result it is *halal* (allowable) . . ."

To reach "the good result" of arousing hatred against the
United States, Cairo Radio built an edifice of fabrications in
which whoppers are piled on whoppers to achieve a towering
mythology of American evil. Ahmed Said devised a special program, "Cherchez l'Amérique," (after the French, "cherchez la
femme") to build such myths.

The underlying, or basic invention—the one on which all
others are built—is that "The United States created the State of
Israel."

As we have seen, the Soviet Union and its satellites not only led the battle for the UN resolution to partition Palestine into Jewish and Arab states, but provided Israel with weapons to help it survive the Arab invasion of 1948. But this piece of history has long since been rewritten in Moscow and Cairo.

Cairo Radio plays the theme of U.S. responsibility for Israel's birth with ingenious and ever angrier variations. A sample from an Ahmed Said broadcast:

"Through terrorization, pressure, deception, and treachery, America succeeded in persuading a small majority of the UN member countries to support its plot, and thus through this devious way it managed to impose its aggressive plan for the setting up of a Jewish state in Palestine." [2]

Since he hears this myth over and over on Cairo Radio, the Arab is as sure of its truth as he is that the muezzin will summon him to prayer at sundown.

On the mythical foundation of Israel's birth, a second fabrication is erected: "Israel is an American imperialist base." This theme, too, is repeated with variations. A sample from Ahmed Said's "Cherchez l'Amérique" program:

"The entire world knows that Israel is only an extension of America and a base which it set up by force in the Middle East to impose its domination over the area and extend its imperialist influence to every corner." [3]

Or, with less heat:

"Israel is a bridgehead of American imperialism in the Middle East."

With foundation and ground floor in place, Cairo Radio then builds a structure of legends to prove American plots against Arab nationalism and "Arab socialism." Here, the Arab radio listener learns things about the CIA that Americans don't know. A sample from a "Voice of the Arabs" broadcast, March 7, 1967:

"Press investigations state that a great and massive army is being used . . . for implementing the CIA's aggressive plans against the peoples' aspirations and against the causes of revolutionary

[2] "Voice of the Arabs," June 15, 1967.
[3] "Voice of the Arabs," June 16, 1967.

struggle." (The "press investigations" are not identified.) "This army has a new setup, a new weapon, and a new tactic" (these, too, go undescribed). "The biggest resources of this army no doubt are directed at the Middle East; most of its funds are being spent essentially on its agents in the Middle East; the best experience of [CIA] espionage work and political piracy is undoubtedly being mobilized in the Middle East."

"Why? . . . to cooperate with Israel in the extreme . . . to bolster Husayn's (King Hussein of Jordan) traitorous efforts and . . . to make plans for Faysal (Feisal of Saudi Arabia) . . ."

When Nasser closed the Strait of Tiran on May 22 (1967), and President Johnson tried to open them through diplomatic means, Cairo Radio's listeners were well-conditioned to interpret this effort as "imperialist counter-revolution."

Cairo Radio, May 24:

"The feverish, mad, and hysterical defense of what the United States terms Israel's right to shipping in the Gulf of Aqaba has unmasked it as the leader of counter-revolution and the symbol of neo-imperialism throughout the world . . . If by doing so, the United States imagines that it can subject the peoples of the world to its oppressive wishes, to the rule of steel and fire and the dollar, to the self-conceit and self-delusion of its statements, to the stupidity which marks its policy and the cowboy mentality which dominates it, then it is completely mistaken."

A week later, Cairo Radio had a better idea: the American effort to find a peaceful solution to the crisis "stabbed freedom right in the heart."

Cairo Radio, June 1:

"The United States, the head of the imperialist snake, is moving to protect Zionist aggression to usurp the Gulf of Aqaba (i.e., to sail through it with other nations as it had done during the past decade). Under the cover of what it calls "freedom of navigation," it (the United States) tries to stab freedom right in the heart . . . this is not surprising . . . the United States has always been an enemy of freedom."

When war and defeat came in June, Cairo propaganda piled

new "big lies" on the old to build a Homeric fable of American perfidy: United States direct intervention in the war to "crush Arab socialism." Defeat is unpalatable to any nation, but in the Arab World (as in Nazi Germany) wars are never lost. In 1948, the Israelis— many of them ill-armed boys and girls—didn't defeat six sovereign Arab nations. Victory was snatched from the Arabs by "inferior weapons." (Actually, as sovereign nations, the Arab countries had access to world arms markets, and Egyptian planes roamed unchallenged over Israel for much of the war.) In Israel's Sinai victory of 1956, Egyptian soldiers took off their shoes and ran, just as they were to run a decade later. But, as Nasser told Arab students studying in Moscow in August, 1965, the Israelis didn't flight in the Sinai alone.

"On the first day of the battle (of the 1956 Sinai campaign)," Nasser said, "our air officers stated that the planes fighting on the Israeli side actually were greater than the number of planes owned by Israel and that Israel must have obtained foreign assistance."

The identical line was dusted off almost word-for-word on the "first day of the battle" in the June war. Israeli planes struck Egyptian airfields, turned around, and came back so fast that Nasser again reasoned "that the planes fighting on the Israeli side actually were greater in number than the number of planes owned by Israel, and that Israel must have obtained foreign assistance." In the Arab World, thinking "something must have happened" quickly evolves into "something *did* happen." So was born the big lie that Arabs were defeated not just by little Israel, but by the mighty United States and Great Britain. Thanks to the ubiquitous Cairo Radio millions of Arabs will believe this as long as they live.

The fantasy was launched on radio in an official communique on June 6. It read:

"Brother citizens, the Supreme Command of the armed forces in the U.A.R. announces that it has now become certain that, in a comprehensive manner, the United States and Britain are taking part in the Israeli military aggression as far as the air operations are concerned. It has been fully proved that British and American aircraft carriers are carrying out wide-scale activity in helping Israel. The American and British planes have created an air umbrella over Israel. . . . These planes are playing an actual role against the Jordanian forces . . . Jordanian radar screens clearly showed this air activity in support of Israel."

By the next day, Ahmed Said was in full cry with the new line:

"The United States is the enemy. The United States is the hostile side in the battle. The United States is the force behind which Israel is taking shelter. Israel is the United States, and the United States is Israel. The United States is fighting us in the air and trying to prevent us from disciplining Israel, from liquidating Israel.

"The United States saw Israel about to collapse under the blows of Arab massings which were surrounding it, preparing to deal the blow of death. The Chicago gangs moved; the state of gangsterism moved; it moved in order to protect its aggressive base in the Middle East.

"Our battle is against the United States, firstly, secondly and thirdly. Lastly it is against the Zionist bands, very much lastly."

Not content with the fabrication about American planes, Said discovered on his "Cherchez l'Amérique" broadcast that the June war had been planned in the White House. Here, Said used a Radio Cairo technique that has been driving news agencies, newspapers, and magazines wild for years. Said fabricated the story of American plotting and quoted the magazine *Newsweek* as an authority.

From Cairo's "Voice of the Arabs," June 16:

"Reports emanating from America itself confirm its collusion with Israel and prove that it was America that planned the aggressive conspiracy and participated in its implementation. On 12 June 1967, all world news agencies, headed by the American news agencies themselves, quoted a report published by the American *Newsweek*, which is known for its close contacts with American official circles. The report said the chairman of the Joint Chiefs of Staff, General Wheeler, had informed American President Johnson of the proposed plan for aggression a week before its implementation at a meeting that was also attended by the CIA director *who also approved the plan*." (*Newsweek*, of course, carried no such story.)

In the fall of 1967, when the hard-beset Nasser started to make conciliatory moves looking toward reestablishment of diplomatic relations with the United States, he sacked Ahmed Said as program manager of the "Voice of the Arabs."

But Cairo Radio continued to talk of "the tripartite aggression" that had defeated the Arabs in the June war. And it continued to do so even after Nasser grudgingly told *Look* magazine in an interview published in early 1968 that he had been mistaken about the participation of American planes.

Headquarters, Cairo

A former American ambassador to Egypt told this writer, with some satisfaction:

"Despite all that the Russians have invested in Nasser, Egypt still hasn't gone Communist."

In Washington, senior diplomats like to point out that Nasser "has no use for Communists; he puts them in jail." As further proof of Nasser's anti-Communism, they point to his speeches.

"The Arabs' disagreement with Communism is basic," Nasser has said. "The Arabs believe in religion first, and will not accept Communist atheism. They refuse the 'dictatorship of the proletariat' because Arabs refuse the dictatorship of any one class."

Yet, behind this facade of anti-Communism, some curious things have gone on in Egypt.

Nasser's lone political organization, the Arab Socialist Union, which is modeled after Hitler's National Socialist Party and Mussolini's Fascists, has sent delegates to international Communist Party conclaves in Moscow. Here they have been greeted collectively as a "fraternal party," and have participated with communists from all over the world in planning insurrection and subversion. Sometimes, when Nasser's top aides visited Moscow, officials of the Soviet Union's Central Committee of the Communist Party provided personal briefings. Cairo became the transmission-belt for the Moscow line. It was also headquarters for international communist fronts in Africa and Asia, operated in tandem by Russians and Egyptians to further the Kremlin objective of pushing developing nations into the Soviet orbit.

"Cairo has been transformed into a world center of political activity," Alexander Shelepin, one of the Soviet Union's four most powerful men, observed with satisfaction in a speech to Nasser's National Assembly. "Just this year," he went on, "four important international conferences took place in Cairo." Although Nasser popped some Communists into jail, he ensconced others inside his Arab Socialist Union to serve as a "secret" or "core" party to guide and control it. Nasser supports a Marxist magazine which roots for "scientific socialism," i.e., Marxism. And no Communist has worked as hard as anti-Communist Nasser to align the "nonaligned" Third World with the Soviet bloc.

At a Kremlin dinner in honor of Nasser in August, 1965, Leonid Brezhnev praised Nasser as "one of the outstanding national liberation leaders" in Africa and the Middle East. The accolade was well deserved. Few communist capitals can boast the spate of International Communist Front organizations that make their headquarters in Cairo.

With Soviet backing and guidance, Nasser organized the Afro-Asian Peoples' Solidarity Organization (AAPSO). An Egyptian secretary-general, Yusel as Sabai, operates it from offices in Cairo. He arranges quarterly conferences in neutralist or pro-Soviet capitals that seek to mobilize professional groups, student organizations, and other opinion-makers behind whatever Moscow line is going at the time.

In Nasser's own words at a Kremlin banquet, "The Afro-Asian Peoples' Solidarity Organization aims to mobilize in the international arena as many forces as possible and to awaken these forces to take more radical measures, in addition to condemnation (of the West)."

With Fidel Castro, Nasser formed the Three Continent Organization which has secretariats in Havana and Cairo and seeks to link Latin American leftists with those of Asia and Africa.

Every half-year, the Three Continent Organization engineers a "Vietnam Solidarity Week" to organize anti-U.S. street demonstrations and cover walls and fences with anti-U.S. slogans.

One communist front to which Moscow and Peking attach such importance that they have fought bitterly over its control is the Afro-Asian Writers Bureau. The Russians formed it as a means of influencing journalistic opinion-makers in Asia and Africa. When the Communist Chinese captured the organization and harnessed it to Mao's thought, Nasser came to the Kremlin's rescue. He formed a split-away group of Afro-Asian writers with headquarters in Cairo, naming as its director the same Yusel as-Sabai who operates Nasser's Afro-Asian People's Solidarity Organization.

Throughout all this, Nasser maintains his amateur standing as an anti-Communist through the device of chivvying his own Communists. Early in 1966 Nasser put eleven Communists on trial for plotting to set up a "Peoples' Republic." Two of these told the court they had been tortured. But a month after the trial ended with a life sentence for the ringleader, Nasser permitted pro-Communist leaders inside his Arab Socialist Union to convoke a "seminar of Arab and African progressive forces" in Cairo, attended by Arab and African Communists. The aim of the seminar, as the Arab Socialist Union's own magazine put it, was to form a "common platform of alliance of all the progressive forces working for the progressive way of development for the Arab States," i.e., Communism.

But to keep the record of anti-Communism straight, Nasser had the seminar's organizers hauled up before his secret police for interrogation.

It takes a quick eye and stamina to make out who is doing what to whom in Nasser's relations with his communists.

During Khrushchev's first visit to Egypt in 1964, Nasser released some communists who had rotted in jail without trial. The most prominent of these found their way at once into jobs where they could influence public opinion, chiefly on the staffs of newspapers. The Egyptian Communist Party's chief theoretician, for instance, joined the editorial board of *Al Gomhouria*, a government-owned newspaper. Others went into university teaching jobs.

In 1964, at a secret Communist Party meeting in Moscow, Egypt's communists were told to disband. Egypt's communists then went into Nasser's Socialist Union where, they said, they could participate directly in the political life of the country. Here, they served as Nasser's watchdogs against dissidents. They also formed, within the Arab Socialist Union, a "revolutionary vanguard party, consisting entirely of socialists . . . who are imbued with the ideas of scientific socialism."

Often, Nasser's party-within-a-party visited Prague to exchange ideas with Czech Communists.

The ideas developed at these meetings got considerable mileage from the transmission belt of International Communist Fronts in Cairo.

With Josip Broz Tito of Yugoslavia and Mrs. Indira Gandhi of India, Nasser dominated the thought and world outlook of the "non-aligned" countries of the Third World. Indeed, before the June war, Nasser took the lead in organizing "summit conferences" of such nations, and two such meetings were held in Cairo, one of them attended by fifty-seven heads of state and prime ministers. To these conferences, thanks to Soviet Communist Party spadework, Nasser was an incomparable conduit of Kremlin policies. It was only natural that resolutions adopted at the "non-aligned" summit meetings should ring with Communist jargon and slogans, and that the "non-aligned" should align themselves with the Soviet bloc.

Laid end to end, Nasser's services to the Soviet Union added up to a vast communist hoax against the western world. To the Soviet Union, the West, and to Nasser himself, Nasser was a nationalist leader who pursued "Arab Unity" and his own ambitions. To the Soviet Union, he was also an instrument of deception, a proxy behind whom the Kremlin could pursue a vast dream.

6

GRAND DESIGN

From their lookouts on the Mediterranean, the Red Sea and the Persian Gulf, Turkey, Iran and Israel watched with growing anxiety in late 1966 as seemingly unrelated Soviet moves added up to a grand and ominous design. The Soviets were seeking to shift the balance of world power in their favor by securing the Middle East as a base from which to pressure and break up the Atlantic Alliance.

As a first move, the Soviet Union—as we've seen—had wooed Nasser with lavish gifts of arms in 1955. Seemingly, the Kremlin feared a Western reaction, for the weapons were delivered in the greatest secrecy. The Soviet Union didn't even show its hand: Czechoslovakia served as proxy for the arms deal. Historians now feel that had the U.S. intercepted a Czech weapons vessel—as President Kennedy later intercepted Russian vessels bearing missiles to Cuba—the Soviet Union would have backed away. But the U.S. made no move. The Soviet Union won a valuable proxy, and the Russian Bear thrust his nose into the Arab tent.

The second move, in 1960, seemed a mystifying dead end. With Nasser as salesman for Soviet weapons, the Kremlin secured a foothold in Somalia, a desert wasteland of 2 million scattered inhabitants, freshly carved from Mussolini's old African empire on the rim of the African Horn. On the thirty-thousand-man army of Somalia, the Soviets lavished enough jet fighters, tanks, and helicopters to outfit an army four times that size. What were the Russians up to?

The Soviet's third move, soon after, shed light on the mystery. With its proxy, Nasser, the Soviet Union moved into Yemen, a wild mountainous country that lies at the southwestern tip of the Arabian peninsula. Its strategic importance is apparent from a glance at a map. With a pro-Russian Yemen on the Red Sea's eastern shore, and a pro-Russian Somalia at the southern exit of the Red Sea, the Soviet Union could turn the Red Sea into a Red lake, and menace the West's southern approaches to the Suez Canal and Israel's outlet to Asia and Africa.

The Soviets had sought a foothold in Yemen as far back as 1956, when they offered the feudal Imam (ruler) there economic aid and a secret arms deal to be handled by Nasser. At the same time, Nasser tried his own, more direct route to power. His agents made repeated attempts on the aged Imam's life—the last just two weeks before the Imam died of natural causes in 1962. A plot hatched in Cairo, with the knowledge and consent of the Soviet Union, promptly overthrew the Imam's successor, his son Prince Badr. A Soviet-Egyptian puppet took power as head of a "republican regime," and Russian transports began to ferry an Egyptian expeditionary force from Cairo to support the puppet against an uprising by Royalist tribes.

The Kremlin did more. It intervened directly in the civil war. Soviet pilots flew long range TU 16 (Tupolev) bombers from Cairo, dropped their bombs on Royalist targets, then returned to Egyptian bases. Meanwhile, Russian technicians built an eleven-thousand-five-hundred-foot jet runway near the capital city of Sana. At its completion, Egyptian pilots who lacked the training to fly the big Tupolev bombers, now took over the bombing missions in the smaller IL 28 (Ilyushin) bombers that could reach targets from the new runway. The direct Russian intervention lasted four months and taught Western observers a lesson. The Soviets enter a war of liberation directly only if a confrontation with the West seems unlikely, and—even so—return to indirect action, via proxies, as soon as possible.

The Yemen war taught Western observers something else, too.

The lesson came in the form of a new Russian transport plane, the Antonov. Its debut was regarded as an event of the greatest significance. For this was a plane built to carry a heavy load and to take off and land on relatively short runways. For lack of such a plane, the Russians had failed in the Congo uprising of 1963. Seemingly, the Russians had raced to produce one for use in wars of liberation far from Russian shores.

As the war raged inconclusively in Yemen, the Russians dug in. They built a port at Hodeida on the Red Sea, a power plant, and a radio station with which they could beam the Moscow line to the country round about. Some five hundred technicians and their families moved into houses built by the Russians. Visiting correspondents took to calling the place a "Russian city." In Hodeida, the Russians now had a base and a "fall back" position in case the civil war went against the puppet regime.

Indirect action, by proxy, in the Yemen paid important dividends to the Soviet Union. So little did the United States appreciate that the Kremlin was the principal actor in the Yemen intervention, that the State Department extended recognition to the Soviet-Egyptian puppet regime, although the Imam's army claimed control over more than half of the country. Inexplicably, the recognition came at the very time that Soviet pilots were flying combat missions to support the Egyptian-Soviet puppet regime.

The Soviet's proxy strategy saved the USSR even greater embarrassment as the Yemen intervention unfolded. When Soviet Ilyushin bombers, maintained by Soviet mechanics and flown by Soviet-trained Egyptian pilots, dropped Russian poison gas bombs on Yemen villagers, no official Western voice put the blame where it belonged—on the Kremlin. Indeed, while the Kremlin aided and abetted the gas outrage in the Yemen, it raised a cynical outcry against American bombing of military targets in Vietnam.

Nasser and his Russian military advisors turned to gas when their Yemen invasion began to bog down in mid-1963. Because remote villages were chosen as targets, the nature of the Egyptian-Russian horror did not emerge until January, 1967. Four doctors, three Pakistanis and one Saudi Arabian, made their way to the mountain village of Ketaf in northern Yemen where they treated one hundred fifty villagers suffering gas poisoning symptoms such as: "difficult breathing and a harsh cough, vomiting and retching, bleeding from nose and mouth."

A *Baltimore Sun* correspondent, Thomas T. Fenton, who reached Ketaf soon after, reported:

"Ahmed Al Amin, a Ketaf farmer, lost nine relatives, including his son, who were in his three-story mud house when a bomb fell on a nearby stable.

"Mutladh Ali Zaid, a quiet little boy of ten, lost his entire family of fourteen.

"Saleh Mosied, forty, was tilling his garden on the east of the town when the bombs hit. He threw his kaffiyeh headgear over his nose and mouth and ran upwind. When he returned, the village resounded with the sound of coughing people and animals. He saw townspeople die one after another."

The symptoms described at Ketaf pointed to the use of World War I mustard and phosgene gases which burn and blind and cause a lingering and tortured death. The Egyptians had started in 1963 with tear gas, but in such concentrations that it caused blindness and some deaths. They had gradually escalated the deadliness of the gases until early in 1967, when a new horror was introduced. Western intelligence agents obtained canisters with Cyrillic (Russian alphabet) letters containing a new gas. Tested, it turned out to be a nerve gas which attacks the nervous system, causing nausea, cramps, convulsions, and death by suffocation.

Since the Soviets were using Yemen as a testing ground for future military action, the discovery of the Russian nerve gas raised grave concern among western intelligence services.

Would the Soviets give the nerve gas to the North Vietnamese for use against American troops in South Vietnam? Fortunately, the International Committee of the Red Cross intervened to bring the gas to world attention and so, presumably, discouraged its use in Vietnam.

The International Committee of the Red Cross usually keeps its field activities secret to avoid impeding aid operations in the field. But here the ICRC took the unprecedented step of publishing a report on the use of poison gas in Yemen.

"On May 11, 1967," the ICRC reported, "The International

Committee of the Red Cross delegation in Jidda (Saudi Arabia) received appeals for assistance from the two villages of Gadafa and Gahar (in Yemen). According to these appeals . . . inhabitants . . . had been poisoned by gas dropped from raiding airplanes."

The ICRC organized a medical team of two doctors and a male nurse, and loaded a two-truck convoy with food and medical supplies. The ICRC then gave "due notice of the convoy's line of march and time-table to the Egyptian authorities." Nevertheless, the well-marked and well-advertised ICRC mercy convoy was bombed so severely by Egyptian pilots that its mercy mission was delayed for two days.

"It was not until the night of May 15–16 that the mission reached Gahar," the report continues. "This village is situated atop a hill some five hundred feet in height. According to the inhabitants seventy-five people were gassed (and died) during a raid in the early hours of May 10.

"The account given by the survivors is as follows:

" 'The bombers circled the village for some time, then dropped three bombs on the hillside, east of and below the village, two or three hundred yards away to the windward. No houses were damaged. The explosions were relatively mild. The bomb craters were about eight feet in diameter and twenty inches deep, smaller than the usual craters.

"Along with the human casualties, almost two hundred cattle, sheep, goats, donkeys, and numerous birds were also killed. The surviving villagers buried the dead animals in a large pit west of the village, whilst the seventy-five humans killed were buried in four large communal graves.

"The head of the mission had one of the four communal graves opened. There were fifteen corpses in it. An immediate autopsy by Dr. Brutschin and Dr. Janin left no doubt that death was due to pulmonary edema (effusion of fluid into the air cells of the lungs).

"The seventy-five gas casualties were either within range of the gas when it was released or were within its path as it was blown by the wind.

"The four survivors . . . are all in pain from their eyes and almost blind. All have pains in the chest and none has any wound.

"The delegates were later informed that on May 17 and 18 (while the ICRC was in Gahar!) the villages of Gabas, Nofal, Gadr, and—for the second time—Gadafa were raided with gas bombs and that two hundred forty-three persons were killed."

The reason behind the gas bombing emerged at about the same time when British correspondents reported that the Egyptian-controlled Sana radio was broadcasting warnings that poison-gas bombs would be dropped on any areas harboring Royalists.

Duncan Sandys, a member of Parliament, wrote in the *London Daily Mail*: ". . . menfolk who are serving away from home with the Royalist forces are threatened by radio and leaflets with the death and mutilation of their families if they do not lay down their arms."

The use of poison gas has been barred by international agreement since 1925. Such use by Mussolini against barefoot Ethiopian warriors in 1935 evoked storms of indignation. Yet the UN and the West remained strangely silent about the Russian-Egyptian partnership's use of poison gas in the Yemen.

Pressed to speak out, Secretary General U Thant of the UN said that since everyone knew that he and the UN opposed poison gas, why say anything about it? And anyway, Cairo denied the charges. It would therefore be improper to take up the matter in the Security Council!

The United States Department of State took a reserved attitude even after the International Committee of the Red Cross spelled out the Yemen atrocities. Condemnation of poison gas in the Yemen, U.S. officials felt, would be regarded by Nasser as a "pro-Israel maneuver!"

By hiding behind its proxy, Nasser, whom the West was reluctant to antagonize, the Kremlin could "liberate" Yemeni women and children with poison gas yet escape without a word of censure.

For Nasser, Yemen in 1965 was an unrelieved disaster. It chewed up men—an estimated five thousand were dead and missing—drained Egypt's meager resources, and tore apart the Arab world Nasser was trying to unite. King Feisal of Saudi Arabia,

Yemen's neighbor, seeing himself as the next Communist victim, rushed arms to the embattled Imam.

So, in September, 1965, during a state visit to Moscow, Nasser told his Russian partners he had had enough. He wanted out. Here, the Kremlin revealed beyond doubt whose war it really was—and who had the chief stake in it.

Yemen was a key position in the Middle East, Brezhnev and Kosygin told Nasser. The USSR had invested heavily in arms, technicians, and money to hold it. Nasser could not quit now. The Russians requested Nasser to remain to "protect our joint interests." As the poker-faced Nasser remained silent, Brezhnev and Kosygin offered an inducement. The Soviet Union would forgive $200 million worth of debt owed by Nasser if he continued to co-operate! At this, the necessitous Nasser said yes.

What the "joint interests" were that warranted so big an inducement, soon emerged in the next Soviet-Egyptian move. Yemen became a staging area for a "war of liberation" against the neighboring British protectorate of Aden. Here, British troops, naval vessels, and aircraft stood guard over the oil riches of the Persian Gulf to the east. This oil accounts for two-thirds of the non-Communist world's oil reserves. Income from investments there help the British meet their balance of payments. With Yemen as a base, Soviet-armed Egyptian guerrillas, trained by Soviet instructors, crossed over into Aden and plunged it into a bloody war to drive out the British.

By 1966, Party Chairman Leonid Brezhnev and Premier Alexei Kosygin could look south of their borders and regard their Middle East backyard with satisfaction and quickening hopes. Three historic windfalls, coming in conjunction, virtually assured that all of the area would soon topple like a ripe plum into the Russian Bear's lap.

To begin with, in February of that year the Soviet Union acquired a second proxy. Young Syrian army officers, representing a leftist sliver of the extremely nationalist Ba'athist Party, seized power in a bloody coup. Since it was the eighteenth attempt in seventeen years, the new regime was expected to last only a few months. But the Russians were in Damascus with weapons, military instructors, and cash while the young putschists were still jailing the last of the old regime. The young officers hung on, and the coup turned out to be different from any of its predecessors. Prodded by their Russian benefactors, the new regime took two communists into the cabinet. They permitted Khalid Bagdash, the Arab World's leading Communist, to return to Syria from exile in Prague, Czechoslovakia. Under his direction—and on orders from Moscow—Syria's communists joined a united front with the Ba'athists. Young Ba'athist leaders went to Moscow for training in party leadership. The new regime nationalized virtually all of Syria's business enterprises, so reducing contacts with the West. The controlled press took to publishing articles on the Marxist-Leninist "road to national development."

To the jubilant Kremlin, Syria was on its way to becoming the first Communist Arab state. The Russians felt so secure here that they erected a giant communications and nerve center for Soviet operations in the Middle East and in Africa. Suddenly, the Soviet Union had a base on the eastern end of the Mediterranean which could be harnessed to strategic military needs if necessary.

Soviet technicians and intelligence experts manned the electronic and monitoring equipment. It served both as an intelligence clearing house and relay center for Moscow messages to operatives, military personnel, and diplomats from Algiers to Beirut on both ends of the Mediterranean, to Somalia and Yemen at the Red Sea, and to Kuwait and Iran on the Persian Gulf.

With the consent of their new Syrian friends, the Soviets introduced something new into the Mediterranean. At the Syrian port of Latakia, Soviet marines took to holding beach assault exercises from shiny, new amphibious craft, never before seen in Mediterranean waters.

The second historic windfall for the Soviets was the growing American involvement in Vietnam. While American eyes were fixed on the South China Sea, the Soviets made their boldest Middle East power move: they built a fleet in the Mediterranean.

Here, the American Sixth Fleet with its fifty vessels, its jet fighters, and twenty five thousand Marines had ruled alone for years. But in 1963, the Soviet Union began its buildup. A handful at first, the Russian fleet was expanding swiftly prior to the Arab-Israeli war, and already numbered some twenty vessels.

These included destroyers with remote-control guns, submarines, and ballistic missile-launching ships, built specifically for use against American aircraft carriers, thought capable of hitting a target at one hundred miles.

The Soviet vessels had become increasingly audacious in "monitoring" and harassing the Sixth Fleet. Once, a Soviet cruiser, flying the flag of an admiral, kept cutting in so dangerously across the bow of the American fleet's flagship, that the fleet commander, Vice Admiral William E. Ellis, ordered his jets to aim a series of sonic booms on the Soviet vessel.

"Don't stop!" the Soviet admiral signalled back. "We have strong nerves!"

Equally worrisome to the West were the sophisticated missiles that the Soviets gave to their proxy navies, those of Algeria and Egypt. (By providing the deadly Styx-type automatic homing missile to the volatile Egyptians, the Soviets caused the sinking of the Israeli destroyer *Eilat*. Without risk to themselves, the Russians also demonstrated to the West—via proxy—their new naval striking power.)

The third Russian windfall in 1966 promised to transform the Soviet's cautious penetration of the Mid-East into a galloping conquest. This was the British announcement that its garrison could no longer cope with the Russian-Egyptian war of liberation in Aden. The protectorate, as the London *Economist* put it, was a "bloody mess." The British said they planned to pull out their five thousand troops, jets, and naval vessels by 1968. (Since the British decision to quit Aden came only five months after the Soviets' $200 million deal with Nasser to remain in neighboring Yemen, the question arises whether Russian intelligence had advance knowledge of the British announcement. Once the British left, Nasser could move his Egyptian troops into Aden and set up a Soviet-Egyptian puppet there.)

Now, Israel's Foreign Minister Abba Eban and Shah Pahlavi of Iran began to knock urgently on Washington doors.

The point of no return was swiftly approaching for the West, the Israelis pleaded in Washington. And the Shah spelled out the danger to Secretary of State Rusk in a personal plea at Teheran. Britain's withdrawal from Aden would give the Soviet foreign legion, Egypt's expeditionary force in Yemen, a clear road to the oil sheikdoms on the Persian Gulf—and endanger Iran as well.

For years, Nasser had waged a propaganda campaign to break away Iran's chief oil-producing province, Khuzistan. Cairo Radio called it "Arabstan" because of the Arab minority there. The Egyptian General Intelligence organized two national liberation fronts to foment an insurrection. With a Soviet proxy established in southern Arabia (now known as South Yemen), the Shah feared that a war to "liberate" the oil wealth of Iran's Khuzistan would almost certainly follow.

If the Soviets gained a foothold in southern Arabia, the Shah argued, Saudi Arabia would be imperilled, too. Egyptian pilots, flying Soviet Ilyushin bombers, had already bombed Saudi villages from Egyptian-Russian bases in Yemen. Early in 1967 Yemen-based Soviet Antonov transports dropped an equipment "pack" for one thousand Egyptian guerrillas inside the borders of Saudi Arabia—an apparent bluff at invasion. It didn't materialize, but King Feisal knew that he was a top priority on Nasser's "war of liberation" list.

The Israelis conveyed to Washington their own reasons for anxiety.

While Israel's immediate concern is with the actions of its Arab neighbors, it is concerned also with the maintenance of a Western presence in the area, and particularly with the fortunes of the Sixth Fleet. For even if the Sixth Fleet does not intervene to help Israel in a war, its presence deters the Soviets from intervening.

Ever since the Soviets had begun to build a presence in the region, the Israelis had harnessed their best brains to the study of the strategy and tactics of Soviet foreign policy. Basic Communist literature and Western analyses of the Soviets' protracted conflict for world revolution have been required reading at Israel's War College, and of course, at Israel's foreign ministry. To the Israelis, then, the Soviets' aims in the Mediterranean were clear: to push out the American Sixth Fleet, and to replace it with Soviet naval power that would menace America's NATO allies from their southern flank.

Nor was this all. As the Soviet Union and its satellites captured Middle-Eastern export markets, they could apply a further squeeze on the European countries that depended on this trade. Chief target, apparently, was West Germany. Lenin's concept of world power was to marry Germany's highly skilled "proletariat" to the "Soviet people" and so overcome the inefficiencies of the Soviet economy. If you tie West Germany to the Soviet bloc, the world balance is completely changed.

These alarms plunged Washington into a four-way debate that raged two full years prior to the Arab-Israeli war.

The Pentagon reflected Secretary McNamara's publicly stated belief that the Red Sea area and the African Horn were of strategic military importance to the United States. Spokesmen urged that the United States assert its world power status in the area, ship more arms to pro-Western nations there, and warn the Soviet Union through diplomatic channels that the U.S. meant to protect its interests. The intelligence community, speaking through the CIA and painfully aware of the Soviet's piecemeal incursion into the Middle East behind proxies, sided with the Pentagon.

In the Department of State, Arabists—Arab experts who had served in diplomatic posts to Arab countries—dominated State Department Middle East policy. They refused to see Nasser as a Soviet proxy. They argued Nasser had proved his hostility to communism by purging communists and by his statements that Communism and the Muslim religion don't mix. They felt that despite Nasser's actions and words, he could be wooed and won. Through him lay the key to friendship with the rest of the Arab world. They argued against arming Nasser's enemies; that would antagonize him.

In the White House, President Lyndon B. Johnson—like his predecessor, John F. Kennedy—was heavily committed to the idea that a détente with the Russians existed. The Russians had looked into the abyss of nuclear war during the Cuban missile crisis and longed for peace, he felt. In this, the President was supported by Vice President Hubert Humphrey, Secretary of State Dean Rusk, and Averell Harriman, his Ambassador-at-Large. In the light of the Vietnam war, the President was eager to show one major achievement toward peace: a nuclear non-proliferation treaty with the Soviet Union. He hesitated to rock the boat by challenging the Russians.

Growing American preoccupation with Vietnam in early 1967 undoubtedly contributed to lethargy elsewhere. Yet this diplomatic malaise ran so deep that for the three crucial months when war was brewing in the Middle East, the U.S. had no ambassador in Egypt, the eye of the storm.

To Brezhnev, then, in the spring of 1967 things were going well, indeed. Egypt was virtually a vassal state, bound economically and militarily to the Soviet Union. Syria was moving toward the status of a satellite. A Russian-Egyptian puppet held Yemen, and another would soon hold Aden. Geo-political plums were ripening in the Red Sea, the Indian Ocean, and the Persian Gulf. The royal regimes in Saudi Arabia and Jordan were living on borrowed time.

Soon, there would be a Soviet grouping of pro-Russian Arab states, pursuing the road to "socialist national development." The West would be driven from its markets, investments, and bases. It would be the biggest victory in the "protracted conflict" since Stalin's occupation troops thrust Communism on Eastern Europe. Brezhnev was encouraged to take a bold and significant step.

On April 24, 1967, he told European Communist Party delegates that the time was ripe to demand that the United States withdraw the Sixth Fleet from the Mediterranean!

Only one cloud darkened Soviet prospects in the Middle East. It was a country inhabited by Jews, whom the Lord himself had described as "a stiff-necked people."

7

ROAD TO WAR

On May 27, 1967, the Soviet Ambassador to Israel, Dimitri Chuvakin, called on Israel's Prime Minister, Levi Eshkol. The time of the call testified to its supreme urgency. It was 2:40 a.m.

The 72-year-old Eshkol had tumbled into bed at his Hotel Dan suite in Tel Aviv only an hour before, after a cruel day. Up at 6 a.m., he had listened gloomily to intelligence reports of Egyptian concentrations on Israel's Sinai borders and to intercepted Egyptian battle orders that spelled war. Then he had participated in an agonizing cabinet debate as to whether to fight or wait. The decision was to wait. In a painful session with his chiefs of staff, Eshkol defended this inaction while the generals warned that every day of hesitation would cost hundreds and perhaps thousands of Israeli lives. Before he went to bed, Eshkol assumed a cheerful face to play host and money-raiser before affluent co-religionists who had just arrived, posthaste, from the United States.

Now, Eshkol, heavy-lidded, barefoot, and with his pajama tops pushed hastily into his trousers, faced the correctly togged-out Soviet ambassador and the young first minister of the Soviet embassy.

With Eshkol was his male secretary and shadow, Aviad Jappe, also in pajama tops, and a foreign ministry man who, hastily summoned from a nearby suite had, nevertheless—and quite inexplicably—materialized in a proper dinner jacket and black tie.

Like most Soviet representatives abroad, Chuvakin, a portly figure with a broad Slavic face, had served in the Soviets' intelligence apparatus. The Soviet delegation he headed in Tel Aviv was the biggest one there, and Israeli counterintelligence knew that this oversized staff had, as its chief job, the gathering of intelligence both for the Soviet Union and for Israel's Arab enemies. In fact, the Soviet embassy had been caught red-handed in several attempts to turn Israeli citizens into Soviet espionage agents.

The day's cabinet meeting and Eshkol's session with his chiefs of staff had not escaped Soviet eyes and ears. Reported to Moscow, it had triggered the night visit.

Chuvakin, blank-faced as always, apologized courteously for rousing Eshkol from bed, then went straight to the point.

"Will you promise me that you won't fire the first shot?" he demanded.

Eshkol was a bear of a man with a creased, jowly face, a deep voice, and a hearty laugh. He migrated to Israel from his native Poland at eighteen and brought with him the warmth and lack of side characteristic of the Eastern European ghetto Jew. Eshkol resorted to an East European Jewish custom of answering a question with another question.

"What is the first shot nowadays?" Eshkol wanted to know.

"Here, they're shelling our villages—isn't that the first shot? They're mining our roads and murdering our people. Isn't that the first shot?"

Chuvakin persisted doggedly with his question. Just as doggedly, but with many more words, Eshkol took evasive action. He offered to go to Moscow to state Israel's side. He inquired whether the Soviet Union would free its Jewish citizens to migrate to Israel. He demanded to know why the ambassador, whose mission was to improve relations with his host country, sided only with its enemies.

When the Soviet ambassador had stated his question three more times, his young aide said, "Mr. Ambassador, you have asked him the same question four times, and he hasn't answered it once."

Here, Eshkol exploded.

"When it comes to fighting for our survival," he shouted, "you can't hold us back!"

War came six days later. It was a war no one wanted.

The Soviets tried to prevent it after precipitating the crisis that made war inevitable. Nasser had other things on his mind than war, when he ordered his troops into the Sinai. The United States had an emissary in Cairo as late as two days before the war, trying to "cool it." And half of Israel's cabinet voted against military action only eight days before military action began.

Let's follow the road to the Six-Day War with those who travelled it.

Our journey begins fully fifteen months before the Israeli-Arab War.

Leftist army officers had just seized power in Syria and, turning to the Soviet Union, moved toward the status of a satellite state. To the Kremlin, then, Syria was a special prize. Equally important, the Kremlin had visions of linking Syria and Egypt to three other "progressive, socialist states"—the military dictatorships of Algeria, Iraq and Yemen—to form an Arab pro-Moscow Internationale. With Nasser at its head, the Kremlin hoped to use the "progressive bloc" to undermine and "liberate" the conservative states of Jordan, Saudi Arabia, Morocco, Kuwait, and Lebanon.

To speed the split in the Arab world, Radio Moscow, echoed by Nasser's Radio Cairo, sowed suspicion and hatred with a campaign that had two themes:

"Imperialism is hatching dangerous plots against the "progressive Arab states."

"The imperialists are using the conservative bloc as tools in these plots."

At the same time, the Kremlin raised a special alarm over "imperialist plots against Syria."

The alarm was rooted in these developments:

The first use the Syrians made of their freshly delivered Soviet weapons, including the 130 mm cannon that could fire seventeen miles across the waist of Israel, was to plant them on the Golan Heights above Israel's Huleh Valley and rake the villages below.

From time to time, the Syrians zeroed their Soviet guns in on individual villages and pounded them for hours. While the loss of life was low, the loss of homes, orchards, schools—built painfully over the years—was high. The emotional scars on the children were beyond measurement. To the shelling were added terrorist raids and the mining of Israel's public roads. The Syrian regime openly boasted of these and in one case presented a terrorist with a money prize for "service to his fatherland." The service consisted of the murder of a Jewish fisherman in the Sea of Galilee.

When Israel responded with commando raids against Syrian army installations, the Soviet Union thundered in press and radio —and in the UN—that "imperialists are encouraging Israel to attack Syria!"

Bloodcurdling threats by Syria's rulers provided an ironic counterpoint to the Soviet allegations:

President Atassi in an address to Syrian soldiers in May, 1966: "We raise the slogan of the people's liberation war. We want total war with no limits to destroy Israel!"

The Soviet periodical, *Mezhdunarodnaia Zhiznj*, (International Life), June 6, 1966:

"Under pressure from the USA, the militarists of Israel have intensified their provocative activities (against Syria)."

Syria's Defense Minister, Hafiz Asad, May, 1966:

"We have resolved to drench this land in blood, and to throw you (Israel) into the sea for good!"

Pravda, July 20, 1966:

"Israel has borders with several Arab countries. (But) . . . the provocation is against the Syrian Republic. Someone in Tel-Aviv, as well as in certain imperialist circles beyond the ocean, does not like the course of progressive development chosen by the Syrian people."

The Kremlin seemingly believed its own press clippings. After all, didn't Great Britain and France join with Israel in the Suez War of 1956? In the fall of 1966, the Soviets took a fateful step along the road to the next war. To protect Syria's regime, they induced Nasser to sign a mutual-assistance pact with Syria.

Simultaneously, the Moscow line on Syria took a more incendiary turn. To prod Nasser to make a show of force against Israel —and to discourage its "plotting"—the Kremlin began to discover that the Israelis were massing troops on the Syrian border.

Here, the Soviet Union indulged in a luxury available to a superpower when it deals with a small nation. It began to bully Israel with warning notes.

In October, 1966 (eight months before the Israel-Arab War), Israel's Premier Eshkol read with amazement a note from the Soviet ambassador Chuvakin. It read:

"According to information in our possession, concentrations of Israeli troops can again be discerned along the Syrian frontier. Preparations are being made for an air attack, so that in its wake Israeli troops may penetrate deep into Syria."

Premier Eshkol invited the Russian ambassador to get into a car with him. "Take a ride with me—after all, this isn't such a big country. You can't hide units in your pockets. Show me where our troops are concentrated."

"You are being pushed by the imperialist powers," Chuvakin replied.

The Israeli premier and the Russian ambassador never did take that ride together. Two weeks later, a virtually identical Soviet note asserting "the Soviet Government has proof of concentrations, etc.," was again handed to Eshkol. The notes kept coming until the war.

Meanwhile, the same Soviet reports of Israeli troop concentrations kept streaming to Nasser in Cairo, who was bound by treaty to defend Syria. One day in May, 1967, Nasser chose to take one such warning seriously, and started to move Egyptian troops into the Sinai.

While Nasser put a torch to the incendiary pile the Russians had set, he didn't want war.

When Nasser first moved his troops into the Sinai on May 15, the target was not the ostensible one—Israel. It was the United States. The motive was not conquest. It was blackmail.

The evidence is clear.

True, Nasser dreamed one day of humbling Israel. It was his central preoccupation.

But he wasn't in a hurry.

At summit conferences in 1964 and 1965, Nasser told fellow Arab leaders that it would take at least ten years to prepare for war with Israel. He cooled off Arab hotheads who urged a *jihad* and forbade fedayeen raids against Israel from the Egyptian-controlled Gaza Strip. For two years prior to the June War, there were virtually no border incidents that might provoke Israeli retaliation.

And as late as April 8, 1967, Nasser warned Syria's prime minister at a meeting in Cairo to stop terrorist raids, too. He told him angrily that his mutual assistance pact with Syria did not cover "border raids, no matter what their origins or importance." [1]

And three months after the war, one of Nasser's closest advisors told a correspondent:

"Our mistake was to believe that we could speak two different languages: a conciliatory one for the outside world, and a demogogic, uncompromising one, for our own people. *As a matter of fact, we didn't want war!*" [2]

What, then, did Nasser want?

The answer lies in Nasser's desperate financial fix in early 1967.

Two of every three loaves of bread that Egyptians ate during the past decade came from American foreign aid. Since 1955, the United States had provided Nasser with $879,900,000 worth of wheat. Since Nasser paid for most of this in Egyptian currency on a deferred payment plan, Nasser saved $120,000,000 to $150,-000,000 yearly in hard cash which he would have had to spend on wheat imports.

Three American presidents had swallowed Nasser's insults and Nasser's proxy activities in behalf of the Soviet Union. But in 1966, President Johnson scribbled on a scratch pad on his desk an ultimatum to Nasser. There would be no more American wheat unless Nasser gave up his quest for long-range rockets and limited his armed forces to their current size.

Nasser refused. In June, 1966, an American vessel unloaded the last cargo of American wheat at Cairo.

[1] Eric Rouleau in *Le Monde*, Paris: December 27, 1967.
[2] *Le Monde*, December 27, 1967.

Now came another blow. Western commercial banks and the International Monetary Fund told Nasser that he had come to the end of the borrowing road. There would be no more loans unless Nasser stopped spending more than he earned.

Nasser faced one of the most serious crises of his turbulent career. He lacked cash to feed his people or import spare parts and raw materials for his factories. Short rations and spreading unemployment worsened the growing popular discontent and threatened Nasser's regime.

But all was not lost. For in Nasser, Egypt had a material resource not found in the geography books: a magician who materialized hard cash, food, and military gear by feats of legerdemain outside his borders, i.e., via his foreign policy. One observer has described this as "Strength through mischief." [3]

Nasser's closest friend and chief explainer, Muhammed Hasanain Haikal, put it this way:

"Foreign policy has become one of Egypt's . . . major resources. Egypt needed arms, development funds for the future, food for the present," Haikal once wrote in *Al Ahram*. "Well, thanks to Egypt's foreign policy, the USSR and the United States supplied them."

How?

Let's listen to the candid Haikal.

"We carry weight and significance in our world. We are able to influence the course of events in it and therefore are in a position *to do harm or good*."

With an eye toward forcing the United States to resume its role of Uncle Samaritan, Nasser now proceeded to show what harm he could do.

On February 23 (1967), Nasser touched off a propaganda attack against the United States with his most virulent anti-American speech since 1964. At that time he had told the United States to "go drink the Red Sea" (Egyptian for "go jump in the lake."). Now, after citing a long list of unsuccessful American efforts to restrain him, Nasser said, "Let them burst with frustration!"

[3] James Morris, *The Atlantic*, October, 1965.

Nasser's propaganda machine took up the angry refrain. Cairo Radio announcers told the Arab World: "The United States is the chief enemy." Editor Haikal of *Al Ahram* spelled out an indictment eight articles long.

At the same time officials closest to Nasser let American diplomats in Cairo in on a State secret:

Unless the United States "proved it was not hostile to Nasser," the United States faced trouble.

What kind of trouble?

The then highest officer in the American Embassy, David G. Nes, a deputy chief of mission, spelled it out in urgent memorandums to the State Department. There were five possibilities:

An attack on Israel.

Or against King Hussein of Jordan.

Or against King Feisal of Saudi Arabia.

Increased pressure against Libya to close the American Wheelus Air Force Base there.

Sedition in Lebanon to upset the precarious political balance between Christians and Muslims.

Nes, as acting head of the Embassy, took these threats so seriously that he began to bombard the State Department with urgent appeals for "some kind of gesture . . . which would assure Nasser that the United States was not hostile." But although the State Department was willing, Congress and the President were not.

When Washington didn't respond, Nasser turned to the first of his five mischievous options: the threat of war against Israel.

Although Nasser had chosen to ignore, for more than a year, the recurrent Russian cries of wolf about "Israeli forces massed on the Syrian border," he found it convenient—on May 14—to believe Russian intelligence reports after all. He heeded Russian demands for a show of force. Next day, he began to parade troops ostentatiously through Cairo on their way to the Sinai, not to start a war, but to execute—as Cairo later called it— "Operation Dissuasion." Proof that a show of force was all that Nasser had in mind lay in his limited request to the United Nations peacekeeping forces in the Sinai: partial withdrawal to the

Egyptian-held Gaza Strip to provide a corridor for Egyptian troops in the Sinai.

Instead of the partial withdrawal, Secretary General U Thant of the United Nations decided to pull the UN's "Blue Helmets" out of the entire area, including Sharm el-Sheikh on the Strait of Tiran. (U Thant seems to have had no choice. Nasser's friends, Tito of Yugoslavia and Mrs. Indira Gandhi of India ordered their contingents to pack up and go home, even before U Thant made his decision.)

Here, events moved with such speed that Nasser found himself in the position of a gambler who bets a hundred dollars and finds himself with a jackpot of a million dollars on his hands.

Since UN forces no longer intervened between Egyptian artillery at Sharm el-Sheikh and the Strait below, Nasser took his first big gamble.

On May 22, he ordered the Strait of Tiran closed, depriving Israel of its outlet to Africa and Asia and its access to some 90 percent of its oil needs.

The United States, France, and England had promised Israel in 1957 that the Strait would be kept open. Israel, itself, had said that closing the Strait would be regarded as an act of war. Yet, day after day passed and no one acted, neither the Big Powers, nor Israel.

Nasser had stood up to the great powers and the hated Israel. Without firing a shot, he had snatched from Israel its only gain in the 1956 war. Overnight, Nasser was a hero to all of the Arab World.

With this pile of diplomatic and strategic winnings before him, Nasser upped the stakes. He began to talk of war and of squeezing Israel back into the territory it held before its 1948 victory over the Arabs. Seemingly, he won again. His old enemies, Kings Hussein of Jordan and Feisal of Saudi Arabia rushed to Cairo to put their armies under Nasser's command. Now, overnight, he had won his cherished dream of uniting the Arabs against Israel, and the biggest payoff of all—economic concessions from the United States—seemed within reach, too.

President Johnson had dispatched a special emissary to urge Nasser to drop the blockade and cool off the crisis. Nasser, it turned out, could be induced to compromise. Out of the discussions came a Nasser promise to permit Israeli ships to transit the Strait under some small face-saving arrangement. Perhaps the Israelis could fly the Panamian flag. Nasser would discuss a general settlement with Israel. In return, the United States would work out a modus vivendi with Egypt. Nasser said he would send his Vice President, Zakaria Mohieddin, to Washington to discuss details. The United States, in turn, would send Vice President Hubert H. Humphrey to Cairo.

At a press conference on May 28, Nasser startled reporters with newly found praise for the United States. He described the United States as the "greatest world power." He praised its "traditional anti-colonialism!"

Seemingly, Nasser had reason to believe the United States would resume its role of Uncle Samaritan again.

But the United States and Egypt never exchanged vice presidential visits. Nasser had taken one gamble too many. The military pact with Jordan had encircled the Israelis and convinced them that they must strike first or be strangled.

For a third important traveller on the road to the June War, President Lyndon B. Johnson, the journey was painful emotionally and frustrating officially.

Like many Americans, Johnson warmly admires Israel's people and their achievements. This feeling has deepened through friendships with men who are interested in Israel's progress and survival. When Johnson was Senate majority leader in 1956, he joined with the then Minority Leader William F. Knowland to talk President Eisenhower out of sanctions against Israel after the Sinai campaign. Later, as President, Johnson once reassured a group of anxious Israeli diplomats by rising to his full height and saying:

"I am six foot four inches tall. And every one of those inches is for you people."

To these feelings, during the crisis that preceded the war, strategic considerations were added.

Israel is, in effect, an ally in the global conflict. As Professor Strausz-Hupé, head of the University of Pennsylvania's Institute of Foreign Relations Research, puts it:

"Israel, along with Sweden and Switzerland, is one of our three best NATO allies. Of course, none of these small nations are NATO members. But they play indispensable roles in preserving NATO. Sweden, for instance, is a northern anchor for NATO. As long as it stands ready to fight, the Soviets can't outflank Europe from the north (in a conventional war). Switzerland is the center. Now that France is virtually out of NATO, Switzerland is the only land bridge between NATO members West Germany and Italy. We must depend on the forebearance of the Swiss to overfly their country, since France no longer permits it.

"Israel, the strongest military power in its region, is the southern anchor for NATO. As long as it remains friendly to the West, it helps maintain the status quo in the Mediterranean—provided, of course, the Sixth Fleet remains there. This is because Israel regards any attempt by the Soviets to form a unified pro-Moscow internationale of Arab states as a threat against its own security and will fight to prevent encirclement and defeat."

On the other hand, Johnson had to consider a dilemma that has plagued every president since Harry Truman. Aid to Israel outrages the Arab world. As a result, the United States has been extremely reluctant to provide Israel with arms, preferring when possible to encourage others to do so: Canada, West Germany, and France.

To add to all this, the war in Vietnam, coupled with Congressional reluctance to get involved elsewhere, not only barred aid to Israel—it forced Johnson to break his solemn word to Premier Eshkol.

When Eshkol visited Johnson in 1966 and discussed the unsettled conditions in his region, Johnson said (as Eshkol later recalled):

"Don't be afraid. If something happens, we'll be with you within two hours." Johnson, according to Eshkol, then added, for emphasis:

"You must know that I always keep my promises."

Now Johnson not only couldn't be with Israel in two hours, he couldn't even rally other nations for a collective effort to open the Strait.

As the May crisis escalated toward war, Johnson asked the Pentagon, the CIA, and the State Department to predict the outcome. The opinions differed only in the estimate of the number of days it would take Israel to win. The Pentagon thought it would take four days.

Here, the record must await clarification by future historians. In Israel, this writer was told by the highest sources that President Johnson sent word indirectly through mutual friends several days before the war, that Israel had his blessing if war came. Implied, if not specifically stated (according to Israeli sources), was the message that the U.S. would try to keep the USSR from intervening and that there would be no repetition of 1957, when the U.S. joined with the Soviets to force the Israelis out of conquered Sinai before a durable peace was negotiated.

At the White House, however, in an interview fifteen months after the war, this writer was told otherwise. President Johnson insisted that the Israelis had been warned *not* to go it alone.

Journey Into Loneliness

For Israel, the road to war was a journey into loneliness. Not since Czechoslovakia yielded to Hitler had a small nation felt so abandoned.

This was the fourth time the Jews of Palestine had faced annihilation.

In 1942, before statehood, Rommel's armored corps, moving across North Africa toward Palestine, threatened to bring Hitler's "final solution" with them. But the Jewish settlers, although menaced, had the British at their side.

In the 1948 War of Independence, as we've seen, the Communist bloc rushed arms, while the Soviet Union played for time in the UN, winning truces that were utilized by the hard-pressed Israelis to organize their forces and import weapons.

In 1956, the Israelis routed the Egyptians in the Sinai. But they didn't have to worry about Egypt's air force. The British and French simultaneously attacked the Suez area.

But in 1967, not one great power so much as raised its voice against the threatened destruction of Israel.

On May 23, one day after Nasser closed the Strait of Tiran, Israel's Foreign Minister, Abba Eban, set out for Paris, London, and Washington, as he recalls, "to probe the meaning and content of the West's solemn commitments to protect Israel's waterway rights." He wanted to sound out the West's commitment too on the general issue of survival, to see if Israel had support—military or political.

"The first shock concerning the erosion of the West's position was in Paris, when I saw De Gaulle," Eban recalled. "All had melted away. France had promised the most precise backing to Israel's sovereignty and security. But that was in 1957 BCG (before Charles de Gaulle)—now, therefore, invalid, not to be honored."

In London, Eban found sympathy, but no action. In Washington, President Johnson said he needed time to rally international support for re-opening the Strait of Tiran.

But there was no time.

In his pocket as he talked to President Johnson, Eban had a cable, just received, from Premier Eshkol.

"Emphasis is no longer on Strait of Tiran," it read, "but on Sinai. It is flooded with Egyptian forces and tanks."

There were now seven Egyptian divisions facing Israel on her southern borders. The question no longer concerned the opening of a waterway, but the fate of Israel itself.

On May 27, the day after Eban returned empty-handed to Jerusalem, Israel's cabinet voted whether to go to war. The vote was 9–9, a standoff. As the meeting broke up, a messenger handed Premier Eshkol a letter from President Johnson. It told Eshkol that Premier Alexei Kosygin had warned he would go to the aid of the Egyptians, if they were attacked.

"Wait!" President Johnson cautioned.

The spectre of Russian intervention haunted subsequent meetings of the cabinet and the Knesset's security committee.

The aged lion, David Ben-Gurion, now eighty-one, who had led Israel in its last two wars, argued against war. In its other wars, Israel had the support of great powers. Now, it wasn't only alone, but a great power stood ready to intervene on the other side.

As June came, two developments tipped the scales for war.

As we've seen, King Hussein put his army under Egyptian command. Nasser's Cairo Radio liked to call Hussein "the dwarf from Amman." Hussein reciprocated the compliment by calling Nasser, "the evil canker of the Arab world." Now, as "dwarf" and "canker" embraced, the Israelis faced an Arab unity—never before achieved—and a new peril: three hundred thirty miles of Jordanian-Israeli border to defend.

On June 2, General Moshe Dayan entered the cabinet as defense minister, "and from then on," as one cabinet minister recalls, "we could feel things firming up toward a decision."

Dayan had visited Vietnam during the preceding fall, where he had studied Soviet weapons. Later in Washington, he had explored the possibility of Russian intervention in an Israeli-Arab war and had come to the conclusion that the Soviets did not yet have the mobile power, the aircraft carriers and marines, with which to support their proxies.

On June 4, the cabinet decided that Israel's armed forces would take advantage of the next provocation to launch an "anticipatory counter-offense," i.e., a preemptive first strike.

When Levi Eshkol went to bed at 2 a.m. that night, he knew that in five hours and twenty-eight minutes the war would begin.

8

AND THOU SHALT
FIGHT THY WARS
WITH GUILE

—PROVERBS XXIV:6

As it turned out, the piece of the globe that the Soviets covet most was precisely the area they understood least. They didn't understand the Jews. And they didn't understand the Arabs. The result was one of the costliest bloopers in Soviet history—a $2 billion misunderstanding that cost the Russians a ten-year outpouring of arms, plus a humiliating nuclear confrontation with the U.S.

Where was the highly-touted and universally respected Soviet spy network that reached, reputedly, into every nook and cranny of the globe? The Soviet network was at work in Tel Aviv, all right, and in Cairo, and in Damascus and Beirut. Indeed, in all these capitals, the Soviets maintained the biggest embassies and presumably the biggest spy networks of anybody.

Trouble was, an Intelligence Service is no better or worse than the society it serves. As a part of the Soviet system, Soviet Intelligence looked out at the Israeli and Arab worlds through restrictive blinkers.

Being authoritarian, the Soviet system prevents the Intelligence agent or diplomat from mingling with the locals. Big Brother—the KGB—is watching. As non-minglers, how could the Russians grasp the Jews' fierce pride in their past and the attachment to their present piece of land which, as Deuteronomy teaches, the Lord Himself set aside for them? Being a religion with a dogma, Communism bemused the Russians with the idea that the Israelis are "lackeys of Western imperialism." How could they stand up to the "progressive" Arabs who had the "historic forces of revolution" on their side? And being materialistic, the Communists were certain that the heaviest battalions always win. How could a Communist Intelligence officer report to his comrade boss back home that the Jews had an army far more potent than its numbers, because its fighting concepts were rooted in the Bible? That with these concepts today's Jewish few, like their ancestors, could overcome the many?

The Making of the Israeli Army

For years, as future commanders of Israel's army studied in the staff school near Tel Aviv, they could see inscribed on a wall the sixth verse from the twenty-fourth chapter of Proverbs: "And Thou Shalt Fight Thy Wars with Guile."

This is a reminder that modern Israel's military problems, like those of ancient Israel, are so towering that solutions can't be found in orthodox military teaching. The solutions must be original.

First, there is the problem of numbers—2,400,000 Jews against 65,000,000 Arabs.[1] Then there is geography. Israel is a coastal strip, the size of New Jersey, pitted against a subcontinent; a thin wedge, seventy miles across at its widest point—jammed between the two halves of the Arab World. Surrounded on three sides, Israel has 590 miles of land frontier to defend. And there is

[1] Israel's pre-war population was 2,650,000—2,400,000 Jews, and the remainder Moslems, Druzes and Christians.

the political problem. Israel's neighbors refuse to make peace and are forever seeking more weapons and building up their armies for The Day.

Four remarkable men found answers to these problems. They included an Englishman, Orde Wingate, who believed as an article of faith that the Jews are the Chosen People, and a scholar, Yigael Yadin, who kept bucking for a degree in archaeology while laying the foundations for Israel's unique defense system. Both looked to the Bible as a military manual. Moshe Dayan, who routed the Egyptians in less than 100 hours in 1956, and Major General Yitzhak Rabin, the chief of staff in 1967, went on to hone a modern fighting force which, as military historian Barbara Tuchman put it: "Carried out (with the June War) the most nearly perfect military operation in modern history."

Late in 1936, there came to Palestine a thirty-three-year-old British captain by the name of Orde Wingate who acted in so un-British a manner that the Jews at first set him down as a spy. The proper British attitude, as set by the Mandatory authorities, was to be pro-Arab and anti-Jewish. Yet here was an Englishman who, soon after his arrival, announced he was a passionate Zionist and proclaimed it a privilege to help achieve a Jewish State.

Wingate was a man of five feet six inches, with an ascetic's thin face and an enthusiast's burning eyes. He carried a Bible at all times, which he read in Hebrew.

Once, while travelling with a Jewish friend through the Jezreel Valley enroute to Haifa, Wingate became agitated as he studied the topographic features of the countryside. As Wingate's biographer, Christopher Sykes, tells the story, Wingate cried out:

"But why was he defeated? He ought to have won this battle. The man was a fool!"

"What man?" Wingate's startled companion asked.

"I mean Saul," said Wingate, and then went on: "That man had all his army there . . . up there on the heights of Gilboa, south of his water supply, which was there (pointing)—imagine the folly of that when his enemy was to the north there, in Shunem."

When Wingate's companion asked whether it mattered today what Saul did then, Wingate burst out:

"Matter! Of course it matters! By his incompetence, Saul threw away the greatest position a man could occupy in history. He was King of the Jews! He had been elected to rule over the most wonderful people in the whole world, the only people who had discovered God!" [2]

Despite this suspicious behavior, and despite Wingate's job as captain in the hated British Intelligence, Orde Wingate in time became "Hayedid"—the friend—to Palestine Jews.

But when Wingate came up with the pioneering idea that was to provide the basic concept for Jewish fighting methods thereafter, the Jews of Palestine would have none of it.

The Jewish settlers had defended themselves against Arab marauders from behind their stockades and barbed wire.

Wingate proposed special units to go out by night to attack the Arab raiders in their home bases. He proposed further, that these units be composed of Jews as well as British, a repugnant idea to both. The Jews could not see themselves fighting side by side with the British. The British, in turn, were loath to see Jews kill Arabs. But the young British captain with the fiery eyes had his way. So were born the historic "Special Night Squads."

These gave Palestinian Jews their first opportunity to fight Arabs as part of a legal military unit.

From Wingate, Israel's future generals now began to learn warfare methods as unconventional as Wingate's idea that Jews make great soldiers.

General Moshe Dayan, one of Wingate's Special Night Squad fighters, told this writer:

"Wingate was my great teacher. His teaching became part of me and was absorbed into my blood. He taught that numbers don't matter. Even if we were three against a hundred, or even one against fifty, there was a way to win.

"You studied your enemy. You outwitted him. Since you were always the few against the many, you used the cover of night.

[2] *Orde Wingate,* by Christopher Sykes, Collins, St. James Place, London.

You extracted the last ounce of surprise from the timing, the place, the method, and the weapon."

From the Bible, the British captain would cite ancient Hebrew tactics to underline his instruction.

There was Gideon, for example, who—with only three hundred picked Jewish warriors—put to rout a vast host of Midianites. Wingate liked to go into details. Not only did Gideon attack by night, but he chose the moment when the Midianites had just changed the guard. Gideon also deceived the enemy into believing they were surrounded by a great host by having his handful of men raise a great clamor, with trumpets and the breaking of pitchers, which concealed torches. Wingate was so taken with Gideon's guile that once, in an attack on an Arab base, he re-enacted the Gideon tactics, but with bugles instead of ram horn trumpets.

Although the Israelis have been producing a master ruse, straight from Gideon, in war after war, the Arabs never seem to catch on.

For example: during the June War, Israel's three destroyers (one an ancient frigate captured from the Egyptians in 1956), three old submarines (one couldn't submerge), and eight motorboats had to keep Egypt's seven modern destroyers, twelve submarines, twenty missile-carrying boats, and forty PT torpedo boats from raising havoc with Israel's populous Mediterranean coast. Guile did it.

For a full week before the June War, the Israelis made believe in broad daylight that they intended to storm the Egyptian garrison at Sharm el-Sheikh and free the Strait of Tiran. They brought down four landing craft and, with the Egyptians watching, loaded them aboard a ship at the Israeli Red Sea port of Eilat. But at night, the Israelis unloaded the landing craft, removed them to the desert, then repeated the loading performance the next day and for several days thereafter. The Israelis also sent motor boats charging up the Red Sea coast at thirty knots, ostensibly on re-connaisance. This so convinced the Egyptians, that they moved 40 percent of their Navy down through the Suez Canal to protect Sharm el-Sheikh. There they remained, bottled up in the Red Sea during the war, when Nasser blocked their exit route—the Suez Canal.

After all the surprising places in which the Israelis had shown up in previous wars, they could still surprise the enemy in the June War. To crush the Syrians lying atop fifteen-hundred-foot high escarpments, the Israelis sent their tanks up the steepest incline, a seemingly impassable route.

Syrian prisoners said later: "In our wildest and most horrible dreams, we didn't think the Israeli tanks would come up where they did."

Night fighting, as taught by Wingate, became so fixed a habit of Jewish military operations that, as one Israeli general told this writer:

"If dawn came before we finished an operation, we all felt naked. The thing that frightened me most during the War of Liberation [1947–49] was to be caught out somewhere during daylight."

It wasn't only the cover of darkness that the numerically inferior Israelis were after. They knew that the Arabs abhor night fighting, and the hand-to-hand combat it entails. So, few Israeli attacks, no matter how complicated the operation, have been launched except at night.

Wingate helped create the Israeli army tradition that an officer leads his men into battle—he doesn't follow. Wingate would stride ahead of his night fighters and, while they waited behind, would prowl an enemy village to get information on numbers, disposition, and arms.

Twenty percent of all casualties during the 1967 Six-Day War were officers—up to the rank of colonel—who were in the thick of the fighting with their men.

In the climax to the battle for Jerusalem—the assault on the walled Old City—the brigade commander, Col. Mordechai Gur, led the dash through the Lion's Gate, although Jordanian snipers still mounted the walls.

The Israeli officer isn't up front only for morale. He is up there "to see and to solve," as the June War's chief of staff, General Yitzhak Rabin put it. In contrast, senior Egyptian officers sat at headquarters well to the rear. By the time reports from the fighting fronts filtered up to them through channels, were digested, and new orders issued—there weren't any Egyptians around to execute them.

From Wingate, too, came the Israeli officers' easy, first-name informality with their men. The Jewish squadsmen called their captain *Hayedid* (the friend) or simply by his first name, Orde. At an Israeli base camp in the Sinai after the June War, I watched animated clusters of officers and men pursue the favorite Jewish sport, political argument. All were on a first-name basis. Often the men addressed officers by nicknames.

A reporter who went looking for a Colonel Y. at the Defense Ministry in Tel Aviv during the June War, was told by the colonel's pert young girl-soldier-secretary that there was no such Col. Y.

"But I talked to him only an hour ago," the reporter protested. "The colonel was sitting right there. He's a short man."

"Oh!" the secretary exclaimed, "You mean 'Djook' (cockroach)!"

Nor is there any nonsense about saluting. I traveled some four hundred miles through the Sinai in the company of a major and a captain. No enlisted men saluted them at checkpoints, camp entrances, anywhere.

Top brass gets the same treatment. An Israeli correspondent told of a visit to a Sinai camp with Chief of Staff Rabin. Only the sentry at the camp's gate raised his hand in casual salute. Several dozen soldiers who lounged nearby merely mumbled "Shalom," and got a "Shalom" in reply from the general. General Rabin then talked to a group of soldiers who had just returned from a night assault. One man, lounging easily, answered the general's questions about the battle. Then, in the middle of a sentence, he seemed to decide that the Chief of Staff required some military courtesy. Casually, without interrupting his answers, he brought his feet together to "attention." General Rabin flicked his wrist and said, "That's not necessary."

Inquiry revealed there is no Hebrew equivalent for the "Sir!" with which enlisted men usually address officers. The closest an Israeli soldier comes to it is with a "Yes, commander!"

Orde Wingate inspired his Jewish soldiers to believe they were far superior to their Arab enemies. He underlined this belief with the constantly expressed hope that he would someday lead an army of Jewish soldiers.

Wingate never realized this dream. The British in Palestine finally tired of this Englishman's Zionism and transferred him out, forbidding him ever to set foot in the Holy Land. Wingate was a major general when he died in an airplane crash during World War II. Winston Churchill said of him in the House of Commons:

"He was a man of genius who could have become a man of destiny."

Churchill didn't know it, but Wingate *had* become a man of destiny. What Wingate taught his Jewish soldiers was destined to help defeat the Arabs in the guerrilla wars of the 1930s and to have world consequences later.

The Ancient Map that Won a Modern Battle

It remained for a bookish soldier, who later became a world famous archaeologist, to convert Orde Wingate's precepts into victory in Israel's War of Independence. This was Yigael Yadin who somehow managed to blend two passions, the study of the art of warfare and the study of archaeology, and to reinforce one with the other, to achieve success in both. Yadin, now a professor of archaeology at Hebrew University in Jerusalem, is the author of two classics on Biblical warfare: "The Scroll of the War of the Sons of Light Against the Sons of Darkness," and "The Art of Warfare in Biblical Lands." His researches helped win two decisive battles in Israel's War of Independence and inspired Israel's present system of defense which can materialize a powerful striking force of reservists virtually overnight.

In his teens, Yadin, like Moshe Dayan, fought with the underground Haganah and with Wingate's Special Night Squads. As World War II approached, and with it the threat of Nazi invasion, the Haganah leaders created a special fighting force, also underground, the Palmach. Yadin, then in his late twenties, took charge of training Palmach officers at a clandestine school, hidden in the hills near Nazareth.

Where did the archaeological student Yadin get the savvy to train military officers?

"We had the best military manuals in the world," Yadin told this writer. "American, British, Russian, French. We used to translate them into Hebrew, and we took out of them what we thought was best suited to our needs." And, of course, Yadin had Wingate's teachings.

As chief of operations in Israel's War of Independence, Yadin relied on his scholarly researches to apply Wingate's dictum: "Extract the utmost surprise from timing, place, method, and weapon."

As Professor Yadin told this writer:

"My studies of the Biblical warfare showed that the use of terrain (in Palestine) hadn't changed in the last three thousand years.

"When the Moabites and Amanites (today's Jordanians), the Assyrians (today's Iraqis), and the Egyptians invaded ancient Israel, they used certain roads dictated by the terrain. In the War of Independence, then, I could anticipate the invasion route of the Syrians, because they would use the same roads and defiles their ancestors used."

One bit of anticipating involved the fate of the entire northern front. The key to its defense was the Jewish settlement, Degania, which lies just southwest of the Sea of Galilee.

As Yadin had anticipated, the Syrians passed the Yarmūk River in their planned assault on Degania. They numbered six thousand troops as against one thousand Israelis. Here Yadin extracted surprise from the weapon used as well as the place.

A day before the battle, four 65-millimeter cannons of 1870 vintage, without sights, arrived in Israel by ship. The then Prime Minister, David Ben-Gurion, wanted to rush them to Jerusalem to help lift the siege there. Yadin argued they were needed at Degania.

"We argued for hours over those pathetic cannon," Yadin recalls. As a compromise, two of the four guns went to Degania. The two "pathetic cannon" couldn't do much damage. But they could deceive the Syrians into believing that the Israelis had substantial artillery.

"The cannon arrived at the last moment," Yadin recalls. "Our men immediately began to fire them. Some of the shells fell into the Sea of Galilee. Some squirted off sideways." But the ruse worked. The Syrians expected neither cannon, nor waiting Israelis, and took to their heels.

Yadin liked to line the walls of his operations room with Roman maps of ancient Palestine. This scholarly hobby helped beat the Egyptians and end the 1947–49 war.

"We had a terrible time with the Egyptians," Yadin recalls. "They held most of the Negev, thanks to their control of the two main roads in the area: the Via Maris along the coast, and the road leading south from Beersheba into the Sinai. There was no use attacking the Egyptians frontally. They guarded the roads with tanks, and we had none."

Yadin took to his Roman maps, and was rewarded with the discovery of an ancient road that led across the Sinai sand dunes to a spot called Ahuja el Fahir, just behind the Egyptian encampment south of Beersheba.

A young lieutenant, Yitzhak Rabin, later chief of staff, was dispatched with a squad of engineers, to search out the ancient road. A man of few words, he reported:

"Difficult, but passable."

That night, Israeli engineers levelled off the worst stretches of sand that had drifted the road, laid down planks on other portions. Before dawn, a motorized brigade using ancient half-tracks negotiated the Roman road and emerged in the rear of the Egyptians. Here, Yadin had extracted surprise from place as well as method. The surprise was so complete that the commanding Egyptian colonel was captured in his pajamas.

"Where in the world did you come from?" he wanted to know.

"We thought we had all the roads blocked."

Thanks to this piece of guileful warfare, armistice negotiations began soon after.

At the end of the War of Independence, Prime Minister Ben-Gurion named Yadin chief of staff and presented him with a challenge as big as any he had faced during the war. This was to devise a defense system for a country that was neither at peace nor at war. The Arabs had signed armistice agreements but no permanent peace or border treaties. They regarded themselves as legally at war with Israel and openly prepared for the "next round."

Yadin's task was to create a defense system which would spare Israel the burden of maintaining an armed camp. It had to permit the people to go about their business, develop their country, absorb immigrants, yet secure Israel against invasion and annihilation.

Yadin borrowed partly from the modern Swiss and a good deal from Kings Solomon and David, to come up with a system based both on reservists and on border settlement strongholds manned chiefly by civilians.

Yadin had found that David's army was composed of two separate formations—the regular army and the militia. This militia was a people's army of reservists, called up only in time of emergency. The rest of the time, as Professor Yadin wrote in his *Art of Warfare in Biblical Lands*, they lived at home, pursuing their peacetime occupations, except for a minimum period of reserve service once a year.

"It is no accident that the modern defense forces of Israel established after thousands of years of exile," Yadin has pointed out, "should today be organized on a pattern similar to that of the armies of David and Solomon. The Israeli forces of today are also based on a relatively small regular standing army and a large militia founded on exactly the same principles that governed the formation of David's militia."

Core of the Israeli system is the drafted boy or girl of eighteen, called up for thirty-six and twenty-four months of duty, respectively. Only the mentally and physically handicapped, and members of some religious sects, stay out. And even some of these are drafted for office work. Married girls are exempt. Girls studying to become teachers are deferred.

During peacetime, this army of draftees serves as a training ground and as a deterrent force. Since Israel is forever repelling Arab guerrilla raids or mounting retaliatory expeditions into Arab territory, it is a rare draftee who doesn't come out of service without some combat experience. Once out, he keeps his uniform, his rifle or Uzzi (an Israeli submachine gun), and reports for yearly training that may last as much as forty-two days. Like a volunteer fireman, he's ready to race to his post at any time, day or night.

To keep costs down, Israel drafts civilian equipment, too. All vehicles that can be used in war—bulldozers, milk tankers (for water), buses, automobiles—are registered with reserve units, inspected regularly by the army, and are called up during war, like soldiers.

The professional force consists of a small number of senior officers and of Israeli Air Force pilots. So, in war, 80 percent of the Israeli Defense Forces are reservists.

"It is quite clear that if the future of the country depends on such a bizarre system," Professor Yadin told this writer, "it had to be tested and re-tested so that it was provably workable."

So, in 1950 and again in 1951, over the protests of many cabinet ministers, Yadin conducted nationwide shadow mobilizations.

"We had the greatest peacetime maneuvers ever," Yadin recalls. "Once we called up a hundred thousand troops, and virtually the entire economy ground to a halt."

The mobilization of reservists was rehearsed over and over until the mobilization time was whittled down to two days. By the time of the Six-Day War, Yadin's "bizarre scheme" worked with routine perfection.

In Cairo, or Amman, or Damascus, life went on much as usual during the June war. Buses, cars, and trucks jammed the streets. Crowds thronged the sidewalks. Shops were open for business. Except for sandbags piled before public buildings, and crowds gathered before radio loudspeakers, a visitor might not know there was a war on.

Tel Aviv, Haifa, and Jerusalem, on the other hand, bore the aspect of deserted cities. Streets were empty of buses. They and their drivers had gone to war. So had the taxis and *their* drivers. So had the trucks and truck drivers. Starting on May 15, males from eighteen to forty-nine (and in many cases, over) began to disappear. Boys and girls under eighteen took over from the mailmen. Wives took over from shopkeepers. When this wasn't possible, the shop was closed, and a sign posted:

"Off on a guided tour through Egypt. Back soon."

Once, when General Moshe Dayan explained the Israeli reserve system to a French general and told him that Israel's soldiers ride to a battlefront in civilian buses and wear their own civilian overcoats in winter, the French general was nonplussed.

"I could sense he was conjuring up an army of the Eighteenth Century," Dayan wrote later, "capable of mounting the barricades with their flags, but not able to conduct a desert campaign with armored vehicles and cope with the maintenance of long supply lines."

The French general would have boggled even more had he seen how the mobilization machinery went into action and who some of the reservists were. Drafted into service, besides buses, trucks, and taxis, was virtually anything that could roll on its own power: laundry and ice cream delivery trucks, Volkswagens, Volvos, and Fords. Some were pressed into service on such short notice that there was no time to daub them with camouflage paint. The infantry brigade that fought at Um Katef in the Sinai, for instance, rode to the edge of the sand dunes in shiny blue tourist buses.

The reservist listened to the radio for code words that called up his unit, or a runner brought him the news at his home. If the reservist wasn't in, a red slip was tucked under his door. The reservist was out of his house or apartment in minutes, lugging his rifle or Uzzi, and racing for a waiting truck within a half-mile from his home. This hauled him to a larger assembly point, where a convoy of trucks waited to take him to his camp. If the reservist missed the truck in his neighborhood, he hitchhiked to his camp.

The reserve system worked so well that in some units 110 percent of those listed showed up. No one was turned away.

"We accept them," a general said. "Who's surplus, only the computer knows, later."

Many argued their way in.

One fellow in his thirties, who didn't believe in serving during peacetime and had evaded service since the 1956 war, now pleaded:

"It's true I've been evading service. But now I want to go. You can put me on trial later."

A fifty-seven-year-old grandmother of seven, once a nurse with the Red Army, had been too old for service when she came to Israel. Now, she kept a grocery store in Tiberias. When her delivery truck was drafted, she insisted on her rights under the regulations.

These provide that a reservist whose vehicle is called up can serve as its driver. It was stretching a point, but the grandmother was allowed to go in with her delivery truck, and was assigned to a medical unit on the Syrian front.

Another, who won his argument to get in, was a thirty-year-old teacher, Eitan Yahalom, who has but one eye and was exempt under an "invalidating classification." The teacher demanded and received a medical examination for re-classification. He made it.

The reservists ranged from privates to generals.

Big, earthy Brigadier General Abraham Jaffe, who led a tank brigade that sealed off the Mitla Pass and trapped thousands of Egyptians, directs the Society for the Protection of Nature in Israel during peacetime. Two weeks before the war, he was lying in the swamps of southern France, bird-watching. General Jaffe's deputy, Lt. Col. Issahar Shadmi, manages a Tel Aviv skyscraper.

At a captured Egyptian camp in the Sinai, this writer found that the captain in charge of brigade operations was an administrator in Tel Aviv's school system. The deputy brigade commander—a lieutenant colonel who, incidentally, conducted a press conference in Hebrew, English, French, and German—was a fire alarm manufacturer.

Along with the reserve plan, Yadin organized a parallel system of militarily self-contained border settlements. The border kibbutzim or villages go about their day-to-day agricultural and industrial business. But during war, they become military strongholds. Since the younger men are in the army or are called up as reserves, the fighting is left to men beyond the reservist age of forty-nine. A commissioned officer, one of their own neighbors, commands them. The Army quartermaster corps supplies rifles, machine guns, bazookas, and barbed wire, and helps prepare deep concrete shelters for the women and children.

New settlements, particularly exposed and vulnerable to attack, are "manned" by boys and girls from Nahal, an organization that trains boys and girls for farming as well as fighting.

The Making of the Israeli Soldier

At a captured Egyptian base camp in the Sinai, soon after the June war, I had my first acquaintance with Israel's fighting men. They were a curiously unmilitary lot. In the desert heat, comfort had supplanted spit-and-polish. No two pairs of headgear, pants, or shoes were alike. One warrior wore a yarmulka, the skullcap worn during prayer; another affected a forage cap, and another a jaunty Australian campaigners' hat with feather. One original had on a Russian tank crewman's felt headpiece with earlaps to keep out the noise. Footgear and pants were equally diverse. Some affected Egyptian sandals, others tennis sneakers. A few wore their Army issue boots. Most had shed their camouflaged dress and put on dungarees. Others wore tennis or track shorts.

As striking as the diversity of get-ups was the human diversity. No American melting-pot could top this ethnic mélange: blonde, tall, straight-nosed types whose families had lived for generations in Germany and Russia; swarthy, aquiline-nosed youths from Morocco, Tunisia, Iraq and Egypt; dark, squat, and bearded young

men from the Yemen who seemed to have just stepped out of a
stylized mural of Babylonian or Assyrian charioteers. Plus a
sprinkling of tall, fine-featured and dusky youths from India.

Truly, this was a human Joseph's coat of many colors, patched
together from the offspring of a hundred and one countries. More
than half of them were "Islamic Jews" from the Arab world.
They had been born in the ghettos of Baghdad and Damascus,
Cairo and Algiers, or were the children of parents born there.
These parents had brought a part of the Arab world with them to
Israel: oversized families, poverty, lack of schooling. Yet their
sons had fought while their Arab counterparts took off their
shoes and ran away. Through some hidden alchemy, Israel had
transmuted the Islamic Jews—and Western Jews alike—into military gold.

This process begins in nursery school where the child starts to
acquire a unique mental baggage, drawn from the Bible, that will
set him apart later from other countries' soldiers.

I have heard Israeli children of four singing nursery rhymes
such as these:

> "One morning when Pharaoh woke up in his bed
> There were frogs on his nose
> And frogs on his head.
> Frogs were jumping everywhere.
> Frogs were here, frogs were there.
> Frogs were everywhere."
>
> [REFRAIN]
>
> "No, No, No, I will not let you go!"

In the second grade, as soon as the pupil has mastered the
ABC's, he reads simplified Bible stories. Thereafter, the Bible is
central in his education. It is a manual for teaching history, geography, and literature.

The visitor to Israel is struck by the number of open trucks he
sees on the roads, outfitted with benches and jammed with children. These are school kids on their way to a history lesson: to

Mt. Tabor where Barak defeated Sisera, the King of Hazor; or to Eshtaol, where Samson was born. Or to a hundred and one other Biblical sites.

In Israel no new kibbutz, settlement, or town may be named by the settlers or town fathers themselves. A committee of scholars and archaeologists delves into Biblical lore to determine the name of the site in Biblical times. This, then, becomes the name. The object is to show that today's Israel is a continuation of three thousand years of history.

The history that proves this continuity, as the Israeli school child can see, preoccupies all Israel. Weekly, in the home of Israel's president in Jerusalem, a select study circle of learned men meets to discuss the Bible, and to listen to research papers. One such paper, read by ex-Prime Minister David Ben-Gurion, contended that only six hundred Jews left Egypt with Moses, not six hundred thousand. This precipitated a bitter debate in the press and radio that lasted for months. Yearly, in Jerusalem, a Bible contest, open to children and adults alike, is followed throughout the country with the same interest that Americans follow the World Series.

Before graduating from high school, the student takes final examinations that may qualify him for university entrance. Five areas are covered. One is the Bible.

The army picks up the youth's Biblical education where the schools left off. Here, a "Knowledge of the Land Department" takes over.

"We wanted to call it the 'Love of the Land Department,'" the Army's educational director, Col. Mordechai Bar-On, told me. "But it sounded too sentimental."

"Israel is a country which is pervaded by the past," Col. Bar-on said. "The Bible is concealed behind the slightest elevation of the soil. Ancient echoes may be heard clearly in its valleys and deserts. Every single stone has its story to tell."

The Israeli Army trains a corps of women teachers to tell the soldier that story. He takes long marches to study the battlefield, near Jerusalem, where the Maccabbee brothers stood off the Greeks. Soon after starting his military service, he marches to

Masada where one thousand Jews withstood ten thousand Romans for three years, then committed suicide rather than surrender. In a torchlight ceremony, he hears the Israeli Army's chief of staff recount the story of Masada, and he takes the oath. "Masada shall not Fall Again."

Mrs. Golda Meir, Israel's onetime foreign minister, once explained why to this writer.

"If another country loses a war," Mrs. Meir said, "say, like Belgium, it is occupied, but the people remain. Finally, the invader moves out, and life as an independent country begins again. Not so with the Jews. Twice when we lost wars in Biblical times, we were dispersed all over the world.

"To rebuild this country, make it ours, we had to come back almost one by one. Today, defeat in war wouldn't mean only dispersion, it would mean genocide. And if you added Israel's 2,400,000 Jews to the 6,000,000 murdered by Hitler, there just wouldn't be enough left to try again. It's our last chance.

"And every boy, every corporal, sergeant, and general, knows this."

9

HOW THE SIX-DAY
WAR WAS WON IN
FOUR DAYS

At the turn of 1964, the Israeli cabinet's defense committee met in Jerusalem to hear how the next war with the Arabs would be won. The newly named Chief of Staff, forty-two-year-old Major General Yitzhak Rabin, gave the design for victory and the preparations it would need. He said a war against the chief enemy, Egypt, could and must be won in four days. Three and one-half years later it was.

General Rabin is a sturdy citizen with a thatch of red hair, steady blue eyes, and a face that might belong to a Russian general—or an Iowa farmer. Rabin uses few words, and these have added weight, because he booms them out slowly in the voice of a basso. With his elders in the Israeli cabinet, Rabin carried further weight. He had been fighting enemies of the Jews since he was fourteen. Rabin's exploits as an underground fighter against the British in Palestine inspired the novelist, Leon Uris, to model the hero of the book, *Exodus*, after him. Rabin had fought in all of Israel's wars since. Now he had been chosen to prepare Israel for its biggest test—the coming showdown, not only against the Arabs, but against the latest Soviet weapons and against Soviet training as well.

Tersely, Rabin outlined the military doctrine, tailored to Israel's special needs, on which Israel would have to rely. Rabin had a phrase for it: "the anticipatory counter-offensive." You hit the enemy at the precise moment he's winding up to hit you. You beat him to the punch.

In war, Rabin explained, Israel has two enemies. The Arabs in the field are one. Time is the other. If the Israelis can't win a short war, they can't win one at all. With Israel's reservist system, virtually all the work force goes to war, and the economy grinds to a halt. Israel must win swiftly, too, or else the big powers step in to save the Arabs from disaster. (When the U.S. goes to war, as in Vietnam, nothing on this planet can stop it, General Dayan once told this writer. But Israel is like a mouse that waits at the hole to dart out for a piece of cheese. "We have to move fast," he said.)

Israel, then, must plan for a war that it can fight and win in four days, even three days, Rabin told the Cabinet.

Israel must attack, "take charge of the war, conduct it," Rabin said. Yet it can't fight a preventive war; that would offend world opinion. Israel must let the enemy mobilize, gather on Israel's borders, proclaim to the world that this time the Jews will be annihilated—then hit the enemy with an "anticipatory counter-offensive," just before he starts to make good his threat.

In the three and one-half years between Rabin's talk to the cabinet and the June War, Rabin harnessed Israel's best brains—those of its scientists and scholars, professional soldiers, politicians, and industrialists—to the job of rethinking Israel's military plans, reorganizing, re-equipping, and retraining its army.

The Israelis relied on intelligence with a little "i" to win the coming war. But they began their preparations with Intelligence with a big "I." If you wait to hit the enemy until the precise moment he is about to hit you, it's a risky business unless you have an Intelligence service that knows the enemy's intentions as well as it knows its own. In the coming war, Intelligence would have an additional job. It would have to find out what the Russians were teaching the Egyptians and how well the Egyptians were learning it; what the Russians were giving the Egyptians and how well the Egyptians were using it.

Spy or Die

Just before the Israelis attacked the Jordanian stronghold atop Augusta Victoria in East Jerusalem—during the Six-Day War—a messenger ran up with an Intelligence packet. It contained information about the Jordanian major who commanded the hill. It was a curiously detailed personal study.

The Jordanian major, so the Israeli commander read, was a thirty-seven-year-old Palestinian, a city-bred Jerusalemite. Between the major and his colonel, a Bedouin, the report said, was distrust and enmity. The major had lied to his colonel in the past to cover up errors in judgment and, in the coming battle, probably would lie again. The major, so the report went on, had left his wife who had since gone to live in Kuwait. An expert in Arab calligraphy had studied the major's handwriting and had deduced from it that the officer was emotionally unstable. He might even break and desert his men under fire. The report was prophetic.

As the Israelis prepared to storm the Augusta Victoria Heights, two cars, a Jeep and an Opel, left the Jordanian positions and made their way down toward Jerusalem. A bazooka knocked out the Opel. The jeep got as far as a garage on the road that ran along the foot of the Heights. Five men jumped out and were shot as they fled. One was the Jordanian major who commanded the Heights.

Israel's Intelligence, as deputy chief of Army Intelligence, Colonel David Carmon told this writer, "is the safety valve of our entire defense system. If you depend for eighty percent of your army on reserve callups, Intelligence must sound the alert. It must be on a war footing three hundred sixty-five days per year, twenty-four hours a day. We in Intelligence work harder in-between wars than we do during war."

The famed Israeli Intelligence actually embraces five secret services.

Army Intelligence gathers military and political information. This ranges from the study of the Arab mind, to the gathering of information on the foibles of Arab military commanders.

Shin Beth handles internal security. For years, Shin Beth supplied King Hussein with names and whereabouts of Egyptian and Syrian terrorists who based themselves in Jordan for raids into Israel.

Central Intelligence is a counterespionage organization which heads up directly into the Prime Minister's office. Its agents sent bombs through the mail to the German scientists working on missiles for Nasser. They "liquidated" others and so terrified the rest that no first-rate German scientist would remain. Nasser turned to charlatans who wasted Egypt's substance in wild goose chases for nuclear weapons. These, of course, Shin Beth did not touch.

The other two secret services include Police Intelligence and a modest information-gathering service in the Foreign Ministry. But, it's on Army Intelligence that Israel depends for its knowledge of the enemy.

Army Intelligence gets first call on Israel's ablest university graduates, including specialists with advanced degrees.

"We keep our people in the same job for long periods, so that they get to be experts in their fields," a senior Intelligence officer said.

One Israeli Intelligence officer who specialized in Jordanian military strategy, politics, and economics, was indignant when a superior challenged an economic appraisal, saying it differed with that of the Jordanians themselves.

"Of course I know better than they (the Jordanians) do," the Intelligence officer said, "I've studied their methods longer."

Israel's Intelligence has a redoubtable tradition to draw on, for the Jews of Palestine have always had to spy or die. Before Israel became a state, the underground Palmach trained an "Arab Company" of Jewish boys and girls of Islamic origin to live as man and wife in Arab villages. They tilled the soil like fellaheen; some wandered the country with nomadic Bedouin tribes. And they sent back word when Arab marauders meant to call.

Today, no Arab commander or politician can know for sure that Israeli ears aren't listening.

For three years prior to 1965, Israeli Army Intelligence knew every decision of Syria's chief of staff. They knew the secret discussions of Syria's ruling party, the Ba'ath. Israeli Intelligence knew of every shipment of Soviet arms to Syria months before it left Russia. Intelligence had a detailed catalogue, gun by gun, man by man, of the forces lodged on the Syrian Heights above Israel's Huleh Valley. Israeli Intelligence knew all this, because they had planted a quiet, Egyptian-born Israeli into the highest levels of Syrian political and military life.

The spy, Elie Cohen, was a tall, dark haired man who had an actor's talent for losing himself in a new identity. Intelligence trained Elie Cohen for two years in Intelligence work and the nuances of Syrian Arabic, in its special idiom and figures of speech. Cohen was drilled and drilled again in the multitude of details that transformed him into "Kamal Amin Taabes," supposedly born in Syria of parents who took him as a child to Lebanon. As Elie Cohen sank deeper and deeper into the identity of Kamal Amin Taabes, it took a powerful effort of will to answer to his own name and act himself, when he came home to his wife and two children in a suburb near Tel Aviv.

Israeli Intelligence sent Cohen—or Taabes—to Argentina where he established himself as a Syrian expatriate businessman. Cohen-Taabes then "returned" to Damascus where he set himself up in an apartment opposite the office of the Syrian Chief of Staff, where he could know in minutes if exceptional activity was afoot.

As a free-spending young "Syrian importer," Kamal Amin Taabes' apartment soon became the center of gay life. The Israeli spy—who maintained a quiet reserve and never spoke an extra word—became an intimate friend of the Syrian Chief of Staff's nephew, a lieutenant, who revealed the inside doings of the Syrian high command and who took him to inspect the highly restricted military area atop the Syrian Heights. Cohen-Taabes stored in his photographic memory the details he would soon pass on by short wave radio to his compatriots across the border. Through other Syrian friends, Taabes won access to secret military files.

Indeed, the quiet but seemingly brilliant Kamal Amin Taabes established himself so firmly as a Syrian patriot and man of good judgment, that Ba'ath Party leaders sought his counsel and urged him to take a hand in the party's leadership. This Cohen-Taabes side-stepped as too risky.

For five years, through Cohen–Taabes, Israeli Intelligence knew much that the top Syrian military and political leaders knew. Elie Cohen was discovered when the Damascus police, making a routine check of amateur wireless transmitters (hams) sent out a notice to all licensed operators to maintain silence on a set day. Cohen-Taabes had no license and received no notice. He continued his daily wireless report and so was detected. Israel offered to give up all the Syrians it held, some 19 terrorists and spies, for Elie Cohen. Israel sought the help of France and other powers to prevent Elie Cohen's execution. He was tried and hanged. But to the Israelis and to the Arabs, too, Elie Cohen lives as a symbol of Israeli Intelligence's ability to infiltrate agents anywhere in the Arab world, including Arab armies.

When Israeli disposal squads went into the Sinai battlefields to clear away the dead after the Six-Day War, they sent one body clothed in an Egyptian officer's uniform back to Israel for burial with military honors. It was that of an Israeli Intelligence agent known merely as Samil. His body was found inside an Egyptian tank.

"The Arabs had no surprises for us," an Israeli Intelligence officer said. "We knew what they had, and where they had it."

This included the location of thirty SA-2 (SAM) missile sites, built on both sides of the Suez Canal at a cost of about $300 million. The Israeli Air Force destroyed about half of these. Others were spared, and their missiles were hauled away later.

Israeli Intelligence also knew of secret Soviet shipments of sophisticated weapons to the Egyptians, so new that they had not yet been released to the Soviet's Warsaw Pact partners. Israeli Intelligence leaked news of these shipments to the world to induce western powers to sell similar equipment to Israel.

The study of the Arab mind and temperament occupies some of the most gifted analysts in Israeli Intelligence. General Y. Harkabi, a former Army Intelligence chief, has pointed out that the Arab is a loner, mistrustful of his fellows, quarrelsome in his home. He does not involve himself in the collective team effort to win wars.

There is a lack of cohesion in Arab society, General Harkabi has found, that reaches down into the family. This lack emerged when journalists probed the family background of Sirhan Bashir Sirhan, the man accused of murdering Robert F. Kennedy.

The *New York Times* reported:

"Despite their living together most of the time, the Sirhan family—mother, five brothers, and a sister—seemed always to be apart from one another and from their surroundings. They pursued different careers and made different friends. They seldom communicated with each other, in English or in Arabic . . . the father, Bishara Sirhan had left the family (after its arrival in America) and was not heard from again until the (Kennedy) assassination."

The Arab's self-interest and lack of concern for the other fellow, even his kin, as General Harkabi pointed out, showed itself in the June War when Egyptian officers abandoned their men in the burning Sinai. In some instances, the officers took their soldiers' water and food with them. Perhaps the cruelest disregard of their own was the Egyptian High Command's decision to cut off the flow of water to the pipelines in the Sinai while Egyptian soldiers were still straggling home. The aim was to deprive the victorious Israelis. But hundreds of Egyptian soldiers died tortured deaths from thirst. The International Red Cross pleaded with the Egyptians to turn on the water. In vain.

Knowing this lack of cohesion in Arab society and the Arab's tendency to go from euphoria to despair when things go wrong, the Israelis could plan to hit the Arabs as hard as they could at the outset, to shift the fortunes of war immediately.

The Israelis take advantage of another known flaw in the Arab character: the Arab tendency to hide unpleasant reality beneath a dream or a lie. In anticipation of exaggerated Arab claims of victory, General Moshe Dayan ordered a blackout of war bulletins during the first day of the war. The Egyptians claimed such exaggerated victories over the Israeli Air Force that—with no disclaimers from the Israelis—the Russians stalled UN moves for a ceasefire. By the time the Russians learned the truth and pressed for a ceasefire, it was too late to salvage the Egyptian armies.

When Gen. Rabin took command as Chief of Staff, he had to

fit the Israelis' knowledge of the character of the Egyptian soldier and his officers into a new situation, created by the Russians.

When the Israelis chased the Egyptians out of the Sinai in less than one hundred hours in 1956, the Russians realized that arming the Egyptians was not enough. Around 1961, Israeli Intelligence learned that the Russians were reorganizing the Egyptian army. They were teaching the Egyptians to wage war according to the Moscow Doctrine.

"Up to that time, we had no knowledge of the Moscow Doctrine," a senior Intelligence officer said. "We started studying it; we collected everything we could lay our hands on—Soviet military manuals and service journals; the reports of military attachés."

Israeli Intelligence especially mulled over reports on Russian teaching and Egyptian learning from agents inside the Egyptian army.

The Moscow Doctrine is a defensive concept evolved from Russian experience. It employs massive troop concentrations and relies on heavily fortified positions. With special photographic equipment developed by Israeli scientists and with high altitude planes, Intelligence minutely photographed the defensive positions the Russians were helping the Egyptians perfect in the Sinai.

"We studied, and we thought, and we analyzed," a senior Israeli Intelligence officer said. "We asked ourselves how well the Arabs understood the Moscow Doctrine.

"We worried that the Egyptians would tailor the Moscow Doctrine to the character of their officers and soldiers. We felt, had they done so, it could have been a turning point in Arab fighting ability. But we found out they were just copying the Moscow system without adapting it to Egyptian needs and to the desert terrain.

"This opened new possibilities to our fighting forces," the Israeli Intelligence officer said.

Intelligence prepared a book on the Moscow Doctrine. It not only detailed the Russian method of fighting under the Doctrine, but ways to cope with it. The book contained scale drawings to the inch of the newly-built Egyptian fortifications in the Sinai that embodied Moscow Doctrine defense principles. Prize exhibit was the seemingly impenetrable belt of fortifications, three miles wide and five miles deep, at Um catef in the Sinai, thirty miles from Israel's border.

Book in hand, the newly-installed Chief of Staff Rabin began to fashion an answer to the challenge posed by the Russians.

First, Rabin staked out a substantial area in Israel's Negev Desert. Then, going by the book supplied by Intelligence, Rabin's engineers built a model of Um Catef fortifications. They dug trenches, three lines of them, like the ones at Um Catef. They used barrels and crates to simulate bunkers, tanks, and artillery positions. Flag markers indicated minefields. The distance between trenches, the location of mock bunkers and artillery, the minefield areas were exactly the same as in the defense complex at Um Catef. The Israelis called their mock fortifications, "The Russian Positions."

"The Russian Positions" now became the central concern of the Israeli Defense Forces. Officers' schools, Armor and Infantry Schools prepared their own manuals of exercises to solve problems posed by "The Russian Positions."

"We confronted ourselves with every problem we could think of," General Rabin recalled. "What techniques to use in a night assault, what to do by day, what support to get from the engineers.

"We relied a great deal on exercises. The Egyptians carry out small-scale exercises and vest the understanding of an operation only with the senior officers. We acquainted all units from brigade to platoon level—and every man from general to private— with what they would find when they attacked. Our maneuvers simulated the kind of large-scale battle that would be necessary to take the Um Catef positions. Sometimes, in our maneuvers, we used as many as three hundred tanks."

After three years of exercises, as one Israeli officer put it, "I could have found my way blindfolded through Um Catef." Others said, after the June War, "When we broke into the Um Catef positions, it seemed to us as if we had been there before."

10

"BOYS, WE
CLOBBERED
THEM!"

At 5:30 a.m., June 5, 1967, in a briefing room of an Israeli air base, a squadron leader grumbled at his fighter pilots, freshly tumbled from their bunks.

"Anybody don't feel good?"

"Anybody go to bed late? No? Good!"

Then he turned to the briefing room blackboard, cleared a space and wrote in Hebrew:

$$H = 7:45.$$

At other Israeli air bases, at precisely the same time, other squadron leaders chalked up the same electrifying message. At Hour 7:45 a.m., Israel's Air Force would smite the Egyptians.

In Israel's doctrine of the "anticipatory counter-offensive," the Air Force was the swift sword that would strike the first blow. Everything in that air force—pilots, planes, ground crews—had been moulded and prepared for years for that blow.

To provide the highly skilled professionalism this air strike would need, Israel's pilots, unlike the rest of the defense forces, stayed on after their thirty months of draft duty to become career airmen.

They were trained and trained again to fly long distances at virtually ceiling zero—hugging the earth or the sea—to avoid radar detection. Officers and men studied, developed, then rehearsed techniques for attacking planes on the ground. Once a day, the Israeli pilot loaded his cannon and machine guns with live ammunition and flew one sortie against dummy planes lined up on desert runways. Israeli pilots engaged in mock dogfights with an actual MIG 21-C. A defecting Iraqi Air Force officer flew it to Israel in the fall of 1966. Israeli pilots flew it to gain firsthand knowledge of what it could do and how to cope with it.

And with an eye toward a future assault inside Egypt, Israeli pilots learned how to take evasive action against the Soviet anti-aircraft missile, the SA-2. Known as SAM, it travels at three and a half times the speed of sound, tracks down and blasts enemy aircraft out of the air.

When the Israelis bought Mirage fighters in 1957–58, they asked the French to redesign them for the use of cannon instead of missiles. In vain the French protested that missiles were today's sophisticated weapons. The Israelis knew what they wanted. They wanted cannon that would kill planes on the ground. And they got them.

Ground crews, too, were trained for the big punch. When a plane came down from a practice sortie, the ground crew swarmed over it with the urgency of a pit crew servicing a car at the Indianapolis Speedway. On the eve of the June War, Israeli ground crews could refuel, reload, and check out a plane in an average 7.5 minutes. Only the deck crews on American aircraft carriers could come close to this performance.

Israel's scientists developed propellants for a special runway-destroying rocket. The bomb penetrated the asphalt surface of the runway, then burrowed like a mole into the crushed rockbed below. A timing device delayed explosion so that the buried rocket tore a crater five times greater than that achieved by the ordinary bomb, but exploded at irregular intervals to frustrate repair work.

The indispensable Israeli Intelligence worked for the day of the attack.

"We knew everything about the Egyptian Air Force," General

Mordecai Hod, Israel's Air Force commander said later. They knew from reconnaissance photos and other sources about Egyptian airfields, ack-ack batteries, missile sites, the location of Migs and of Tupolev bombers, even the location of wooden dummy or decoy planes. Intelligence also supplied details of the Egyptian pilots' daily routine, the precise hour at which they flew morning patrols, when they had breakfast, how long it took them to get up in the air after an alert. (It took as long as 25 minutes as against an unspecified but substantially lesser time for Israel's pilots.)

Many Israeli pilots seemingly knew far in advance of the big day, the specific Egyptian field they would one day attack. They boned up on the agriculture and history of the Nile Valley or other areas they would fly over, seeking bits of information—the site of a historic landmark, perhaps. They read avidly about Egypt, from its industry to its mythology. Some consulted the Encyclopedia Britannica.

All had been prepared. All had been rehearsed a thousand times.

Now, a little before 7 a.m., the Israeli planes took off for eleven Egyptian bases in the Sinai, at Suez, and in the Nile Valley. The two-engined Vautour fighter-bombers, mounting four cannon each, had the farthest target: Luxor on the Nile, almost twice the distance to Cairo. The single engine Mirages, mounting two cannon, headed for the nearest target at El Arish in the Sinai and elsewhere. Whatever their targets, all had to arrive over them at the same time, 7:45 a.m. Israel time, 8:45 a.m. Cairo time. The Vautours took off first, in flocks of four. The others followed at staggered intervals, carefully calculated.

Israel had staked virtually all on one roll of the dice. Only twelve planes remained behind, against potential air strikes from Jordan, Syria, and Iraq. In an underground command bunker at Tel Aviv, the Air Force brass, cabinet ministers, Intelligence, and Defense Chiefs who had made the final decision, waited in silent knots for the outcome.

For three men, the dragging minutes of radio silence that would be observed until the planes were over their targets, bore down with agonizing weight.

One was the Air Force Commander, General Mordecai Hod.

On his mustachioed face, as he watched the radar screen for enemy planes, the long-legged Hod mirrored confidence. But beneath his balding pate, nagging questions intruded. Only a year before, at thirty-nine, Hod—or "Moti" as everyone called him —had taken over the Air Force from the man who had built it, the redoubtable General Ezer Weizmann, nephew of Israel's first president, Chaim Weizmann. Hod had perfected the final plan for the air strike and had convinced a hesitant Prime Minister Levi Eshkol to take the win-or-lose-all gamble.

The plan's daring was pure Hod, who has lived dangerously all his life. Hod took his first solo flight after only two hours of instruction, when he was a youthful Haganah agent in Italy. Exuberant as well as confident, he took off for the suburban home of his girl friend and sent her family scurrying for safety out of doors as he buzzed the house. Hod got his Air Force Wings in 1949, one of the first batch of fliers to do so. He takes a fierce pride in his Air Force, starting telephone conversations with colleagues with the question:

"What's doing today in the best Air Force in the Near East?"

Now, Hod had an overriding worry. Surprise was at the heart of his plan. The Egyptians, guarding only against a traditional dawn attack, sent their patrols up at sunrise. They returned to base around 7:45 Israel time, when they thought all danger was past. They had breakfast and loafed in their ready rooms. That is why Hod had selected the 7:45 target hour. Still, the war crisis had been building up during the last few weeks, and the Egyptians—already on a war alert—might take it into their heads to increase their patrols well into the morning. Flying low, the Israeli planes were almost certain to avoid radar detection. But what if, in their final leg over Egypt, they were spotted from the ground? General Hod chewed on his unlit cigar and waited for the end of the radio silence that would give him his first clue as to how things were going.

Premier Eshkol, huddled in the bunker with his military advisor, Professor Yigael Yadin, had other worries.

Top priority in the air strike were the Soviet TU 16 (Tupolev) bombers whose three-thousand-mile range placed every Israeli city and settlement at their mercy. They were Egypt's first strike force, and Israel's pilots had been ordered to kill those Tupolevs first, to pay no attention to anti-aircraft batteries, to leave SA-2 and radar sites alone, and to go in for the kill.

But while Israel's Air Force was occupied, what about Syria's twenty-eight Tupolevs and Ilyushins, Iraq's forty-four Soviet bombers, and Jordan's thirty-six American Skyhawks? These could plunge Israel into a bloodbath. In 1948, Egyptian planes, roaming Israel's skies unchallenged, dropped bombs on Tel Aviv's bus station during the evening rush hour, killing forty persons. Although the bunker's airconditioned interior was cool to the point of discomfort, Eshkol wiped perspiration from his forehead.

Inside the bunker, Chief of Staff Rabin, a stoic man, sweated too. To his commanders, poised on the Sinai border, he had promised friendly planes in the sky during their own great gamble—the four-hundred-mile charge through a desert choked with enemy armor.

If the air strike failed, it would be the Israeli armor that would be naked to enemy strafing.

A plan is only as good as the men who execute it. For their execution of Hod's win-or-lose-all gamble, Israel's pilots won the reputation as being among the world's best.

Flying the mirror-smooth Mediterranean at fifty to thirty feet altitude, virtually altitude zero, is a hazardous business. Water and sky blend to create a numbing monotony, requiring a nerve-wracking exertion of will to maintain altitude and avoid ditching.

But electronic eyes were scanning the skies all over the Near East for the very feat the Israelis were now pulling off. These included the radar-laden Russian Intelligence vessels similar to the ill-fated USS *Liberty*; radar-bearing aircraft from the Sixth Fleet's carriers, the British communications center on Cyprus, as well as twenty-three Egyptian radar scanners, sixteen of them in the Sinai. Under the eyes of all these electronic watchdogs, the Israelis streaked undetected toward their targets, flying the last perilous miles over Egypt at palm-tree level.

Over their eleven separate targets at the appointed time, the

Israeli pilots climbed to thirty thousand feet, then dived to three hundred and two hundred feet. They lowered their landing gear, as rehearsed, to slacken speed, and the massacre of the Tupolevs and the Migs began.

At 8:45 a.m. Cairo time, as Israeli Intelligence had predicted, the Israeli pilots could see Egyptian patrol planes taxiing to a halt after their patrols. Pilots were leaving the planes or were walking across airfields. Anti-aircraft crews, too, had been caught by surprise, away from their positions, and the first attack wave had little ack-ack to deal with.

The planes made four passes over their targets, taking their planned seven minutes to drop their burrowing rockets to crater the runways, then bombing the trapped Egyptian aircraft. Ten minutes after the first attack wave came the second, and ten minutes after that the third.

As the Israelis made for home, the terrifying SA-2 anti-aircraft missiles came up to intercept some of them.

Here is how a military writer described one Israeli pilot's encounter.

"Major Ury was first to see it (the SAM). Suddenly, about a mile away, he perceived something rising slowly like a huge white bear, only it was a huge white light. Within a few seconds, it looked like a flying cigar. As Ury watched what he knew to be the second or "active" stage of a radar-guided missile, it turned its nose down and began to chase Ury's Vautour, slowly at first, then faster and faster. Nearer and nearer it came, a lunatic robot pursuing him with murder in its electronic brain. 'Break!' Ury found himself shouting into the mouthpiece, and the Squadron Leader instantly turned the aircraft into a brutal dive-and-pitch which compressed their suits with a force of three or four G's and nearly broke the plane in the process. The flaming SAM, attempting a similar turn, but unable to complete it as fast, hit the ground in thwarted rage some distance away." [1]

As the first eighty minute phase of the air strike ended, and

---

[1] "Operation Sons of Light," by Schlomo Borer, Israel Universities Press.

Hod pieced together the returning pilots' stories, he shouted to the jammed command room:

"Boys, we've clobbered them!"

Not long after, the full, incredible picture emerged.

In one hundred and seventy minutes, Israel's Air Force had destroyed all thirty of Egypt's Tupolev bombers, along with two hundred and sixty Migs—three hundred of the three hundred and forty aircraft in Egypt's Air Force. Now, the Israelis were free, on the very first day, to turn their attention to the Iraqi, Syrian and Jordanian Air Forces, too.

As the first results of the air strike began to come into the Command Bunker, General Rabin's assistant chief of operations put in a telephone call to the Commander of the southern front —whose armored columns lay like a coiled spring on the Sinai border. The assistant chief of operations uttered but three words:

"Good Luck. Act!"

11

THE RUSSIAN
POSITIONS

At 4 a.m. on June 6, barely twenty hours after the Six-Day War
began, Brig. General Ariel Sharon knew that the war was won.
His paratroopers, infantry, and armor had overrun a five-mile-
deep belt of fortifications that blocked a chief road into the Sinai.

The fortifications, located some twelve miles from the Israeli
border at a point called Um Catef, were the most formidable that
Russian brains could devise. They bristled with the most modern
armament that Soviet arsenals could supply. Years of Russian instruction had gone into the twenty-five-hundred-odd Egyptian
officers and men who held it. Yet, Israeli tanks and supplies were
already racing, unimpeded, through the road the fortifications
once blocked, to cut off and destroy the unsuspecting Egyptian
formations in the desert beyond.

Along with the air strike of the preceding day, and the reduc-
tion of El Arish, the Battle of Um Catef (won without air support) was one of the decisive operations of the war. Sharon, a
barrel-chested, prematurely greying career soldier, had fash-
ioned the victorious plan. His men had executed it. But the
victory truly belonged to Israeli Intelligence and Israeli intelligence. These had raised and answered crucial questions:

What are the Russians teaching the Egyptians?

How well does the Egyptian character and temperament adapt to Russian military methods?

How do Russian military methods adapt to desert warfare? Israeli Intelligence's answers to these questions began with a sure knowledge of the enemy.

Israeli Intelligence officers know, that to the Egyptian soldier and his officers, the Sinai is an alien land. The soldier comes chiefly from villages in the moist, lushly green Nile Delta, the officers from metropolitan Cairo and Alexandria. The Egyptian peasant-soldier is afraid of the desert, feels orphaned, lonely, and far from home in it. Both soldier and officer are uncomfortable in the dry, empty, and glaring furnace of the Sinai by day, and uneasy and fearful in the pit-like darkness and dead silence of the night. (In the weeks preceding the June war, Israel's psychological warfare broadcasters played on these fears with "nature courses" in Arabic that described the "snakes, scorpions and other fauna" to be found in the desert.) The Israeli soldier, on the other hand, was at home in the desert because of years of over-night marches in his own Negev.

The Egyptian soldier abhors night fighting. But night fighting is the Israeli soldier's specialty. With night fighting goes close, hand-to-hand fighting. This, too, doesn't suit the Egyptian soldier.

Israel's Intelligence knows, too, that the Egyptian soldier is no coward. Faced with a situation for which he has been trained—a frontal attack, for instance—he will stand and fight until he dies. But against the unexpected, he is likely to panic. His officers are slow to react and to take countermeasures.

In 1963, Israeli Intelligence had to fit its knowledge of the Egyptian soldier into a new situation.

After the Sinai campaign of 1956, the Russians realized that arms alone were not enough. At first, the Russians sent instructors to teach the Egyptians how to use and maintain the Soviet equipment. Then around 1961, Israeli Intelligence noticed that Russian and Egyptian army brass were shuttling increasingly between Moscow and Cairo. The Russians, as we've seen, were teaching the Egyptians to wage war according to the "Moscow Doctrine."

The Moscow Doctrine relies on heavily fortified positions, and calls for a counter-strike force held in reserve. At the critical moment when the enemy gets into a fortified position, but does not yet have the momentum for a speedy thrust forward, the counter-strike force overpowers and destroys him.

In the defense concepts of the Moscow Doctrine, the Russians felt they had the means of containing Israel's type of offensive warfare. Once contained, the Israeli's could be rolled up by superior Arab counterattacking forces. Here, in the Moscow Doctrine, was Egypt's means of squaring accounts with the Israelis.

Classic embodiment of the Russian Doctrine as we've seen was the seemingly impenetrable belt of fortifications, three miles wide and five miles deep, at Um Catef.

The Sinai is not a table-flat desert, a sea of sand on which armies can maneuver unimpeded. It is, rather, a wasteland of rough, broken ground intersected by granite mountains that can rise, as in the case of Mt. Musa (Mount Moses), to a height of eight thousand feet. Mediterranean winds have sculpted the Sinai sands into dunes that rise gently from the seaward side to a towering one thousand feet, then drop sheerly like a wall on the other side. Mountains and dunes restrict troop movements through the Sinai to a few roads and passes. The oldest route through the Sinai runs along the Mediterranean coast. The Roman Legions that thundered over it on their way to conquests in biblical Palestine called the coast road Via Maris. Alexander the Great's chariots and Napoleon's Grand Army used it.

During World War II, the Shell Oil Company transformed an old caravan and smugglers' route to the south into an asphalt covered road. It ran from Beersheba, then in British mandated Palestine, through Nitzana—now on the Israeli-Sinai border—then through the village of Abu Agheila and on to the Suez Canal. It became the main route through the Sinai.

Here then, near Abu Agheila, at a point on the road called Um Catef, the Egyptians had dug trenches and put up gun emplacements as far back as the 1948 war with the Israelis.

By 1956, the Egyptians had so fortified these positions that

Israeli forces under Moshe Dayan beat themselves against it in vain. The Israelis never did take the Um Catef positions. The Egyptians evacuated them after the Israelis got into the Sinai via a paratroop drop at the Mitla Pass, far to the rear, and via a mad trek down the eastern rim of the desert to Sharm el Sheikh at the entrance to the Gulf of Aqaba. A similar exploit could not be repeated later, for the Egyptians would be waiting—in force.

By 1963, the Russians had turned the Um Catef positions into a desert redoubt on which they lavished every lesson they had learned in the defense of Stalingrad and Moscow.

Heart of the system were three parallel lines of five-foot deep concrete-lined trenches, each about three miles long. Minefields and barbed wire guarded the approaches to the redoubt. If an attacking force negotiated these and broke into the first line of trenches, it would then have to fight foot-by-foot through a three-hundred-yard belt of concrete bunkers spewing fire from heavy machine-guns, as well as fire from bunkered-in tanks. If the attacker reached and cleaned out the second line of trenches, there was still another belt, five hundred yards deep, of additional bristling armaments. Beyond the third trench lay ninety heavy Soviet tanks, poised for a counterattack. Behind the final trench, too, stood six artillery regiments with 122 mm. Soviet guns calculated to devastate the attacking force as it approached. A full Egyptian brigade manned the redoubt.

Unlike France's Maginot Line, the Um Catef redoubt had no exposed flank through which an attacker could sweep. To get at Um Catef positions from the flank, an enemy had to bring men and guns over the rock mass of the Dalaf Mountains which stood sentinel on the right. Steeply sloping dunes guarded the left. In 1956, the Israelis had sent infantry into these dunes in a flanking attempt. The foot soldiers floundered knee-deep in the sand for a while, then lost their way altogether.

In 1964, the year Israeli Intelligence wrote the book on the Russian Doctrine and its Egyptian defense system, Israel's generals knew that, in a future war, Um Catef would somehow have to be breached. There could be no detour. It would take too long and be too vulnerable. Nor would it be enough merely to break into the Sinai through the other gateway, the one at El Arish on the coastal road. To fight the usual swift Israeli war—which requires that the enemy be destroyed before the UN Security Council can intervene—the Israelis had to smash both gateways and send tank columns racing into the Sinai to encircle and cut off the enemy.

Actual battle plans for conquering the "Russian Positions" were continually invented, mulled over, and revised until one week before the June war.

Brigadier General Avrohom Yoffe once likened the process by which Jewish officers arrive at a battle-plan to the daylong debates of Talmudic scholars over some point of religious practice. General Yoffe said:

"When a hen laid an egg on the Sabbath, when all work is forbidden, Talmudic scholars would debate for days what to do with it. They would examine the problem from the scores of angles posed by rabbinical precedent. In the same way, Israeli officers will study and re-study all sides of a military problem—the taking of a hill, for instance. They'll look at it from one hundred different angles. And do you know what? They'll find something new and interesting every one of those one hundred times. It's a Jewish trait."

In drawing up the final plan for the assault on Um Catef, Israel's thinking men took into account the "Arab traits," they knew so well. This is where they used intelligence with a small "i."

The battle plan for breaching the Um Catef positions called for a night attack. It also called for plenty of the unexpected. Helicopters would transport paratroopers by night to a point in the desert some four miles behind the redoubt's rear artillery positions. The paratroopers planned to march through the dunes, which the Egyptians believed to be impenetrable. They planned to surprise and knock out the artillery teams in hand-to-hand combat.

Israeli infantry, too, would march through the dunes and come out of nowhere to hit the Egyptian trenches on the flank.

While paratroopers and infantry silenced artillery, trench

and bunker fire, engineers would be clearing the minefields in front of the redoubt. Tanks would then rumble forward to break into the fortified area and take on the Egyptian counterstrike force to the rear of the Um Catef trenches.

In Israel's Defense Forces, battle plans are chosen by the commanders who carry them out. The man assigned to the Um Catef assault was Brig. General Sharon who, until the eve of the war, was in charge of Army training. Sharon likes to wear his purple paratrooper's beret under a shoulder strap, even at his desk. This gives him a certain military dash which he compromises with a non-military slouch, deep in his chair, when talking to visitors.

The Um Catef plan Sharon chose was about as unorthodox, militarily, as his slouch.

To synchronize the activities of some two thousand men engaged in a half-dozen assignments over a twenty-square mile area; to depend on the on-time arrival of troops, slogging through dunes that had defied previous efforts; to orchestrate the vast scheme in darkness—all this was an undertaking of such daring that it verged on a long-shot gamble.

"No other army in the world would involve itself in such a complicated and confused operation," General Sharon told this writer, happily, after the war. To Gen. S. L. A. Marshall, the military historian, the plan was a "Rube Goldberg design." There was, in fact, so much apprehension about the plan among the chiefs of staff, that General Rabin asked Sharon whether it might not be wiser to hold up the operation for a day to permit the air force to soften up the Um Catef positions. Sharon said "No." He would not trade night fighting for air support.

Victory at Um Catef was crucial to the overall war strategy of both sides.

The Egyptians, as Israeli Intelligence knew, intended to use the Um Catef positions as an anvil on which to hammer the Israeli Army to death. For this purpose, the Egyptians had concentrated a special division of armor just south of the nearby village of Abu Agheila. Another armored division was stationed not far behind. As Israeli forces battered themselves against the Um Catef redoubt, both Egyptian forces would swing north toward the

Negev desert, get behind the Israelis, and pulverize them on the Um Catef anvil. This done, the Egyptian columns would move north along the coastal road toward undefended Tel Aviv. That this was the Egyptian design was confirmed by High Command communiqués during the first two days of the war.

"The Israeli Army is falling into our trap and is being mauled," the communiqués said.

The Israeli strategy was to punch two columns of armor, like mailed fists, through Um Catef and El Arish to the north, then hit and unbalance the Egyptian formation in the desert beyond.

The Israelis had reason to believe that Egyptian officers do not regain their balance or establish new lines readily, or do things they had not learned in advance. Harassed by encircling Israeli armor, the disciplined formations would turn into a rabble. This was the strategy.

The paratroopers, foot soldiers, and tank crews who would storm the redoubt and on whom so much depended were conscripts and reservists. Until only two weeks before the battle, they had been shopkeepers, teachers, bank clerks, kibbutz farmers.

But General Sharon had faith in them. He stood beside the road and watched the infantry file by on its way to the assembly point in the desert from which it would make its nighttime trek through the dunes.

"I looked at those men's faces," Sharon recalls. "I saw such determination, and belief, and will, I felt those troops could do anything."

In the ranks marching by General Sharon was infantry corporal Hanan, a redheaded twenty-year-old with an open face, who might be taken for a Minnesota farm boy. Hanan *was* a farm boy. He tended the cow sheds at a kibbutz not far from Tel Aviv. Freshly graduated from high school, he had left these chores to enter the National Service (Israeli Draft) and had completed only five and one-half months of training when the war came.

For two weeks before the war, Hanan's unit had rehearsed a special exercise. It was called "assault on entrenched positions." But the assault, curiously, was not frontal. It was from the flank. In groups of thirty men each, Hanan and his fellow infantrymen ran along the lip of mock trenches or leaped into them in simulated hand-to-hand combat. The exercise was in fact a dress rehearsal for the infantry's mission at Um Catef.

On June 5, Hanan's company began its trench exercises as usual at 5:30 a.m. These were halted dramatically an hour later when Hanan's lieutenant announced:

"This is it. Grab your gear and get ready to leave."

Hanan thought of his two redheaded brothers, one a radio operator, another an armored infantryman. Were they going into battle, too?

He gulped for air as waves of fear and exhilaration hit him at the same time. The long wait was over.

At an assembly point several hours later, Hanan's lieutenant explained the infantry's mission: to move by vehicle to a point in the desert some five miles from the Um Catef trenches, then cross the dunes and attack.

Israel can't afford military troop carriers. So Hanan found himself riding to battle in a convoy of blue inter-city buses. None were camouflaged in any way. They weren't even daubed with mud to look more military. The first Israeli forces had already passed along the road, and it was now jammed with supply carriers that would have startled observers from other armies: sand and gravel trucks hauling ammunition; bakery trucks bringing rations and fresh vegetables; milk tankers carting water; and fuel tankers bringing gasoline.

Sometimes, when sand drifts blocked the road, Hanan and his comrades got out and pushed. After two hours, the battalion commander decided his troops could move faster on foot. So, still six miles from the dunes, the infantry set out in two files along the road, the brigade commander marching at the head, battalion and lesser commanders directly behind. It was at this point that Hanan and his fellow infantrymen filed by General Sharon—without saluting.

The march toward the dunes had begun at high noon under a furious sun that pained Hanan's eyes with its glare, heated the sands to a 140-degree temperature that burned through his shoes, and turned the dry desert air about him into an enveloping oven.

When the infantry arrived at the edge of the dunes, two and one-half hours later, there were still another four and one-half hours of sun to endure before the blessed, cool night came—and the march through the dunes began.

Hanan carried a bazooka and five bazooka shells, three hand grenades, and a submachine-gun. He broke down and cleaned the machine-gun, a simple, sturdy weapon with a range of two hundred yards, which the Israelis affectionately called the Uzzi —after the Israeli officer who designed it while languishing in a British prison (before Israel became a state). Neither sand nor dirt could jam it, and in recent years the Israelis had worked up a flourishing export business selling it to West Germany, Holland, Belgium, and to several countries in Africa. Charles de Gaulle had bought it for his bodyguard. So had Emperor Selassie of Ethiopia.

With the Uzzi, the bazooka, and ammunition, Hanan was lugging a total of forty-four pounds. Bearing his burden up the gentle slope of the dune was endurable, although the yielding sand soon reached over Hanan's boots and filled them with itching grit. A bigger ordeal awaited on the sheer side of the dune. Hanan and his buddies plunged downward head-over-heels, filling noses, ears and shirts with sand. But, providentially, the march was interrupted every twenty minutes to permit scouts to determine the infantry's position.

At a predetermined point inside the dunes, the infantry would veer sharply south. This required precise navigation in pitch-black darkness. The scouts used compasses and counted their double steps to measure distance. The thud of the Egyptian artillery which kept growing ever louder helped check their bearings and prevented the whole operation from becoming a game of blindman's buff.

Three hours of anxious step-counting in the hostile, sucking sands brought the infantry force to the barbed wire perimeter of the trenches. The scouts probed the area for mines and, finding none, blew up the barbed wire. Hanan and his comrades poured through, each company heading for its appointed trench.

Hanan ran toward the second, or middle, trench area, following the blinking red light on his section leader's shoulder for guidance.

If attacked frontally, the Egyptian soldier, pre-trained for such an attack and covered by the machine-gun inside the bunkers behind him, would make it difficult for his attackers. But the Egyptian soldier didn't get that chance.

Hanan and his comrades ran along the back of their trench, blasting anything inside that moved. When they encountered enemy fire from machine-gun nests in their path, they hit the ground, threw grenades at the machine-gun, sprayed it with their Uzzis and ran on.

Hanan's company suffered not one casualty in the first two hundred yards. But soon after, they ran into a cluster of Soviet medium machine-guns, lodged in a concrete bunker which used green tracers to light up the area, and killed five of Hanan's comrades outright. Hanan's lieutenant ran up to the bunker to try to clean it out with his rifle and was killed immediately. Someone in Hanan's section finally took out the bunker with a miraculous shot. He fired a rifle grenade into one of the bunker's gun-ports from a distance of 80 yards.

Within two hours, Hanan and his battalion were masters of their trench. When the sun came up at 4:30 a.m., the area was secured. Hanan and his comrades rested in the seized trenches, and watched the first Israeli tanks rumble up the road they had freed to take on the Egyptian tanks in the rear. Hanan throbbed with mixed feelings. He had accomplished his mission and he was still in one piece. That was good. But a heavy depression absorbed him. Nine of his friends were dead and eleven wounded.

"And those Egyptian soldiers," Hanan recalled, "they seemed so wretched and mangy, hardly like soldiers at all. I was ashamed for them."

As Hanan settled down in the trench, the roar of the Egyptian artillery to the rear diminished steadily. Hanan wondered how the paratroopers had fared in their mission against those guns.

One such paratrooper, twenty-nine-year-old Uzi, a sergeant in the reserves, was in bed with measles when his call-up notice arrived on May 24th. Uzi breeds fish at the Kibbutz Sha'ar Hagolan in the Jordan Valley, and is so good at his job that he once advised Dutch breeders how to increase their output. Now, he tossed disconsolately in his bed, sick for two days, fearing that he would miss the war. Then, giddy-headed and feverish, he staggered out of his bed, kissed his protesting wife, Nitza, goodbye and hitched rides to get to his unit, stationed one hundred and fifty miles south, near the Sinai border.

Here, Uzi hid his aches as best he could and plunged with other paratroopers into the ordeal of training that was to prepare them for battle. The paratroopers began practice marches into the Negev desert with light packs and only a half-mile walk the first day. Then the packs got heavier and the marches grew longer. After a week, they were travelling eight miles daily under full pack and in the full sun. When war came, Uzi's measles had gone, but every muscle and bone ached from the desert marches.

At 3 p.m. of June 5, Uzi heard what the paratroopers' mission would be: to land twenty miles away by helicopter, then march through dunes to attack the Um Catef artillery positions. At 9 p.m., in the cool of the desert night, the helicopters whirled in from out of the darkness, and Uzi watched with growing dismay as they loaded flight after flight of paratroopers and then took off. After two hours, the Egyptian artillery seemed to have located the helicopter take-off points, for shells began to burst in the area. Some helicopters withdrew and now Uzi feared he would surely be left behind. But Uzi managed to get his men on what seemed to be the last helicopter out. There were nine in the helicopter, plus a medic with his folded stretcher and kit of blood plasma.

Below Uzi during the twenty-five minute flight, tracer bullets —white from the Egyptian guns, yellow from the Israelis'—lit up the desert. For one bad moment, the unarmed and vulnerable Sikorsky-58 came under gunfire, but pitched and tumbled safely through the bursting shells and landed on a sandy knoll outlined by flares.

Uzi reached down and ran the foreign sand of Sinai through his fingers. Strange! It was the same gravelly stuff as that of

Israel's Negev. Soon the paratroopers, about one hundred and twenty in all, were off across the dunes, guiding their steps by the flashes of Egyptian artillery some four miles away.

For weeks after the war, Uzi rubbed his aching back when he recalled that march. In maneuvers, soldiers tend to cheat a little on the weight they carry. But now, going into battle, Uzi lugged a maximum pack, stuffing his pants and shirt pockets with plastic explosives as well. Other paratroopers carried some sixty pounds of grenades, rifles, and submachine-guns in their hands and on their backs, but Uzi's burden came closer to sixty-five pounds. For a man of medium height, weighing but one hundred and sixty pounds, this burden was a cruel one.

Uzi's head was weighted down, too, under the heavy paratrooper's helmet, designed for "drop" mishaps, not marches. Although not religious, Uzi remembered the prayer that the Rabbinate had distributed, and prayed silently. As if in mocking answer, a sandstorm blew up, hammering sand against Uzi's eyelids, and into his nostrils and ears.

As platoon leader, Uzi helped his men as best he could, shoving one, pulling another. Each dune seemed to loom higher than the one before. Three hours had passed since the paratroopers had started out. It was about midnight and the desert had turned cold, yet Uzi's camouflaged battle-dress was as wet as if he had been in a rainstorm. Soon, the paratroopers tumbled down their last dune. Flashing fire before them, some two hundred yards away, were seven batteries of Russian 122 mm. guns, about seventy pieces in all, plus several heavy howitzers. These, Uzi had expected from his training maneuvers and pre-battle briefings. He even knew which gun he would take out. Uzi also expected a guard detachment that would be protecting the gun crews.

But the Egyptians were so certain no enemy could come at them from the dunes that they had stationed no guard unit. Only one rifleman stood at the perimeter. He got off one shot and was soon dispatched. Without pausing for breath, the paratroopers divided into two columns, one for the front of the gun positions, the other for the rear.

To the Egyptian artillerymen, the oncoming Israeli paratroopers, materializing like demons from out of the darkness, must have been a nightmare.

As Uzi ran along the rear of the gun position hurling his plastic explosives, he could see other paratroopers grimly killing Egyptians with hand-grenades, submachine-guns, and rifle butts. The assault rolled on so smoothly that, to Uzi, it seemed little different from the realistic exercises—using live ammunition— with which he had prepared for this moment. Only three paratroopers had been wounded, and these slightly.

But now as the carnage neared its close, two groups of Egyptian trucks came lumbering up out of the desert, seemingly with reinforcements. A paratrooper turned his machine-gun on the lead truck to find, to his horror, that it was loaded with artillery shells. The truck hurled upwards like a flaming matchbox, raining giant shards of shrapnel on the attackers and attacked alike. Soon a second truck blew up and a third. Within moments, six of Uzi's comrades were killed and twenty-two others wounded.

But the job of finishing off the artillerymen went on, and within forty-five minutes after the paratroopers had emerged from the dunes, the guns were silent.

The paratroopers loaded their dead and wounded on stretchers, and—four men to a stretcher—staggered back through the dunes. Since there were not enough stretchers, Uzi and a comrade hauled one shattered corpse under the armpits. It was the body of a friend. Uzi wondered what he would tell his friend's wife.

12

SAMSON'S FOXES

For biology teacher Yosi Levari and for his ninth graders, the lesson in the human circulatory system wasn't going well at all.

During the past two weeks, the thirteen- and fourteen-year-olds' interest in lessons had decreased as steadily as the fascinating new chores outside increased: as they pitched in with the adults to dig new slit trenches to the deep underground shelters of their kibbutz, as they helped lay new communications cables and checked up on food stores.

Many of their big brothers and fathers had slipped away quietly—some without goodbyes—from their chores in the apple orchards, the egg hatchery, the wheatfields. And when the paratroop and tank corps reservists had gone off, everybody in the kibbutz, from its seventy-five-year-old patriarch to the youngest kids, knew that war was not far away.

Now, in Yosi's classroom, the children fiddled with transistor radios in search of the latest bulletins from the Voice of Israel. Occasionally, someone would tune in on Damascus, only thirty miles to the East, where Syrian announcers promised in crude Hebrew, to "kill, maim, burn the Jews." One boy had become obsessed with a recurrent chant from Cairo and had turned it up for his neighbors to hear.

"Butcher! Butcher! Butcher!" went the chant.

Yosi would silence the transistors only to have his pupils pepper him with questions about his adventures in the last war, the one in 1956. With his oversized glasses, his reflective face and his quiet voice—so low his pupils had to strain to hear him—Yosi, now thirty-two, didn't look much like a paratrooper. Yet he had fought in the bloody battle for the Mitla Pass, a near disaster of the Sinai Campaign in which half of Yosi's brigade had died.

Yosi's thoughts were far from the classroom, too. Although most of the kibbutz's able-bodied men up to forty-five—some fifty in all—had been called up, he had been ordered to stay behind to command a fortified position, outside the kibbutz. Through Yosi's mind ran the nagging question—would he be ready?

With a sigh, Yosi gave up and dismissed the class.

The time was 4 p.m., and the day, June 4, 1967. There would be no school the next day, nor for five days after that, for Yosi's settlement, known as Kibbutz Dan, and all of Israel, would be fighting for its life.

Yosi left the classroom and followed a tree-lined lane that led to Kibbutz Dan's outskirts. The trees were the proud, green crown of the settlement. They provided a living testament to the settlers' ordeals, achievements, and aspirations. Yosi knew each by its scientific name. When the Kibbutz Dan founders cleared out the rocks and boulders of the barren land, they had planted the common slash or Caribbean pine, *Pinus caribaea*, that could take root almost anywhere. Later, because it was the Holy Land and the Bible said, "Each man shall sit beneath his olive tree," the settlers had planted the *Olea europaea*. After the Sinai Campaign of 1956, when the Syrians took to shelling the settlement from their Golan Heights, only one-half mile away, the settlers planted scores of eucalyptus and poplars to provide a screening cover.

Under Yosi's urging, the settlers recently had brought in the wild native trees of Israel, the Oak of Mt. Tabor—*Quercus taborensis*—under which Deborah must have sat when she directed her victorious battle against the Philistines on Mount Tabor, twenty-five miles to the southwest. And, of course, Kibbutz Dan had brought in the Jerusalem pine, *Pinus helepenens*, from the hills of the Holy City. Only in Israel, Yosi could reflect, with its forty-one varieties of climate squeezed into an area of twenty thousand seven hundred square miles could there be such a diversity of growing things: of purple blooming jacaranda trees beside the oak, of bougainvillaea and the palm beside the candle-like cypress, of cotton fields beside apple orchards. Nor was the diversity of human beings far behind. Yosi's kibbutz boasted immigrants and descendants from several dozen nations: from Poland—like Yosi's father—to Hungary, Rumania, Germany, Tunisia and the Yemen.

Yosi negotiated the triple line of eucalyptus trees on the eastern approaches of the kibbutz and emerged into the hedgehog of concrete bunkers and newly-dug trenches which he would command if the Syrians attacked.

In the silvery light, Yosi took in the fields of wheat, yellow and dry, and lifted his eyes to the gloomy escarpment of the Hagolan Mountains that rise straight up four thousand feet to the triple peaks of Mt. Hermon. Near this mountain, only a mile or so away, the tribe of Dan, fleeing the Philistines, had settled. Yosi's kibbutz had taken its name from that Biblical site. From Dan to Beersheba once measured the length of ancient Israel. Today it was from Dan to Eilat, about one hundred sixty-five miles farther south. Unlike the tribe of Dan, the people of Yosi's kibbutz—with the Syrians towering above them to the east, and the Lebanese to the north—had no place to flee. And this was the story of all Israel, too, wedged in between six hostile nations and the Mediterranean, and only fifteen miles wide at its waist.

The Hagolan Range was Israel's woe. From here, the Syrians —dug into a chain of Maginot Line-type fortifications—regularly raked the settlements of the Upper Galilee and the Huleh Valley below. On a November Friday in 1964, the Syrians had poured five hundred shells into Kibbutz Dan in the space of two hours, leveling the schoolhouses, setting the chicken hatchery and dairy on fire. Safe in their shelters, none of the settlers were harmed. But the children had nightmares for months.

The shellings had continued with such regularity that the border settlers, with the wry humor that Jews wrap around themselves in adversity, took to calling it "Syrian rainfall."

Yosi inspected the two lines of slit trenches, waist high, that he and his men had dug under cover of night and camouflaged with eucalyptus branches. As a paratrooper, Yosi didn't like to be confined in a bunker. It was fine for standing off an attack by machine gunners, but tank cannon could demolish it from a distance of a thousand yards. Besides, the Syrians would never expect the Israelis to wait for them in open trenches, and would probably hammer away at the bunkers. He decided that he would fight from the trenches. Yosi's reserve rank was only that of sergeant, but given a mission by the kibbutz commander, he had full discretion in how to achieve it.

The rose light that precedes sunset in Israel had turned the wheatfields into russet gold. The wheat was ready for harvesting, but mobilization had left the settlers neither time nor men. It was a lucky thing. For that wheat would save the lives of Yosi and his men, and that of Kibbutz Dan.

War came to Israel at 8 a.m. the next morning, and to Yosi's Kibbutz Dan at 4 a.m. on the day after. On the first night of the war, Yosi had gone to bed in his clothes—walking shorts and open-collared sleeveless shirt. On the chair beside his bed he placed his paratrooper's helmet, his binoculars, and his machine gun, an MG-34 of World War II vintage. So, Yosi was on his feet, groping for his machine gun even before the banging on the door had stopped. It was Kibbutz Dan's military commander, Lt. Israel Ronen, the swarthy, Hungarian-born manager of the Kibbutz Dan's plastics factory.

"They're getting ready to come down," he said.

Yosi's wife, Rachel, and his two children—five-year-old Tamir and nine-year-old Ayelit—were already bedded down deep in the shelters. Yosi paused before the glass container on his porch which housed twelve black-and-white mice—with which he demonstrated animal respiration in his classes. Rachel would not permit them in the house—even during a shelling. Yosi turned and raced for his trench to find that most of his twenty men were already tumbling in.

As his eyes accustomed themselves to the dark, Yosi made out the defenders, and they were a curiously unwarlike lot: Davidka, a diminutive man of fifty-two who worked in the apple orchards; Isaac, also fifty-two, a laborer in the plastics factory; Binnie, fifty-five, who tended a fish-breeding pond; Petah, fifty-four, a gentle teacher of English literature in the high school and Yoram, an eighteen-year-old engineering student at the Technion in Haifa (Israel's M.I.T.) who had come with ten other boys to bring in the hay and had stayed on to fight. More than half the men in Yosi's first-line trench were over fifty, the rest—except for Yosi and the engineering student—in their forties. The second trench, directly behind Yosi, bore no more youthful aspect. The mortar team, about six hundred yards to the rear—on which Yosi would rely for artillery support—consisted of Moshe, a sixty-two-year-old locksmith; Shlomo, fifty-six, the director of kibbutz apple production; and Zeev, fifty-two, a fishpond caretaker.

Elsewhere, in positions in and around the kibbutz, some fifty other men of similar vintage rounded out Kibbutz Dan's defense force.

Most of these men were as full of war experience as they were of years. Some had already fought in three wars, in World War II as well as in Israel's two wars. Their kibbutz was part of the border defense belt, and they were an integral part of Israel's Defense Forces under the orders of the Northern Army Command. The men drew their arms from the kibbutz weapons magazine which was regularly inspected by the Army's quartermaster. In the past two weeks they had "reestablished their emotional ties with their weapons," as Yosi put it. They had taken their rifles and machine guns apart, cleaned them, practiced dry runs with them.

Now, at 5:45 a.m., with the sun rising in a glaring ball of flame over the Golan Heights, the first heavy mortar shell—heralding the softening-up bombardment—exploded in murderous shards of shrapnel behind the kibbutz. Yosi ordered his men into the shelter of the bunkers. Time enough to call the men out to fight when the Syrians came down from the hills.

Yosi, alone in the trench, rested his machine gun on the sandbag in front of him and waited.

In the dim light inside the bunker some twenty yards behind Yosi, Yitzhak Yogev, a lean man of forty-four with a horsey face, a cavalier's moustache, and a brush of reddish-brown hair, brooded over the fate of his charges, the young carp he tended in Kibbutz Dan's five fish-breeding ponds. Even now, shells might be destroying them. Yitzhak, a taciturn man, contemplated his own curious fate, too.

"Why is it," he thought, "that someone is forever trying to humiliate or kill this Jew?"

The humiliation began in Yitzhak's native Hungary at the outbreak of World War II when Yitzhak, then sixteen, was herded into a labor camp with other Jews, some of whose families had been in Hungary for six or more generations. Later, when the Nazis came and crammed Yitzhak into a train bound for an extermination camp in Poland, he escaped and fought the Nazis as an underground partisan in the woods of Poland.

The war's end brought no joy to Yitzhak, only a rising hatred and fury. He hated the Germans who had exterminated all but a remnant of Europe's Jews. He hated his fellow Hungarians who had handed him—and his family, now vanished—to the Germans. Yitzhak hated the Poles who, in 1946, were greeting the few returning Jewish Poles with murderous pogroms. He wanted no more of Europe, and he yearned for a land where a Jew could stop fleeing, and where, if someone wanted to kill a Jew, he would find him with a gun in his hand, with other armed Jews beside him.

Agents from the Haganah, the underground Jewish defense force in Palestine, had mounted a subterranean rescue operation called "The Bridge," to bring out Jewish survivors to Palestine. It had to be subterranean because Great Britain, then governing Palestine, barred Jewish immigration.

For all that, Yitzhak and eight hundred and fifty other "illegals," loaded on an ancient two-hundred-and fifty-ton barque which had accommodations for only one-eighth as many, slipped out of a tiny port in Southern Italy and miraculously ran the British destroyer gauntlet to reach Palestine. But a wintry storm was raging; seas were pouring over the miserable barque and its suffocating cargo; and Haganah men waiting anxiously on shore with small boats could not make it to the ship.

Yitzhak and some of the other young men leaped overboard and swam the three hundred paralyzingly cold yards to shore.

Yitzhak had barely got some hot tea past his chattering teeth in a nearby settlement when British Tommies collared him, and within an hour he was behind the barbed wire of his second concentration camp. Within a week he was transported to still another, this one on Cyprus. That British soldiers instead of Nazis patrolled the barbed wire gave Yitzhak no comfort.

But the ubiquitous agents of the Haganah were inside the camp. They drilled the male prisoners in commando tactics, and even taught Yitzhak to use a machine gun which they had somehow smuggled in. The Haganah helped Yitzhak and twenty others escape via a tunnel. Soon he was on a boat again for Palestine, and this time he made it, just in time to fight in Israel's 1948 war of independence.

Yet Yitzhak's story was nothing special in the Kibbutz Dan. At least one-third of its three hundred adults had tasted concentration camp life. Virtually every man over forty had fought in three wars and some, like Yitzhak, had fought in bloody battles in between, in retaliatory raids against Syrian shellings.

Yitzhak inspected his machine gun, his companion in battle since 1948. An MG-34, it had been manufactured in Czechoslavakia's Skoda Works during the German occupation and still bore a swastika on its barrel. There was some satisfaction in having the swastika decorate a gun that had killed so many Jewish enemies, and Yitzhak had deliberately left it.

Now, Yitzhak ran his hand gently over the swastika and wondered when Yosi would call for him.

About one hundred yards back of Yosi and Yitzhak in a forty-foot deep shelter, Alisa Barlev, a teacher in the elementary school, studied the terrified faces of eighteen five- and six-year-olds and steeled herself for the ordeal of calming and keeping them busy.

Major General Moshe Dayan had visited Kibbutz Dan a week before, eye patch and all, and had told the children:

"If there's a war, this is where I want to be. There isn't a safer place in all Israel."

But now the children worried whether the shelter was strong enough to withstand a direct hit. Alisa had left the heavy steel doors of the shelter open to equalize the air pressure, and as the concussion of a shell slapped the children's faces and hers—as with an open hand—and scattered crayons and papers, one boy, with mouth trembling, said:

"Is it the shelter that's shaking, or is it me?"

"It's you, dear," Alisa said.

Alisa's world had been shaking ever since she was sixteen when Storm Troopers goose-stepped through the streets of her native Hamburg. Alisa's father, a doctor, had won an Iron Cross for his World War I services to the Fatherland, but the family had to flee, arriving in 1939 in a London that was rocking under the Blitz. Alisa's world kept quaking when she reached Palestine in 1948, just in time for another war. Like Yitzhak, she was now living through her fourth one.

So, at forty-four, Alisa had a fragile look and a mouth tightly drawn. Yet for six days she would have to keep from breaking. She would have to forget about her nineteen-year-old son, Israel, running ammunition up there in the open, and her husband, Petah, in the trench with Yosi. She would teach the children geography by following the war on the school maps. She would read to them from the shelter's library of sixty books. She would help the children cut out "color postcards" to send to their fathers and neighbors up front in the kibbutz positions—and laugh when one boy wrote, "Everything in the shelter is very nice. I hope you have nice conditions, too."

Now, as the shells destroyed their homes overhead, Alisa turned her attention to the five-year-old boy who had gone into shock. Alisa wrapped the child in blankets and massaged his all-but-silent pulse. She wiped the boy's clammy face.

"Everything will be all right," she crooned to the child and to herself.

In the shelter for the seventh graders, Gabi Madyan wasn't worrying only for her charges, but for the life of the kibbutz—which she had helped found twenty-eight years before.

Gabi had left her native Poland—not in flight, but in hope—as a pioneer who would exchange the murky ghetto for life on the land, and with fellow Jews would build a new kind of society, a communal utopian one. They would also build a new Jew, one who worked on the land with his hands, and whose children would climb trees "like regular Tarzans."

Gabi was seventeen then, a strong girl, with strength in her bearing and command in her face.

In Palestine's first agricultural school, Mikve Israel, she plunged into the study of soils, irrigation and horticulture with the passion an acolyte might study for orders. Then, one night in the fall of 1939, with thirty other dreamers from Poland, Hungary, and Rumania, Gabi had rolled up to the present site of Kibbutz Dan in a convoy of three trucks bristling with the rifles of Jewish underground commandos—the Palmach—and in six dark hours before dawn had set up the beginnings of a kibbutz.

From one truck, the pioneers hauled prefabricated wooden sections, hammered them together into a square stockade, set another wall just inside it, and filled the space with gravel to form a fort. From another truck, they hauled three prefabricated sections of a tower, set it up in the center of their stockade, hauled electric wires to its top, and with power from a generator below lighted the settlement's first light. With it the settlers could flash a call for help, if attacked by night. By day, they could signal from it with a heliograph.

Sunrise exposed to potential enemy Arab eyes another Wall and Tower Settlement, with two bare barracks for housing. But to the settlers, there was an even more urgent enemy than the Arab: the malarial swamps that stretched the full length of the Huleh Valley in which Kibbutz Dan lay. The ravages of the swamp's anopheles mosquito could be seen in the wasted bodies of the Bedouins, in the Arab village nearby, and in the distended bellies of the Arab children.

Although the settlers installed double doors and double windows to keep the mosquitoes out of their barracks, and topped off their meals with atabrine and quinine tablets—setting them out in bowls on their dinner tables, like candy—few escaped malaria that first winter, and one child died.

Within two weeks of the Kibbutz Dan's founding, the settlers had removed enough boulders from the higher ground—with crowbars, backs, and hands—to plant vegetables. They set to draining the swamp and planted the eucalyptus there—the Arabs called it the Jewish tree—to hasten the process. They lived four couples in a room (the children slept in a communal dormitory) with only a malaria net between them.

Each settler owned only the iron bed and mattress on which he slept—the Jewish Agency's welcoming gift to every immigrant —and shared all else, even the clothes on their backs. On Friday nights, when Gabi and her fellow settlers scrubbed up for the Sabbath, the fresh laundry waited for them. There were three sizes: small, medium, and large. The underthings Gabi put on could have been worn by another, the week before.

The settlers hired no labor, and so all shared the work. Even when Gabi, a born leader, ran the kibbutz as executive secretary, she took turns cleaning up in the kitchen of the common dining hall.

The settlers used no money inside the kibbutz, and received a small allowance, about one hundred and fifty dollars per family a year—for books and vacations—shared from the sale of the kibbutz produce. Everything else was ploughed back to build and build again.

Now, the Kibbutz Dan was a million-dollar-a-year cooperative business. It produced thirteen hundred tons of apples, two hundred and forty tons of carp, 3 million eggs, not to mention wheat, cotton, fodder, and dairy products.

The Jewish idealists had succeeded in a big, practical way where other attempts—Brook Farm, and Robert Owens' New Harmony community in the United States, and the Communists' totalitarian kolkhozy in the Soviet Union—had failed. The kibbutz had been good to its people. It had sent Gabi to Switzerland twice to care for her asthma; it had sent Yosi to the University in Jerusalem to take a degree in biological science.

And the kibbutz idea had been good for Israel. The 4 percent of Israel's population that lived in its two hundred and thirty kibbutzim produced about 28 percent of the country's agricultural produce. The kibbutzim also produced most of the country's leaders, including Moshe Dayan and Yigal Allon, the 1948 war hero and Labor Minister, who on weekends was always to be found taking his turn in his kibbutz's kitchen.

As the Syrian shells smashed into the apple orchards, set the henhouse afire and slaughtered the cows, Gabi thought back to the dark days of the war in 1948, when all seemed lost except the Jews' saving sense of humor.

"Never mind," they would say to each other, "the Jews have a secret weapon. It's called 'No Alternative.'"

Everyone in the kibbutz understood this, from Tzvika the fifteen-year-old goatherd, and Alisa's son, Israel, who ran ammunition, to Shlomo, who had a lung operation and couldn't fight, but dodged the shells to bring hot food to the shelters; from the giant, Binnie, who milked the cows and watered the apple trees until the water pipes were smashed, to the women in the shelters and men in the defense positions.

Alone in his trench, as the blinding sun of the Holy Land rose from behind the facing eastern ridges, Yosi had a last minute worry. It was for the rare specimens of Israeli wildlife housed in the Kibbutz Dan's museum of natural history. Yosi had stowed the specimens carefully in the museum basement. Among them was a griffin vulture with a nine-foot wing spread, the rare long-legged buzzard, and the even more rare Berwick's swan. Yosi had swapped three kibbutz turkeys for it with the reluctant hunter who had shot the swan and wanted to eat it. Yosi had mounted the specimen himself and got an artist friend to paint in a natural life background for the display case. Yosi's specimens and the museum were the pride of the kibbutz, indeed of all Israel, for school classes from as far away as Jerusalem had visited it.

The unexpected shelling of 1964 had scattered the specimens and set the museum afire. It could happen again.

Yosi shielded his eyes from the glare and saw that he had something more immediate to worry about. Coming out of the foothills and the sun were six medium Soviet tanks, 34-tonners! They took up firing positions behind the shelter of the hills, and from one thousand yards, opened fire, each shell heralded by a ball of flame and followed by a cloud of dust whipped up by the escaping gases of the gun barrel. Within several minutes, the tanks had spread out and, moving forward, were beginning to lob phosphorous and smoke shells in front of Yosi's position, harmless in themselves but providing, as Yosi knew, the inevitable cover and prelude to an infantry attack. Yet, where was the infantry?

At this moment, Yosi heard shouted commands from the dried-up streambed beyond the wheatfields. Syrian infantrymen who had concealed their advance by crawling along the stream's bed now clambered from the wadi, four hundred yards away, and advanced at a trot toward Yosi's position.

Yosi swung his machine-gun toward the oncoming Syrians, now about three hundred yards away, and shouted for his men. In a few seconds, Yosi could hear the reassuring clatter of Yitzhak's machine-gun at the other end of the trench, plus the Uzzis and rifles in the middle.

The size and power of the Syrian attack surprised Yosi. Moving toward his front line of ten men were three platoons of infantry, about ninety men, supported by two heavy machine-gun units, numbering another twenty men. Behind them, Yosi could see Syrian artillerymen wheeling two recoilless rifles, capable of piercing tank armor. And behind all these, spitting cannon and machine-gun fire, were the six tanks.

The first blast of Yosi's and Yitzhak's machine guns had bowled over several infantrymen. The charging line faltered, then broke as the men retreated to the safety of the wadi.

Soon, they were out again, and—with the tanks not far behind—were now only about one hundred and fifty yards away.

Instinctively, Yosi wheeled his machine-gun on the lead tank, saw his bullets ricochet harmlessly off its thick steel hide and caught himself—as he later said—laughing at himself for battling a tank with a machine-gun. But Yosi's machine-gun had scored a point. The Syrian tank commanders, who had been directing their tank drivers from open turrets, now slammed their turrets shut and some of the officers, seemingly ill-at-ease with the use of the tank periscope, began to tack wildly, so that their tanks, to Yosi, began to look like scurrying mice.

The infantrymen, for the third time, were coming on again, and Yosi, down to his last belt of ammunition, called for more on his walkie-talkie, and caught himself thinking:

"A good old-fashioned miracle is what we need."

And it came, straight out of the Bible.

Yosi noticed that tracer bullets from his machine-gun were setting some of the wheat afire. He yanked out the regular belt of bullets, replaced them with tracers, and methodically raked the wheat around the maneuvering tanks. There had been no rain since April, and in the hot, dry June day the wheat burst into flames. Within a few minutes the gold of the field had turned into a raging red, and it was swiftly turning into a roaring pyre.

It was the story of Samson and the foxes all over again. Samson had tied brush to the tails of foxes, set the brush afire and loosed the foxes in a field of wheat to avenge himself on the Philistines.

Now, as two- and then four-foot walls of flame licked at the Syrian tanks' gas containers, located vulnerably on the outside, their commanders wheeled them around and fled in panic, pursuing a mad zig-zag course as they tried to steer by periscope.

Yosi and his men let out a wild cheer as a tank tumbled like a beetle into the wadi and lay helpless on its back. Another got as far as the Banias River a half-mile away, where it, too, turned over in the swiftly running waters. A third tank, making wildly and erratically for the foothills, hit an outcropping of rock and stalled. Through the smoke, Yosi could see the crew trying to start the tank, then give up and run off. The infantry and machine gunners meanwhile had abandoned their rifles and guns and fled toward the road that wound up into the Syrian heights. Yosi and his men tried to shut out the screams of the wounded infantrymen who were being broiled alive in the battlefield inferno, and whom no one could help.

Proverbs teaches: "And Thou Shalt Fight Thy Battles With Guile."

Yosi had heeded the Bible by putting his men where the Syrians didn't expect them, in *front* of the bunkers, so that during most of the two-hour battle, the tanks fired over the Israeli heads. He had topped this ruse by setting the wheatfields afire.

Yosi and his men stood guard in their trenches for four more sleepless days and nights, but no further attack came. And they came off virtually unscathed. One man suffered a bloody nose when a ricocheting stone hit him in the face. Another, Alisa Barlev's husband, Petah, got a shell sliver in his leg, while broiling a steak from one of the cows that had been slaughtered in the shelling.

"I'm ashamed to tell you how I was wounded," Petah confessed to his wife.

Although some of the children would show mental scars for years, everybody in the kibbutz—some five hundred souls in all —had come through alive. But scores of homes were in ruins. The henhouse was a mass of twisted tin and charred timbers, and four thousand hens would have to be replaced. The charred remains of twenty cows lay near the dairy, like so many sacrificial offerings; but, miraculously, Yosi's museum was unharmed. So were most of the schoolhouses.

In the burned-out battlefield, Yosi and the kibbutz disposal teams found eight Syrian bodies, charred and distended beyond all recognition. But it was clear from the weapons abandoned on the field and from the shards of shells that the Kibbutz Dan had stood off a more awesome enemy than the Syrians: the Soviet Union that had armed the Syrians with the latest weapons from their factory production lines. Some of the shells had been fired from the Soviets' new 130-millimeter cannon. The Russians had rushed this weapon to the Syrians even before they had made them available to their own Iron Curtain satellites. And as monitors in the kibbutz communications center could hear during the battle, Russian advisors were helping their Syrian protégés range the guns, and zero them in on the settlement.

As Yosi's men hauled away four heavy Gurianov machineguns, sturdy rifles, and two recoilless artillery pieces, Yosi clambered over the burned-out, abandoned tank in the wadi, a Soviet T-34.

It was clear, Kibbutz Dan had been fighting an extension of Soviet foreign policy.

13

THE CHILDREN
OF GADOT

When the Sabbath comes, the children of Gadot, a kibbutz on the Jordan, like to picnic on a new playground acquired during the June war. They can crawl over a real Russian tank, charge into real concrete-lined trenches. Best of all, they like to crawl into a concrete bunker, poke a stick through the gun ports, and aim it directly down at their own Kibbutz Gadot, lying almost within rifle range in the Huleh Valley below. For the new playground is atop the Golan Heights, lying above the northern Galilee.

Until the June War, Gadot lay clearly lined up, naked and vulnerable, in the gunsights of the Syrians. Officers' diaries and other records captured during the war revealed that the Syrians kept tabs on the daily moves of the kibbutz settlers. They knew when the children went to school in the morning, and when they left in the afternoon. They knew when their parents went out to the five hundred acres of grapefruit and apple orchards and to tend the kibbutz's herd of one hundred cows.

At sundown Gadot's settlers would look anxiously at the ridges above them. If the Syrian lights failed to go on, Gadot parents gathered their children and made for the deep concrete shelters. A blackout usually signalled a coming "incident." Incidents, both day and night, had given Gadot little rest in the year before the war. On the eighty children whose habits the Syrian gunners knew so well, and on Gadot's one hundred and twenty adults, the Syrians had rained some two thousand shells.

In the Upper Galilee, dominated by the Syrian ridges, thirty-eight settlements were raked by gunfire so regularly that the settlers called the shelling "Syrian rainfall." But it was Gadot that received most attention. Just two months before the war, the Syrians flattened several dozen homes and smashed chicken runs and cow barns. During the war Syrian guns killed off all of Gadot's twenty four thousand chickens, one-third of its one hundred cows, set wheatfields afire and raised so much havoc with homes and public halls that it took sixty construction workers five weeks to repair the damage. The Syrians were so intent on levelling Israeli settlements that some of them neglected the Israeli tanks and infantry that were moving up the ridges against them. The Israelis, monitoring enemy radio messages, heard Russian gunnery advisors giving angry orders:

"Stop firing on the settlements—fire on the troops!"

After the war, the children of Gadot emerged from their shelters, outwardly as healthy as ever. But their school-teachers told visitors:

"Something has gone out of them. They have lost the joy of childhood."

One ten-year-old refused to leave his shelter when the war was over.

"I won't sleep upstairs," he said. "You can't give me any guarantees." Finally coaxed out, he spent long silent hours by himself. Other children had nightmares.

And in their drawing classes, the children drew gloomy pictures, using only black crayons. A favorite theme was that of a giant figure, presumably an adult, chasing a diminutive one—a terrified child's commentary on the insane world he lived in.

The children of Gadot had been drawing dark and gloomy pictures since 1957. That was the year the Russians came to Damascus bearing gifts—tanks, Migs, mortars, artillery. With similar gifts, the Soviets had infiltrated Egypt. Now the opening of the

Soviet arsenals to the Syrians opened Syria to similar penetration. The Russian presence soon became apparent in the Golan tableland which towers some eighteen hundred feet above neighboring Israel. Known in the Bible as the Land of Bashan, the Golan plateau was once the granary of the Eastern Mediterranean seaboard. Winds from the sea bring more rainfall to this area than to any other east of the Jordan. Its soil, produced by the weathering of the underlying basalt rock, is black and rich. Yet decades of neglect had turned the region into a bleak, sparsely cropped, and sparsely populated region. This land destruction the Syrians completed with Russian help. Into the Golan Heights area—constituting 2 percent of Syria's land—the Syrians concentrated virtually all of their armed forces and military installations.

From the foot of the cliffs to their crown, the Syrians—with Soviet guidance—incised observation posts, machine gun bunkers, anti-tank emplacements, and firing trenches. Atop the ridges, the Syrians dug further trenches and buried tanks in the ground to provide stationary artillery. These were sealed off by minefields and barbed wire. And spread out along some twenty miles of cliffs were the gun emplacements for the 130-millimeter Russian Long Toms which could loose ten tons of shells per minute up to a distance of fifteen miles, and so rake any of the Israeli settlements in the Huleh Valley below.

Behind the ridges, for a belt of some dozen miles, the Syrian military had turned the Golan Heights into a barren wasteland. The fellaheen who lived there huddled in villages made up of primitive mud hovels half-buried in the ground. The occasional patches of sparsely sown wheat were infested with mines. The only spots of color in the area were the gaudily painted portals which once served as entrances to Syrian military camps. On these, against a white background, the Syrians had used brilliant greens, oranges, and purples to paint nationalist slogans and the dream map of an Arab empire stretching from the Atlantic to the Persian Gulf.

With the Soviets serving as armorers and instructors, the Syrians poured 60 percent of their national budget into their armed forces. And with the Soviets providing an economic model, the Syrians nationalized banks, insurance companies, factories. They expropriated land and drove most of Syria's intellectual leaders, as well as middle class professionals and businessmen (some fifty thousand in all), into exile in Lebanon. The resulting economic chaos was deepened when young officers, comprising but a sliver of the ten-thousand-member Ba'ath Party which rules 5 million Syrians, seized power in early 1966. This was the eighteenth attempted coup in seventeen years. To take the people's minds off unemployment and the virtual breakdown of the economy, the new junta followed a classic course. They beat the drums for a holy war against Israel.

Here the Soviets—and the Communist Chinese—provided the ideological jargon.

President Nureddin al Atassi of Syria proclaimed:

"We want a full-scale *popular war, a war of national liberation* to destroy the *imperialist* Zionist base in Palestine. We want a policy of *scorched earth*. It is only through this policy that we can hope to build a new life for the Arab masses."

How scorching Israel's earth could possibly build a new life for the Arab masses, Syria's president didn't say. But the Syrians gave it a try by setting up official government machinery to train and dispatch terrorists to Israel. During 1966, the Syrian police state "built a new life for the Arab masses" with sixty-one instances of mine-laying, sabotage and murder inside Israel.

Over these unremitting outrages, the Soviet Union threw a superpower's cloak of political protection. In vain, Western members of the United Nations Security Council tried to have the UN condemn the Syrians. The Russians called the victims—the Israelis—the aggressors, and vetoed even the mildest anti-Syrian resolution.

When the June War came, it seemed at first that the Syrians, who had taken more Jewish lives during peace and had destroyed more Jewish homes and crops than any other Arab country, would escape unscathed. As the Russian Bear cast a long shadow from the Golan Heights, even that most formidable of Israel's men of valor, General Moshe Dayan, counselled prudence. The Russians would almost certainly intervene to prevent the fall of their Syrian protégés, he argued. Better rest on the victory already achieved against the main target, Egypt.

But the children of Gadot and those of the thirty-seven other settlements in the harassed   Valley had the last word. Their parents, organized in the "Upper Galilee Regional Council," sent a three-man mission down to Tel Aviv.

"You must free Galilee once and for all," they implored Prime Minister Levi Eshkol and his war cabinet.

Israel's kibbutzim are linked to the Histadrut, the country's labor federation, and together they carry a considerable political clout. The army added its voice. General Dayan dropped his objections.

But to deal with the Syrians before the Russians could intervene with Migs or paratroopers, or before the UN could intercede with a ceasefire, the job would have to be done in a hurry.

Defense Minister Dayan gave Chief of Staff Rabin the green light to scale the Golan Heights and destroy the Syrian army.

"But you have only four and a half hours to do it," Dayan said.

There now followed a curious triple play, part military, part political—and all, pure Israeli brass.

At Washington, D.C., Israel's Ambassador to the U.S., Avraham Harman, kept an eye on the UN in New York and calculated from moment to moment when a ceasefire resolution might come. With an ear to pressing telephone inquiries from the White House and the State Department, Ambassador Harman made a still more fateful calculation. The Israeli attack on Syria brought Russian demands—over the Hot Line to Washington—that the U.S. stop the Israelis, or the Russians would intercede. Harman had to calculate whether they meant business. In Tel Aviv, the second participants in the triple play—Prime Minister Levi Eshkol and his war cabinet—kept the telephone open to Washington, and made their own calculations about the UN and the Russians. With each calculation, they doled out additional fighting time to

Chief of Staff Rabin. The Chief of Staff, in turn, didn't know where his next fighting hour was coming from. So he improvised his war against the Syrians as new doles of time came in.

Here, in Rabin's own terse words, is the short short story of one of the most bizarre operations in the annals of warfare:

"At 7:15 a.m. (Friday, June 9) we were ordered to undertake military operations against the Syrians.

"At 11:30 a.m., our units crossed the Syrian border and began to scale the Golan Heights.

"At 4:30 p.m., my four and a half hour time limit was up. We had pushed up the cliffs, but had not yet broken into the Syrian positions. No word came from the war cabinet, so we kept going.

"At 8:30 p.m., we had broken into the Syrian fortifications. But General Dayan told me there was no more time. (A UN ceasefire was expected momentarily.) While our men were still engaged I changed our plan. Instead of pushing eastward into the Golan plateau, I ordered our troops to fan out north and south, immediately behind the Syrian ridge positions.

"At 11 p.m., General Dayan told me we would have until dawn, about 4 a.m. I didn't change our plans.

"At 3 a.m. (Saturday, June 10), I was told, we could probably continue beyond dawn, and might have an additional few hours during daylight.

"At 8:30 a.m., our commanders told me, the Syrians were fleeing all along the line. I asked General Dayan's permission to change the plan again, and to send our troops east toward the Syrian Army's headquarters at Kuneitra, thirty-five miles from Damascus. Dayan said O.K. But we could have only until noon."

(At the UN, and over the Hot Line from Moscow, the Russians were making increasing threats to intervene. The Americans were growing nervous. They wanted assurances the Israelis wouldn't push on to Damascus—which they felt would surely bring in the Russians.)

"At 12 noon, the war cabinet gave us a few hours more time. (General Dayan was working out ceasefire details with General Odd Bull of the UN in Jerusalem.)

"At 3:45 p.m., we entered Kuneitra, our original objective.

"At 4 p.m., the UN ceasefire went into effect."

In twenty-seven hours, the Israelis had finished off the Syrians and outfaced the Russians as well. They had gambled that the Soviets would not risk involvement with the U.S.—and had won.

The Israeli troops who took the Golan Heights wear the green berets and oak leaf insignia of the Golani Brigade and are known as the "Golani Boys." The brigade is famous for its exploits in two prior wars, has its own traditions, songs, and rugged commando training—like the U.S. Marines. Most of the "Golani Boys" are drawn from the Upper Galilee and grew up under the shadow of the Syrian guns.

Some, like twenty-two-year-old Maurice, an Egyptian-born Israeli, had seen friends blown to pieces by those guns during peace time.

Maurice, a corporal, drives heavy earth-moving equipment—bulldozers, tractors—for a living. Each year when he reported for his forty days of reservist duty with the Golani Brigade, a special job awaited him. He drove a tractor plow in the fields of a kibbutz adjoining the Syrian border. He knew he was constantly in the gun-sights of the Syrians above him. But he had learned how to anticipate a Syrian shelling. Maurice kept his eye on the Syrian shepherds in the nearby hills. When they began to gather their flocks and melt away, Maurice would race his tractor to the kibbutz and return with one whose cab was protected by armor. The Syrians had maintained for years that the nearby fields the Israelis were cultivating were part of a demilitarized zone set up under the Armistice agreements of 1949. The Israelis denied this and used Army drivers like Maurice to till the land under Syrian fire.

Maurice had experienced several narrow escapes. Once, in the summer of 1965, a fellow reservist, driving an armored tractor just forty-five feet from Maurice, was burned to death when a shell hit the tractor's fuel tank and pinned the driver under the burning vehicle.

Two years later, when Maurice went into battle against the Syrians, he was as unarmed as when he did his reservist plowing. The military vehicle he drove was a 30-ton Caterpillar bulldozer. He didn't even have the protection of armor. The U.S. officials who carefully screened military sales to Israel under a virtual embargo never dreamed the bulldozer would wind up as an instrument of war.

Maurice's assignment was not much of a surprise to him. During his thirty-month stint as a draftee and during the weeks that preceded the June War, Maurice had practiced taking his bulldozer up steep grades at Mt. Carmel near Haifa and elsewhere. Now, he knew what that training had been for. It was for the present task of clearing a path for tanks and troop carriers that would ascend the wild Golan cliffs. Those cliffs were strewn with giant granite boulders more formidable than any tank traps. It was Maurice's job and that of his seven fellow bulldozer drivers to move those boulders and tame the cliff.

Maurice is one of four sons of a former Egyptian police sergeant who migrated to Israel in 1949. Generations of the family had lived in Egypt, and together Maurice and his brothers made a curious lot. Maurice, a throwback to Polish ancestors, has blue eyes, red hair and a fair skin. His brothers—two older, one younger—are obviously middle-easterners with olive skins, dark eyes, curly dark hair. In his temperament, too, Maurice differed from his brothers. They are volatile; he is phlegmatic—a quiet man, deliberate in speech.

Still, when his lieutenant passed on the electrifying word on Friday (June 9) that the Brigade was to move against the Syrians, Maurice threw his beret in the air and cheered with his buddies.

As the Golani Brigade's tanks, bulldozers, and troop-laden half-tracks moved eastward to the Syrian border through the ten miles of Huleh Valley settlements, the roads were lined solid with crying women, shouting children, and beaming old men. To Maurice, all seemed laden down with fruit and flowers which they pressed on the troops. Near the kibbutz known as Kfar Blum a tank got mired down in the soft loam of a cotton field. The settlers brought stout ropes and tractors and hauled it free.

The Golani Brigade's commanders would have preferred the cover of night for their assault on the Golan Heights. But there was no time. The attack began near high noon. In the glare of the burning sun, the Syrians could see the Israelis toiling up the cliffs to get at them. But they were as surprised as if the Israelis had fallen on them in the dead of night, under the cover of darkness. To achieve this surprise, the Israelis had chosen an attack route so steep, so strewn with boulders, that the Syrians, expecting nothing from that direction, had stationed relatively small defense forces on the ridges above. Some two hundred Syrians held two strong points, a hill called Tel Azaziat and another, seven hundred feet higher up, called Tel Faher. And although the Syrians had ample warning, they could call no reinforcements. For two days, the Israeli Air Force, unchallenged, had rained bombs and napalm on the Syrian ridges. The Syrians, dug in under tons of concrete, held their ground. But not a man could get through to another position. No ammunition could come in, not even water.

Maurice swung his bulldozer behind three tanks that spearheaded the attack up the slope. On foot, in front, a captain from the Corps of Engineers showed the way. The painful ascent began. Within minutes one of three tanks in front of Maurice was hit and aflame.

Some four hundred and fifty feet farther on, the two remaining tanks clanked to a stop. Two man-high boulders blocked the way, and the Engineer Corps captain motioned Maurice to maneuver his bulldozer above the tanks.

Slowly, Maurice inched his bulldozer around so that it backed the boulder. With the steel teeth of his rear blade, Maurice pried into the earth beneath the boulder, loosened it, then turned his bulldozer around and came at the rock frontally. The boulder inched over, then with a roar and a following cloud of debris thundered down the slope. Methodically, as if he were grading a slope on a construction job, Maurice went to work on the second boulder.

The roar of his bulldozer's diesel engine drowned out the racket of gunfire, but Maurice could see below him Israeli half-tracks laden with seven to nine Golani men each, blow up under direct hits. Shards of shrapnel exploded around his cab. But, curiously, Maurice found the present moment less terrifying than his ordeal under fire when he drove armored tractor plows during peacetime. Perhaps it was the concentrated struggle with the boulder that shut out all else. Soon, the second boulder went crashing down the slope. Maurice moved his bulldozer aside to let the two lead tanks through. They moved up the slope to provide cover for the troops that were clambering closely behind, both on foot and on half-tracks.

Maurice now settled down to a prolonged test of nerve and of endurance. This was his secondary assignment: to clear a track along which supply trucks and ambulances could move up the cliff later. Slowly, and wondering all the while why he wasn't being hit, Maurice drove his bulldozer back and forth, hacking away at the granite outcroppings of the cliff and shoving away boulders. The long afternoon gave way to night, and Maurice worked on. By dawn, the main force of the Golani Brigade had moved up the path he had cleared. The usual mad array of Israeli supply vehicles had followed them: laundry and ice cream trucks, moving vans. Ambulances came down with the dead and wounded. As the sun rose higher in the sky on this Sabbath, the sixth day of the war, the Syrian guns fell silent.

Maurice edged his bulldozer down the slope. He knew that when his next tour of reserve duty came around, he would no longer be driving an armored tractor plow.

Five O'Clock News

Hebrew has no equivalent for the Japanese word, kamikaze— suicide mission. Instead, the Israelis have the concept of "ultimate fulfillment," no matter what the circumstances.

In the battle for the Syrian Heights, Lieutenant Aharon, a deputy company commander, knew it was hardly likely that he or more than a handful of his company of sixty men could return alive. His mission was to spearhead the attack on Tel Faher, the strongpoint on the northern flank of the Syrian ridge positions. He had to break through and open the hole in the Syrian dike so the main force of the Golani Brigade could pour through.

Aharon knew the Tel Faher position from maps, photographs, and sand models. Perched atop a three-pronged ridge of volcanic rock, Tel Faher was a defensive system of pillboxes, firing trenches, and underground sleeping bunkers. It was built to withstand heavy bombardment and was held by some one hundred men armed with bazookas, heavy and light machine-guns, mortars, rocket launchers, and Kaleshnikoff assault rifles. Two tanks guarded the position. In front, there stretched a belt of mines and barbed wire fence some six hundred feet across.

For all the mathematical odds against him and his men, Lieutenant Aharon had waited in anguish as the war entered its fourth day without orders to attack. The twenty-three-year-old Aharon lives in a Huleh Valley kibbutz and, just a fortnight before the war, had become the father of a son. Unless the Syrian guns were silenced, the son, like his father, would grow up under their terrifying shadow.

"We hope to go," Lieutenant Aharon wrote his wife two days before the battle, "and we hope to come back."

With his company commander, a major, and with sixty men, Lt. Aharon crossed the Syrian border in seven half-tracks, preceded by tanks and bulldozers. In the five hours that it took to inch their way up the cliff and reach the crown of the bluff, just below Tel Faher some seven hundred feet above, Lieutenant Aharon's company lost three of its half-tracks. Lieutenant Aharon didn't know how many men were dead or wounded. But he knew that instead of the original sixty men in his company, he and his company commander now led twenty-five. Of the nine tanks that were to have provided cover for Aharon's first-wave assault on Tel Faher, six had been knocked out.

There was nothing for it but to push ahead. Lieutenant Aharon, his major, and the twenty-five men jumped from their half-tracks. They divided into two sections, one led by Aharon, the other by the major. Officers and men were heavily weighed down. Most carried Uzzi machine-guns with fifty clips of ammunition apiece. All had wreaths of hand grenades strung around their necks. Each section had a bazooka, and some of the men carried rifles with rifle grenades.

To reach the barbed wire perimeter of the Tel Faher position, Lieutenant Aharon and his dozen men crawled up a slope on their bellies in the face of trench fire. They all made it.

The barbed wire posed no problem. Two of Aharon's men threw themselves flat on it, and the others crossed over on their backs. Aharon now led the way gingerly through the mine field, then plunged his men into the main firing trench of the Tel Faher position. For a half hour they fought with fists, knives, and teeth to subdue the defenders. Aharon lost another three men. His major lost six, then fell dead, too, from a sniper's bullet.

Although the trench was cleared, Syrian bunkers and machine-gun emplacements remained intact above. At this point, after some five hours of climbing and fighting, Aharon and two of his men lay pinned down in a Syrian trench. Behind him, some six other survivors of his company—some wounded—clung to whatever cover they could find. Aharon waited for the Syrians to counterattack and finish him off. But the counterattack did not come. Instead, something so unexpected happened, that Lieutenant Aharon found himself laughing out loud.

Next to the lieutenant, a Golani boy of eighteen fumbled in his camouflaged battle-dress and pulled out a small transistor radio. As Lt. Aharon stared incredulously, the youth fiddled with the transistor. "I want to hear the five o'clock news," he said. The boy finally got Radio Israel, put the transistor next to his ear to shut out the roar of gunfire—then let out a triumphant whoop.

President Nasser had just announced his resignation!

Lieutenant Aharon passed the word on to the men pinned down behind him. From despair, the men went to elation. They felt like lions. By now, more Israeli troops had made their way up the ridge. Some had even worked their way behind the Tel Faher position. Lieutenant Aharon and his men picked themselves up and joined in the final assault. Now, nothing could stop them. Within an hour Tel Faher had fallen. The cost was thirty-one Israelis killed and seventy-eight wounded—one hundred and eight casualties to take a position held by one hundred men. But, with the capture of the neighboring Tel Azaziat, the way was open to the larger conquest of Golan Heights.

A week later, Aharon knelt beside the crib of his four-week-old son, safe in his kibbutz. Disposal squads collected spent shells; workmen installed new windows and patched walls. To all this Aharon was oblivious.

He had kept his vow to his child of Gadot.

14

THE REDEEMERS

The Faithful City [1]

In the religious ecstasy that boiled around the Wailing Wall in Jerusalem's Old City a day after the war, a young Israeli pilot stood off by himself, providing a strange contrast to those about him. While old men in caftans and side curls prayed, cabinet ministers wept, and soldiers in camouflaged battle dress gaped, the pilot faced the ancient stones of the wall at rigid attention, his right hand at his forehead, palm outward, in smart salute.

"I'm not religious," the pilot explained later. "I don't know how to pray. But I had to do something to express the feeling that Jerusalem was ours again—after two thousand years."

In the Sinai and on the Golan Heights, the Israeli soldier and his officers fought with cold fury against Egyptians and Syrians who threatened the Jews with genocide for the second time in two decades.

But in the battle for Jerusalem, the Israelis fought with exaltation and with gratitude to a Providence that had chosen their generation to fulfill ancient prophecies—and erase a modern reproach.

---

[1] To an ancient Jerusalem besieged by the Assyrians, Isaiah prophesied: "And I will restore thy judges as at the first, and thy counsellors as at the beginning: afterward, thou shalt be called The City of Righteousness, the Faithful City."—Isaiah 1:25.

The reproach lay in this:

Although the Jews of biblical Jerusalem had given spiritual gifts to the world which changed the course of history, the Jew of 1967, alone among all peoples, was barred from the city his poets had described as "The City of God, the Holy City."

The modern repayment of evil for good was indeed a paradox.

Here in Jerusalem, some twenty-seven hundred years before western industrial nations passed factory laws to curb the exploitation of wage earners, Jews gave the world the first vision of social justice.

"The spoil of the poor is in your houses," the poet-prophet Isaiah had thundered at the rich from the street corners of Jerusalem. "What mean ye that ye beat my people to pieces and grind the faces of the poor?"

In Jerusalem, too, some three millenia before the United Nations, a Jew had proclaimed the ideal of general disarmament, universal peace, and unity among men.

In poetry that has become the literary heritage of all the human race, Isaiah prophesied:

"And they shall beat their swords into plowshares and their spears into pruning hooks; nation shall not lift up sword against nation. Neither shall they learn war any more." [2]

In Jerusalem, Jews wrote the Bible, to be translated in time into a thousand-and-one tongues to serve as a great unifier between nations, cultures, and civilizations. And here, in Jerusalem, Jesus Christ, known to his fellow Jews as Jehoshua or Joshua (changed to the Latin, Iesus, then to Jesus—to accommodate non-Hebrew tongues) preached a religion of love, individual moral responsibility, and social justice—rooted in the Hebrew prophets —that was to conquer the western world.

From Jerusalem, the ancient tiny Jewish nation had left an impact on modern civilization greater, as Will Durant observed, "than that of Babylonia . . . or Persia . . . perhaps greater than Greece."

Yet, from 1948, when the Jordanian Legion overran Old Jeru-

<hr>

[2] Americans and Russians, Arabs and Israelis can read this inscription on a wall facing the United Nations Headquarters in New York City.

salem, until the war of 1967, no Jews could visit their holy places. Christians could re-trace Christ's steps in the Via Dolorosa; Moslems could pray in the Mosque of Omar from which, according to Moslem tradition, Muhammad ascended to heaven. But Jews were barred from the site of the ancient Temple built by Solomon, whose memory had helped keep them intact as a people through two thousand years of dispersion.

Indeed, in Arab-held Jerusalem, the years 1948–1967 were the years of Roman Emperor Hadrian all over again. After the Jewish uprising of 135 A.D., Hadrian had sought to erase Jerusalem's memory by building a new city on its site—with a new name, Aelia Capitolina. The Jordanians of 1948 didn't change Jerusalem's name. But as in Hadrian's time, a Jew risked his life to set foot in it. The Jordanians leveled ancient synagogues where Jews had prayed for centuries. Arab workmen desecrated the two-thousand-year-old Jewish cemetery on the Mount of Olives and used its gravestones to build a hotel. On Mount Scopus, where the world-famous Hebrew University was founded in 1922, libraries, laboratories, and classrooms mouldered unused. Here, Jordanians waylaid a busload of professors, students and doctors on April 12, 1948 and massacred seventy-seven of them. Under the 1949 armistice, Mt. Scopus became a demilitarized enclave inside Jordanian Jerusalem. Only a caretaker Israeli police guard remained on Mt. Scopus thereafter. The Jordanians even refused to permit the Israelis to move some 1 million books from the National and University libraries that were stranded there.

"The Jordanians," wrote Christopher Sykes, the British diplomat and foreign correspondent, "showed themselves amongst the worst guardians of other people's rights and shrines to have appeared in the whole troubled history of Jerusalem." Neither Greeks nor Romans, Mamelukes nor Seljuks, nor Crusaders, Turks and British had topped the Jordanians in enmity toward the Jews.

Against Jewish fighters fired by ancient memories and recent wrongs, then, the Jordanian defenders stood no chance. The Bedouin battalions that held Old Jerusalem did not take off their shoes and run like the Egyptians. They were the best that Jordan's

Arab Legion could boast, and the Arab Legion was the best the Arabs could boast. It was, in fact, the only Arab army that could claim a victory over the Israelis—the conquest of Old Jerusalem and the West Bank of the Jordan in 1948. Yet, flesh and blood and bravery alone could not stand against demons who came at one with guns and knives—and nails and teeth—and thought that to die in this battle was a privilege and a "mitzvah" (a good deed in the eyes of God).

Jerusalem witnessed the bitterest fighting of the war. Of the two brigades—one of paratroopers, the other of infantry—that took East Jerusalem, two hundred died. This was one-fourth of all Israeli deaths during the Six-Day War. Of the four hundred men (two companies) who stormed the bunkers and trenches atop the strong point known as Ammunition Hill, only sixteen walked away without hurt. Sixty-three died; two hundred twenty-one were wounded.

And they possessed his land
This side Jordan . . . toward the sunrising.
— DEUTERONOMY IV:47

On the morning of June 5th, as Israel's planes attacked Egypt's airfields, Prime Minister Eshkol sent a note to Jordan's King Hussein, via General Odd Bull who was in charge of UN peace-keeping forces in Jerusalem. It read:

"We shall not initiate any action whatsoever against Jordan. However, should Jordan open hostilities, we shall react with all our might."

The Israelis regarded Hussein as the most moderate of the Arabs. Through the years they had made friendly overtures to him.

Israel's government had offered Hussein a corridor to the Mediterranean, technical help and economic cooperation, in return for normal, peaceful relations. Moshe Dayan, while a member of Israel's Knesset (parliament), had suggested that the two countries exploit the waters of the Jordan together and work jointly to increase tourism. Dayan had also suggested a Swiss-type confederation with Jordan.

When Hussein chose war, he extinguished a spark of hope that Arabs and Jews could live as friendly neighbors.

Hussein's grandfather, King Abdullah, had kindled that spark eighteen years before. He had sat down in amicable and even festive confab with representatives from the infant State of Israel and had hammered out the borders of modern Jordan.

Abdullah, like his grandson Hussein, was small in body. But he was big in vision, and had great gifts of leadership to go with it. When the Jews of Palestine proclaimed the State of Israel in 1948, Abdullah, then ruling four hundred thousand Bedouins in the east-of-Jordan kingdom known as Trans-Jordan, promptly crossed the Jordan with his British-trained Arab Legion and gobbled-up much of the area known today as the West Bank. This was the territory the UN had set aside in its Partition Resolution of 1947 for the creation of an independent Palestinian Arab State. Abdullah's Arab Legion also drove the Jews out of their quarter in Jerusalem and secured Old Jerusalem, with its holy places, for Trans-Jordan. He then changed his country's name to Jordan.

When the UN called for a halt to the war between five Arab states and Israel in 1949, Abdullah sent secret word to the Israelis inviting them to come to his winter palace at Shuneh, near Jericho, to talk. The doings at Shuneh provide a sunny footnote to the otherwise cheerless saga of Arab-Jewish fratricide.

Israel sent its brightest young men, among them Moshe Dayan and Yigael Yadin, both to become world-famous, one as a general, the other as a biblical archaeologist. To avoid detection—and possible mob violence—the Israelis disguised themselves as UN observers and came under cover of dark, travelling the twenty miles from Jerusalem under the protection of Abdullah's bodyguards. They talked all night and departed before sunrise.

At the first meeting, Abdullah presented the Israelis with a splendid sword worked in silver; it adorns a wall in Israel's Foreign Ministry to this day. The Israelis, in turn, gave Abdullah a Bible of exquisitely tooled leather. Then, at a banquet served on gold and silver service, Abdullah spoke eloquently—to his own assembled cabinet as much as to the Israelis. Abdullah praised the Israelis as fighters, suggesting that they were quite capable of conquering at least part of the West Bank that Abdullah had acquired. Then, as Professor Yigael Yadin recalls the speech, Abdullah said:

"I'm a Bedouin, and we Bedouins have a saying: 'When you are riding a heavily burdened ass, and you see the enemy approaching, you have two alternatives—to be captured with all your goods, or to try and escape and toss out the goods piecemeal.' I have invited the Israelis here in order to toss out goods."

King Abdullah then retired for the night, leaving his ministers to haggle with the Israelis. Two nights went by without agreement. On the third night, after the usual sumptuous feast, Abdullah gave orders to his people:

"That's it! Tonight we sign." He then withdrew, but returned from time-to-time in his sleeping robe to check up. When the negotiations narrowed down to a contest over a village called Beit Guvrin, Abdullah put his arm around Yadin and pleaded:

"Ya Yadin! Give me Beit Guvrin. Tomorrow is my birthday. Give me Beit Guvrin as a birthday present!"

Yadin, then thirty-two, said to the king, who could have been his father:

"Who am I and what am I? You are a King, and I am a dog. If I were to give you Beit Guvrin, they would throw me out and give you nothing."

To this, the King replied:

"*Tayat* (all right!). Let's go and sign." Abdullah was the only Arab leader ever to cede Arab-held territory to Israelis, trading parcels in order to straighten out borders.

The signing involved an armistice only. For two years King Abdullah and the Israelis continued to meet secretly to work toward a permanent peace and mutual diplomatic recognition, the king treading warily because of Arab hostility around him. But the talks could not be kept secret forever. As news of Abdullah's "fraternizing" with the Jews leaked out, passion won over reason. Abdullah was shot to death in 1951 while praying in the Mosque of Omar on the Temple Mount of Jerusalem. Hussein, then sixteen, and at his grandfather's side, escaped miraculously. Abdullah's assassins were believed to have been procured by the ex-Mufti of Jerusalem who had spent the second World War in Berlin, aiding Hitler's holocaust of the Jews. He had returned to Cairo where, under Nasser's wing, he hoped to apply the lessons learned from the Nazis.

Hussein officially became king at the age of eighteen, because his father—Talal—mentally ill, couldn't rule. Rarely has a teenager assumed so cruel a burden.

The Jordan Hussein inherited from his grandfather was a house divided. The eight-hundred-thousand-odd Palestinians, acquired along with the West Bank, constituted two-thirds of Jordan's population and were a politically-orphaned and restive lot. They owed no allegiance to Hussein's Bedouin Hashemite throne. Young Hussein could never know when his Palestinians would take to the streets in bloody riots against him, or accept bribes from Arab neighbors to finish him off. Hussein had other problems. His reliance on the British-officered Arab Legion and on British handouts stirred Arab nationalist cries that Hussein was "a tool of the imperialists!" Syrian and Egyptian terrorists used Jordan as a base, so threatening to embroil Hussein with Israel. When Hussein sought to restrain them, fellow Arabs raised outraged cries that Hussein hankered after peace with the enemy, just as his grandfather did. All these strains on domestic tranquility were stretched to the breaking point by Nasser who enflamed the Palestinians with radio propaganda and with Mukhaberat agents who were forever trying to kill Hussein.

But with great physical courage (Hussein once confronted mutinous troops and emerged their hero), with a timely rescue by British paratroopers, with help from Israel [3] and with adroit politicking, Hussein nevertheless arrived intact to face the momentous events of the last two weeks of May, 1967.

[3] In 1958, Israel—as we've seen—permitted British paratroopers and American oil to reach Jordan across its airspace, when neighboring Arab states refused.

Part of that politicking had been an occasional dalliance with Nasser. On the eve of the 1956 Suez War, for instance, Hussein signed a mutual assistance pact with Nasser—but was wise enough to stay aloof from the fighting that followed.

Now, in 1967, when he was eleven years older and presumably wiser, Hussein plunged into a war in which victory could be as disastrous as defeat.

Nasser had played the role of Hussein's most dangerous enemy right up to the eve of May 30, when they exchanged fraternal kisses. A fortnight before, Cairo Radio had called Hussein the "traitor King of Jordan," and demanded his overthrow. Not long before that, Nasser, in a speech at Cairo University, derided Hussein as "the adulterer of the Hashemite family." If the Arabs wiped Israel off the map, there would no longer be an Israeli buffer between Hussein and his enemy, Nasser. A triumphant Nasser could then press an old ambition: to replace Hussein's conservative Hashemite kingdom with a "progressive" pro-Soviet regime.

Why Hussein attacked Israel, then, is a royal puzzlement. The answer may lie, at least in part, with a fateful Israeli miscalculation eight months before the Six-Day War.

In late 1966, Israel chafed with mounting anger and frustration as Syrians bombarded Jewish settlements, ambushed farmers, and mined public roads. The UN, hamstrung by Russian vetoes, did nothing. Some of the terrorists crossed over from Jordan where the Palestinian Arabs sheltered them—and Hussein could not or would not control them. Although the Syrians were the prime villains, Israel struck with tanks and armored units against the Jordanian town of Es-Samu'. The Israelis blew up forty houses and wiped out two troop carriers full of Arab Legionnaires who tried to intervene. Why did the Israelis attack Jordan instead of Syria? The answer may be that the Israelis were reluctant to involve themselves with the Soviet Union. In any case, Israeli officials admitted privately later, that the raid had been a mistake. The attack should have been directed at Damascus.

For Hussein, the attack on Es-Samu' fanned old suspicions into a new obsession. He had long suspected that the Israelis had designs on the West Bank and on East Jerusalem. He had only to look at a map to see that the West Bank was a tempting target to his neighbors. It bulged at one point to within fifteen miles of Israel's Mediterranean coast, so squeezing Israel into a dangerously narrow corridor. Any Israeli general would give much to push back that Jordanian border to a more defensible line. As for Old Jerusalem, Hussein knew that for hundreds of years Jews had finished their prayers with the vow: "Next Year in Jerusalem!" After Es-Samu' Hussein became convinced that his neighbor would expand eastward at the first opportunity.

So, when Nasser began to move troops into the Sinai and to rally Arabs to his standard, the stage was set for tragedy for Jordan. For Israel a providential opportunity arose to fulfill a folk dream, the return to ancient Jerusalem.

"Do nothing to provoke Hussein!"

When Jordanian shells began to fall in West Jerusalem and on Israeli settlements on the morning of June 5, the Israelis withheld their fire for four hours in the firm belief that Hussein was only making a gesture toward Arab Unity, and would do no more.

Afterwards, Brig. General Uzzi Narkiss, who commanded the two-and a half-day war against Jordan, said:

"No one imagined there'd be fighting along the whole border of the West Bank."

To the Israelis, Nasser was the chief enemy, and most of Israel's armed strength was deployed on the Sinai border.

Only one brigade of armor, headquartered just east of Tel Aviv was left behind as insurance to guard the Central Front—Israel's populated coastal plain and the tortuous three-hundred-mile Jordanian border. In reserve, too, if the Jordanians or Iraqis attacked from the east, was the garrison in the Israeli part of Jerusalem. The Central Front's commander, Brig. Gen. Narkiss, thought the chances of such an attack were so small that he fretted he was sitting out the war.

The general's fretting eased off a bit when a senior Egyptian General, Abdul Munim Riad, arrived in Amman on June 1 to take charge of all forces in Jordan. And when Israeli Intelligence learned that a full Iraqi Division was on its way to Jordan, Narkiss began to nurture a glimmer of hope. There would be war with Jordan, after all, and the historic opportunity to spend "next year in Jerusalem."

Nevertheless, Defense Minister Moshe Dayan came up to Jerusalem on the Sunday before the war and told Narkiss there would be no change in the disposition of troops.

"Don't do anything to provoke Hussein," Dayan said. "If his people fire, do nothing. Keep silent. If there's war, do the best you can with what you have. Grit your teeth. Ask for nothing!"

Narkiss is a slight man of forty-two, a native of Jerusalem with a pinched face. He learned war at the French École de Guerre. Like most Israeli military men he learned much more by studying Israel's special needs.

To meet those special needs, for instance, Narkiss had pored for hours over historian Josephus Flavius' accounts of the Jewish wars with the Romans. These taught that whoever aspired to conquer or hold Jerusalem must command the ancient Judaean hills inside and outside the city. Should Hussein truly mean war against Israel, he would signal his intentions by assaults on the high ground of two demilitarized zones: Mount Scopus, held by one hundred eighty Israeli police, and the hill of Evil Council, held by UN peacekeeping forces lodged in Government House there. Narkiss also knew that the key to all of the West Bank was the high ground that lay between Jerusalem and the Jordanian town of Ramallah some five miles to the north. In case of war, Narkiss' tanks would have to climb and break through this rugged and roadless terrain. Only a goat could feel secure on the escarpments, and they were abundantly mined, besides.

But, as the morning of June 5 came and Jordanian artillery lobbed shells into Jewish Jerusalem and across the narrow waist of Israel, Narkiss did nothing to "provoke Hussein." He "gritted his teeth," as instructed. He waited.

At an airfield near Tel Aviv, during the same morning, Colonel Mordechai Gur, a handsome thirty-seven-year-old army career man, known to his men as "Motta," chafed also at his enforced idleness as the war rolled on in the Sinai. Scattered across the field was Gur's brigade of paratroopers. Although reservists, most had seen action during Israeli reprisals against Arab terrorists. Yet, all were agog with the scuttlebutt that they would soon jump in the Sinai Desert. But, as the hours passed, the order to board planes did not come. As Col. Motta waited at the brigade telephone, he recalled a curious conversation six years before with the Israeli Army's chief chaplain, Rabbi Schlomo Goren, a bearded patriarch who cut a strange figure in his brigadier general's uniform.

"Motta," the Rabbi had said to Gur, then stationed in northern Israel, "I want to be the first Jew at the Wailing Wall when Jerusalem is redeemed."

"In that case," Motta Gur had replied, straight-faced, "you had better stay on good terms with me, because I'm the man who's going to redeem it."

Almost a week before, on a premonitory impulse, Colonel Motta had travelled up to Jerusalem to look across the border at the enemy's positions and fortifications. Still pursuing his hunch, the young colonel wanted to return to Jerusalem for a further look with his staff and battalion commanders. But friends on the general staff laughed at him.

"Forget about Jerusalem," they said. "Sinai is where you're going. Later, Motta regretted he had listened.

As the morning dragged into early afternoon, the order came through from brigade headquarters. Motta and his red berets finally had their mission. But it was not in Sinai. They were wanted in Jerusalem! Motta and his staff and subcommanders raced for a plane. His paratroopers began to board buses for the forty-mile mountain road trip to Jerusalem. The time was 2 p.m. The war was six hours old.

The Israeli who fought the Romans

On a bus with his paratroopers, twenty-five-year-old company commander, Yoram Zanosch, tried to digest the momentous news of the coming battle for Jerusalem. With orders to head for Jerusalem came news, too, that the Jordanians had assaulted Government House, had hauled down the UN flag there, and were sitting triumphantly atop the Heights. Jordanian artillery was also pounding Mt. Scopus, in preparation for *its* seizure. Radio Amman, in characteristic Arab fashion, announced it was already taken. This meant Hussein had cast the die for war. The paratroopers' assignment was to serve as assault infantry and break into Jordanian fortified positions on the perimeter of Old Jerusalem. Their mission, too, was to assault the Jordanian Legionnaires atop the Heights near Mt. Scopus and from there break into the walled area known as the Old City.

The Old City! Captain Yoram Zanosch closed his eyes and saw its crenellated grey stone walls as if he were looking down on them in the brilliant light of an Israeli summer's day. The Turks had reared these high battlements in the sixteenth century on the foundations of crumbling Roman fortifications, and there they stood like something out of a Middle Ages print. Yoram knew every one of the Old City's six well-known gates: the Jaffa Gate, surmounted by the Tower of David which could be seen from Jewish Jerusalem's King David Hotel; the Zion Gate, a stone's throw from Mt. Zion where King David was believed to be buried; the Damascus Gate and Herod's Gate; the Dung Gate and St. Stephen's Gate, also known as the Lion's Gate.

Through which gate would the paratroopers break into the Old City, Yoram wondered. Probably through St. Stephen's Gate. It opened up on the Via Dolorosa, and from this narrow way there was quick access to the Temple Mount. Atop the Mount was the golden-domed Mosque of Omar. But most important, at the Mount's southwest perimeter—the western wall of Herod's Temple—was the Wailing Wall. Yes, the shortest route to the Wailing Wall was through St. Stephen's Gate.

For Yoram, the study of Jerusalem was a lifelong passion. It started during a primary school trip to the city when Yoram was twelve. He stayed in a hostel with fellow pupils and for two weeks trudged all over the pink sandstone streets of the Israeli part of the divided city. He climbed atop Mount Zion, the site of King David's Tomb—so near the site of the Temple just beyond the barbed wire in Jordan, yet barred to Jews. He visited the three-story cave, carved out of rock, where the judges of Israel's ancient supreme court, the Sanhedrin, lay buried. But what fascinated him most was the view, eastward into ancient Jerusalem, from atop the YMCA Tower, across from the King David Hotel in Western Jerusalem.

Young Yoram loved to play a game. Like every Israeli schoolboy, he had studied the Bible as the history of his country. Jerusalem was the stage on which ancient Jewish heroes had played their greatest roles. So Yoram would peer down on a hill overlooking the Valley of Hinnom, just south of the Old Walled City, and make believe that there, in front of him, King David's Judaean warriors were storming the walls of the Jebusites. Yoram could even imagine the halt and the blind that the Jebusites had placed on those walls in an early psychological warfare effort to strike fear into David with their curses. Or, he could see Judas Maccabee march in triumph up the Valley of Joas toward the Temple he had freed from the Syrians. Or watch Bar Kochba and his men make their stand against the full might of the Roman Empire.

Other boys collected stamps. But Yoram collected tales and pictures of Jerusalem. He returned again and again, bringing easel and paints to set down Herod's Tomb, and the caves of Sanhedria, and the Tomb of Absalom, David's son.

"How beautiful it is," Yoram said of the biblical panorama before him. "Someday it will return to Israel, but I won't be a part of it."

Yoram was wrong. It was he who was the first Jew in two thousand years to stand before a Wailing Wall that was no longer in alien hands.

Yoram grew up to be a strapping six-foot one-inch man. He inherited his long frame from his stately, Italian-born mother. From his German father, Yoram inherited a fair skin, now deeply tanned, straw-colored hair, and blue eyes. But in these eyes was a serenity neither his father, a refugee from Hitler, nor his mother, a refugee from Mussolini, had ever known.

The serenity was the product of Yoram's life in a small,

sheltered universe, the religious kibbutz, Yavne, near the Mediterranean port of Ashdod. At Yavne, in Roman times, there stood an ancient seat of Jewish learning. Of the several hundred kibbutzim in Israel, only twelve are religious. So Yoram was that rarity among Sabras—he was a deeply religious, and observant Jew. At Kibbutz Yavne, the laws which the Lord had instructed Moses "to tell the children of Israel," governed every waking hour.

Yoram started his day at dawn with morning prayer—"Shaharit"—at the kibbutz's *beit knesset* (temple). He put on his silk prayer shawl, and bound the two ritual phylacteries (leathern boxes containing the Ten Commandments) to his left wrist and his forehead, as instructed in Deuteronomy: "And thou shalt bind them (the Ten Commandments) for a sign upon thine hand, and they shall be frontlets between thine eyes." At sunset, Yoram returned to the *beit knesset* for evening prayer, "Mahriv." When Yoram went into the battle for Jerusalem he carried a submachine gun under his right arm, a wreath of hand grenades around his shoulders, and inside his blouse was the small velvet sack with the Star of David on it, containing prayer shawl and phylacteries.

Yoram's work linked him to his forefathers, too. Trained in agricultural school, he managed his kibbutz's cotton production. He could say that, like Saul, he "followed the plough," (i.e., a tractor). Like Jacob, his friends tended the sheep (and the cows, and fishponds, and egg hatcheries). And like Hosea, "they gathered the sycamore."

Friday night was the big night of the week. Everyone scrubbed up and went to services at the *beit knesset*. These consisted almost entirely of songs to the coming Sabbath. The singing continued in the kibbutz's communal dining hall, where the week's most elaborate meal was laid on: freshly baked white bread, broiled chicken, cakes and sweet wine from the kibbutz's own grapes and cherries.

In an age when families are scattered over the face of the earth, the institution of the kibbutz had turned the clock back to a simpler time, when grandparents lived amidst their grandchildren, and a whole clan of uncles, aunts, and in-laws sat down to an evening meal together. Yoram's pert, blue-eyed wife, Nahama, an art teacher in the kibbutz high school, sometimes thought this was a mixed blessing. But it gave Yoram a secure feeling to look around his big table and see his mother and father and Nahama's mother and father. He loved to talk agricultural shop with his Uncle Belli who had taught art history in Rome and now managed the kibbutz egg hatchery, the biggest in the Middle East. Belli had sent a young assistant to Purdue University in Indiana to study egg selection and liked to say:

"The Jews of Israel are great farmers and great fighters, but they're poor businessmen. Here we produce the best and cheapest eggs and chicks in the world, but we haven't got the business brains to dig up markets for them."

The June sun was high in the sky when Yoram's bus reached Western Jerusalem. As he alighted, Yoram could see the angry red flashes of Jordanian artillery from Jerusalem's eastern hills. He strained his eyes north to where the West Bank of Jordan squeezed Israel into a narrow corridor.

From the Latrun Fort, just inside Jordan, to Yavne, this corridor was only a scant fifteen miles across. Yoram wondered whether his wife, Nahama, and their two-and a half-year-old daughter were safe.

Events had marched on. Infantry from the Israeli garrison in Jerusalem had counterattacked Government House. At a cost of eight dead, the infantry had driven the Jordanians from it and had run up the Israeli flag.

The demilitarized zone of Mt. Scopus was under heavy fire. The 1949 armistice permitted an Israeli convoy to transit the Mt. Scopus enclave once every fortnight to change the one hundred-and eighty-man guard there. The Israelis had used this opportunity to rotate the maximum number of officers and men atop the Height. So, over the years thousands of Israeli soldiers and officers had acquainted themselves with East Jerusalem that way. Although the convoy was closely checked by UN peacekeeping troops, the Israelis had also managed—during the last several weeks—to smuggle a considerable arsenal up the height. The "police guard" atop Mt. Scopus, then, was ready to give as much as it took, until help arrived.

Yoram's colonel, Motta Gur took his officers to a rooftop near the Mandelbaum Gate, used by Christian pilgrims and by UN personnel to enter Jordanian Jerusalem. Motta wanted a closer look at the area his paratroopers had to break into. Yoram saw he was up against the most formidable of all combat assignments, the assault on a built-up area.

Inside those squat buildings below, Arab Legionnaires waited behind rifles, machine guns, and bazookas. They waited in concrete bunkers and trenches. Between the Israelis and the enemy were a succession of concrete walls. In among these were mined areas and complicated tangles of concertina barbed wire.

When the paratroop-laden buses arrived from Tel Aviv, brigade officers discovered to their dismay that the paratroopers had gotten off in such a hurry, they had left behind arms and ammunition, and had arrived virtually emptyhanded. The attack on Jordanian Jerusalem had been set for 10 p.m. Now, as the officers scurried to supply their men from the Jerusalem garrison's stores, the attack was put off until midnight. Then, as it dawned on Col. Gur's staff that casualties would be extremely heavy, arrangements had to be made to evacuate the dead and wounded. So, the assault was pushed back again. Now it was set for 2 a.m. This was cutting it mighty fine; the attackers would have the cover of darkness for only a scant three hours.

As Yoram drove through the blacked-out streets of Jewish Jerusalem toward the point from which his battalion would jump off, he mused on the irony of events. Here the Jews were handed one of the most momentous opportunities of their history, the chance to regain ancient Jerusalem. Yet, in contrast to the usual meticulous Israeli planning, this historic operation was improvised at the last minute. Many of the younger officers knew nothing of the terrain they would be fighting over; they became acquainted with it via hastily prepared Intelligence instruction sheets, which they studied just as hastily by the beams of their flashlights. As zero hour approached, the confusion almost escalated into disaster. One of the ten buses bringing the paratroopers to the rendezvous point got lost. Five jeeps had to be sent out to bring it in. Then, as the Israeli tanks clanked up, shattering the quiet of the night, Jordanian artillery in the Joas Valley below opened up on the disembarking paratroopers. Within minutes, one bus was aflame, and one hundred of the paratroopers were dead or wounded. The first stage of the paratroop brigade's Jerusalem action was the evacuation of dead and wounded. All around him in the darkness and confusion Yoram could hear tough paratroopers sobbing like children. When he visited them in the hospital after the fighting, he heard the same plaint over and over.

"To be hit before I could even lift an Uzzi or fire a shot! What a disgrace!"

Israeli tanks and mortars pounded the mined areas in front of the barbed wire. Jordanian flares lit up the scene as if it were high noon. Israeli demolition squads, armed with bangalore torpedoes, cleaned out the first of the barbed wire barriers and Yoram, following close behind four tanks, led his company down a gentle slope toward the Bedouin Legionnaires waiting below.

The enemy bunkers, reinforced with heavy concrete roofs, seemed to withstand everything but direct artillery hits. There was nothing for it but to take them out with demolition charges or with hand grenades dropped into their portholes from the top, a suicidal business. Sometimes when such charges seemed to wipe out every living thing inside, the heavy machine guns kept firing. For an hour, Yoram and his men fought in alleyways, in cellars, on stairs, and rooftops. One of Yoram's lieutenants, jumped by a huge Bedouin, dispatched the man with his knife. He was so shaken by the encounter, that Yoram sent him down as wounded. As Yoram led his men deeper into Jordanian Jerusalem, snipers in buildings behind them took a heavy toll. Of Yoram's two-hundred-man company, seven were dead and thirty-seven wounded. He took over another company, even more heavily chewed up, and moved on. To Col. Motta Gur, who cut in on communications from time-to-time to ask about the fighting, Yoram said, "O.K. O.K. Everything will soon be all right." By 7 a.m., Yoram and his men were dug-in at a point below the heights of Augusta Victoria near Mt. Scopus. The next part of the plan was to storm these Heights, as a curtain-raiser to the final act of the drama: the assault on the Old Walled City itself.

Elsewhere, two other battalions of paratroopers had carried out their costly assignments and waited, too, for the attack on Augusta Victoria. To the north of where Yoram lay, his friend, Captain Nir, a thirty-three-year-old high school gymnastics instructor, had taken Ammunition Hill, so-called because of the ammunition stores buried in its maze of caverns. Ammunition Hill was ringed by six successive lines of six-foot deep trenches, topped by some forty concrete bunkers. King Hussein, it was learned later, had visited the position a week before the war and had made the Bedouin defenders there swear that they would fight to the death. They did. Of the two companies that defended the hill and the police training school nearby, the Jordanians lost one hundred to one hundred and fifty dead. Forty Israeli paratroopers lost their lives taking the Jordanian police training school.

Meanwhile, during the night the armored brigade that had waited in reserve near Tel Aviv fought its way up the steep ridge between Ramallah and Jerusalem and was now linking up with the paratroopers in the northern part of the city. Israel's Air Force was raising havoc with the Jordanian tanks near Jericho to the south of Jerusalem. This prevented them from coming to the relief of the Jordanian forces atop Augusta Victoria. The first stage of the war with Jordan was over. Arab Jerusalem was cut off from Jordanian forces to the north and to the south.

The order to attack Augusta Victoria came at 8:30 a.m., Wednesday. But Yoram did not take part in it. He was on his way to the St. Stephen's Gate to the Old City, under orders from his colonel, Motta, who was on his way there, too. The Augusta Victoria Heights and the Old City were attacked at the same time. A UN ceasefire hung like a sword over the Israelis, and the liberation of the Old City and its holy places could not wait until the Heights above it were taken.

Yoram's half-track, bearing eleven paratroopers, had barely arrived at St. Stephen's Gate when Col. Motta Gur drove up. With him was the bearded Rabbi Goren in his incongruous brigadier's uniform. With one arm the Rabbi clutched a giant ram's horn, the ritualistic shofar, blown on high holy days and other solemn occasions. In the other, he bore a small scroll of the Torah—the first five books of the Bible. Colonel Motta was keeping his promise to the Rabbi—to be among the first at the Wailing Wall.

Jordanian snipers were still being cleared from the walls. But neither the colonel nor the rabbi waited. A tank smashed the giant wooden gate, pulled back, and the colonel's command car swept in. Behind him came Yoram's half-track, followed by a column of troop carriers.

The column rolled up the narrow Via Dolorosa and made for the Temple Mount. There the colonel and his staff waited while Yoram and his paratroopers dashed for the Wailing Wall to clear it of snipers.

When Yoram arrived at the Wall, he was alone. The giant, square stones, each about three feet across, loomed upwards to a height of fifty-four feet. Against this majestic ruin, about fifty yards long, the Arabs had crowded a mean slum of mud huts, and as an ultimate insult had built several public lavatories in the alleyway in front of it.[4]

Herod had rebuilt this wall as part of the Temple enclosure that Solomon had first erected centuries before. In Yoram's mind, nineteen centuries rolled back. Once again, he played the game he played as a boy when he looked down on East Jerusalem from West Jerusalem's YMCA Tower. Yoram was back in the time of Titus, the emperor who destroyed the Temple and dispersed the Jews. He could hear Roman soldiers shouting, "HEP, HEP!": three letters which stand for *"Hierosolyma es perdita,"*—"Jerusalem is destroyed!" It was a cry that had rolled down the ages, and even the Nazis shouted it in derision of the Jews.

Yoram felt a stab of pain as a bullet whizzed by his ear, hit the wall and ricocheted against his right cheek. He whirled automatically, firing his Uzzi at a sniper some fifteen feet behind him. But Yoram was not killing an Arab. The Arabs were mere interlopers. Yoram was fighting Romans like the Jewish heroes of old.

Yoram shook off the illusion. The occasion required prayer,

---

[4] Lavatories and slum were bulldozed so swiftly—soon after the taking of the Wall—that none of the 2,000,000 Israelis who poured toward the Wall from all over Israel within the next six weeks, suspected they had been there.

not games. He broke out his praying shawl, fixed the leather phylacteries on wrist and forehead, and began to say the morning prayer. But it remained unfinished. Yoram had been at the Wall alone for some five minutes. Now fellow paratroopers came running up. With praying shawl flapping in the wind, Yoram gave orders to secure the area.

This done, Yoram repaid a debt. On finishing his military service at twenty, he had spent one of the happiest years of his life studying the Talmud—a post-biblical book on Jewish law and observances—with two venerable Jerusalem rabbis, famed throughout Israel. These were Rabbi David Hacohen and Rabbi Zvi Yehuda Cook, the latter a remarkably learned man who held, so Yoram heard, a half-dozen Ph.D.'s from as many European universities. To Yoram, no one in Israel was more deserving, because of piety and learning, to be among the first to pray at the redeemed Wall. He dispatched a lieutenant and a captured Jordanian jeep to fetch the rabbis. The lieutenant found Rabbi Cook in his tiny West Jerusalem home, observing a forty-day period of meditation and prayer. The Rabbi had vowed he would not set foot outside his house—"except for an important religious occasion."

How does a rabbi break such a vow?

A rabbinical court of three rabbis, hastily convened from the neighborhood, found a way. The redemption of the Western Wall, they held, was "an important religious occasion." Within minutes, Rabbi Cook and his old friend, Rabbi Hacohen—both in their middle eighties—clambered into the jeep and were rolling triumphantly through the streets of Jerusalem, their shoulder-length, unshorn locks trailing in the wind. At the Wall, they "rent their garments" in classic biblical fashion, and prayed for those who had died taking it.

While the last of the Jordanian defenders were being rounded up in the Old City, the destruction of Jordan's Army and the conquest of Jordan's West Bank moved toward a swift close.

The Augusta Victoria Heights, believed so formidable that the assault had been twice delayed to bring up more tanks and allow for a heavier air strike, fell with virtually no resistance.

With Jerusalem's high ground in their hands, the Israelis struck north and south. From Jerusalem, Motta Gur's paratroops joined infantry from the Jerusalem garrison and the tanks that had fought their way down from the ridges north of the city to race southward to take Bethlehem and Jericho. On their way, the exuberant Israelis liberated a dozen trumpets from Jordanian stores and raised a triumphant racket as they battled their way into Jericho.

When Israeli tanks reached the northernmost tip of the Dead Sea, the tank brigade commander, Col. Uri Ben-Ari, paused to ponder the results of an Arab victory twenty years before. Here, a Jewish kibbutz, Beit Ha'aravah, had stood before the war of 1948. Nearby, a Jewish potash factory had produced fertilizer from chemicals mined from the Dead Sea. The Kibbutz Beit Ha'aravah had won fame throughout Palestine and abroad for the job of regeneration its settlers had accomplished. Yard-by-yard, the Jewish settlers washed the saline, inhospitable desert soil, and so reclaimed one thousand acres. These they had turned into a luxuriant stand of tomatoes and orange groves, a defiant belt of live color in the lifeless desert. Now, not a stone of the kibbutz or the potash factory remained. The once-luxuriant stand of tomatoes and fruit trees had gone back to desert.

The northern half of the West Bank fell swiftly, too. From the Northern Front, facing Syria, the Israeli High Command brought down Israel's most famous infantry brigade, the Golani. Assisted by tanks from the Northern Front, these troops soon overran the high ground around the town of Nablus, and moved on to the Jordan River.

In an open jeep, King Hussein braved strafing Israeli planes in a vain attempt to rally his crumbling forces. But the odds were too great. The Israeli Air Force which had quickly disposed of Jordan's aircraft now pounded Jordan's armor and men mercilessly. The Iraqi Division had arrived on the eve of the war, but remained in the valley east of Jericho and saw no action. The Egyptian general, Riad, had sent a hurry call for two battalions of Egyptian commandos. They had arrived during the fighting, but prudently stayed out of it. In Amman, Hussein toted up the terrible cost of his gamble. He had lost 6,094 in dead or missing, and about 170 tanks and 29 aircraft. He had also lost half of his kingdom and the tourist revenues from East Jerusalem which had accounted for 40 percent of Jordan's $31,528,000 annual income.

A touch of miracle

During the war, the Israelis had their own Churchillian voice to tell them of their finest hour.

It belonged to Irish-born Chaim Herzog, son of the onetime chief rabbi of the United Kingdom. Herzog had chosen a military career in Israel and had advanced to the rank of Brigadier General in charge of Military Intelligence. Now, as military commentator over the Voice of Israel, his daily reports, studded with ancient lore and poetry, rallied the small nation. On the night of the Old City's capture, General Herzog said:

"The hour-glass of events is filling up, and each one of us is living this moment of history. Generations of Jews for thousands of years to come will think of us, of a small and privileged group . . . who created this moment replete with historic significance for all of the Jewish people."

To Israelis, who had come from the depths of despair to total triumph in a few brief days, the victory had a touch of miracle to it.

And it was at the Wailing Wall that Israelis could best savour the mysticism of recent miraculous events. To the religious Israeli, the Wall was the holy place where, one day, the Messiah would come. To the non-religious and religious alike, the Wall was the focus of the reborn nation. It was the symbol of the durability of a people who had made a unique journey, intact, through almost four thousand years of history and—just as uniquely—still spoke the ancient tongue of their forefathers.

The Wall, then, was the scene of the wildest rejoicing. Old men in caftans danced ancient Chassidic dances in which soldiers in battle dress joined. Rabbi Goren was there. He blew a mighty blast on his trumpet; he prayed; he recited earlier Jewish exploits from the Bible.

Prime Minister Eshkol and David Ben-Gurion, framed in his halo of wild, white hair, came within the first hour. So did the Chief of Staff, General Yitzhak Rabin, the architect of the victory, and General Moshe Dayan, symbol of that victory to the world. Dayan is not a religious man. He is in fact known as a "Canaanite," the Israeli term for a non-observer. Yet, in line with religious tradition Dayan wrote a prayer on a piece of paper, folded it, and inserted the prayer in between the stones of the Wall. He then said what every Israeli felt, but did not dare to say so soon:

"We have returned to the holiest of our holy places. I give you my word, we shall never be parted from it again."

Even while Israeli tanks were still racing for Suez, bulldozers moved into Jerusalem and began to smash down the sniper walls and barbed wire that divided the city.

15

COUNTDOWN IN THE
HOLY LAND

While an anxious world watched the Israelis fight long odds to win the Six-Day War, few knew that the United States and the Soviet Union had almost joined that war.

The American people knew only what the White House had told them. President Lyndon B. Johnson revealed that the U.S. and the Soviet Union had used the Hot Line between Moscow and Washington on Monday, June 5, 1967, to reach an amicable agreement to keep hands-off the Arab-Israeli war. Left untold was the subsequent hot exchange on the Hot Line in which the Russians threatened, with growing anger, to intervene against the Israelis. Left untold, too, was the President's fateful dispatch of three Sixth Fleet task force groups, including a battalion of Marines, to the war zone—to cool off the Russians.

The news of the Hot Line confrontation and the near clash between the two world superpowers did not emerge until August, 1968—14 months after the event—when the Reader's Digest published the full story of the hair's-breadth brush with nuclear war.[1]

In the similar, momentous confrontation over the Cuban mis-

[1] "The Week the Hot Line Burned," Lester Velie, August, 1968.

siles in 1963, President John F. Kennedy gave the American people a blow-by-blow account of his "eyeball-to-eyeball" showdown with Nikita Khruschchev.

Why did President Johnson keep secret the even more dangerous showdown with Alexei Kosygin?

In the answer to this riddle lies the answer to the puzzle of American behavior in the Near East since the June War.

Lyndon Johnson set as the top goal of his presidency, a détente with the Russians and an end to the nuclear weapons race. As a senior State Department official put it, Johnson wanted to "move the Russians to the politics of peaceful co-existence."

Disclosure of the Hot Line confrontation would have embarrassed and humiliated the Russians by showing they had backed down before superior American power. It would have shown that the Cold War had never abated, and it would have shattered the general belief, nurtured by Washington, that an era of peaceful co-existence was unfolding between the U.S. and the Soviet Union.

No quest is more urgent than détente with the Russians and an end to the nuclear arms race. The President who succeeds in this search will be hailed as a hero by a relieved world.

The trouble is, it takes two to détente.

John F. Kennedy, who tried hardest to build bridges to the Russians, suffered the rudest disillusionment. After his Cuban missile experience, Kennedy—a wiser man—said of the Communist Chinese *and* the Russians:

"The only thing they disagree on is how they're going to bury us."

Now, after the June War and throughout 1968, President Johnson wooed the Russians at precisely the time they pushed their most ambitious effort to bury us. With treasure, guile, and energy the Soviets drove hard to oust us from the Middle East and the Mediterranean, the most crucial and explosive arena in the protracted global conflict.

In the process, the Soviets set the stage for a fourth round between the Arabs and the Israelis. This could either destroy Israel, or lead—as it did in the third round—to the nuclear abyss.

Let's pick up the story as the guns fell silent in that Third Round.

Paper Bear

As the Russians packed their bags to leave Tel Aviv after the Six-Day War, the Soviet Ambassador Chuvakin, his diplomatic aplomb in tatters, roared at a Western diplomat:

"This little nation (Israel) can't defy the Soviet Union! It must be punished!"

The rage was understandable.

Israel had thumbed its nose at the "historic forces of world revolution," and made a monkey out of Communist dogma. The Egyptian and Syrian "progressive forces," presumably riding the wave of the future, had collapsed ignominiously before "reactionary Israel."

The mini-nation had undone in six days what it had taken the superpower years to build.

First, Israel had deflated the Soviet Union's military stock with the Arabs and restored that of the Americans. Despite implied promises of military support, the Russians stood aside impotently before the greater American power. Militarily, to the Arabs, the Soviet Union was a "paper bear."

Israel showed up the political impotence of the Russians and dramatized that of the Americans. The Russians sent their biggest gun, Alexei Kosygin, to the UN. He demanded the UN brand Israel as the aggressor, punish it with sanctions, and force it to withdraw from Arab territories. But before the Russian Bear's huffing and puffing no house came down. The U.S., supporting the Israeli position of "no withdrawal without a prior settlement," had the votes. In the UN, too, the Soviet Union bowed before the superior American power.

Strategically, too, the Israelis had landed a Sunday punch on the Soviet Goliath. The Soviet's position in Yemen on the Red Sea crumbled. So did the dream of conquering all of the Arabian peninsula.

After the war, Nasser had to pass the tin cup to his rich neighbors—Saudi Arabia, Libya and Kuwait—to replace the loss of Suez Canal revenues. For his contribution, King Feisal of Saudi Arabia exacted conditions:

"I will help my dear Arab brother," King Feisal said. "But my dear Arab brother must withdraw from the Yemen, and stop using it as a base to drive me from my throne."

Agreed.

As Nasser's troops withdrew, the Soviet-Egyptian puppet in Yemen fell, and an independent regime took power. Nasser's withdrawal shattered other hopes. For four and a half years, the Russians and Nasser had used Yemen as a base to drive the British from the neighboring British protectorate of Aden. They had looked forward to the day when the British left and Egyptian troops marched in. But when that day arrived, early in November, 1967, the Egyptian troops themselves were embarking for home. In a twist of history, British and Egyptian troops left southern Arabia at virtually the same time. The Arabian peninsula had won a reprieve.

In the first weeks after the war, the Arabs felt they couldn't look to the Soviet Union to extricate them from the humiliating consequences of their defeat by forcing the Israelis to withdraw. Only the U.S. could change the situation for them. This brought King Hussein to Washington to seek support. It also brought Egypt's Foreign Minister Mahmoud Riad to Washington on the same mission, although the Egyptians had no diplomatic relations with the U.S.

The U.S., thanks to the Israelis, now held the initiative in the Cold War struggle over the Near East.

But within a year, all this had changed. The Russian Bear had not only picked himself up off the canvas. He had the U.S. on the ropes.

In July, 1968, *New York Times* Correspondent Drew Middleton reported from the Near East:

"The predominant feeling among Western and Arab observers in the area is that the Russians have altered the strategic situation at the crossroads of Europe, Africa, and Asia to the marked disadvantage of the United States."

What happened?

To make a comeback, the USSR had to rebuild and reorganize the military establishments of its proxies. It had to build a mobile military capability of its own to deter Israel or support Soviet proxies in some future crisis. The Soviets had to regain lost strategic positions, such as in the Yemen.

All this would take time. Rebuilding the Egyptian and Syrian officers' corps, alone, would take two or three years.

The Israelis had handed the U.S. a golden gift of time to fashion a positive strategy to hold a key arena of the global conflict.

At a Kremlin debate that lasted two days, the Central Committee of the Soviet Communist Party decided to place some heavy bets that the Americans would not use that gift of time.

By the turn of 1968, the Russians had flown in or sailed in to Egypt, Syria, and Iraq virtually all of the equipment Israel had destroyed during the June War.

The new equipment for Egypt came with six generals and three thousand military advisors—five times as many as before the war—and enough to station one Russian officer behind every Egyptian gun and missile in a sensitive position. With these came a new Ambassador, Sergei Vinogradov, whose senior status was underlined by his prior assignment—that of Ambassador to France. In Vinogradov, the Egyptians soon had a pro consul, as one correspondent reported, "highly reminiscent of the former British High Commissioners before the Anglo-Egyptian independence treaty of 1936. At every social or political gathering, he is the most honored guest." Vinogradov had access to Nasser at any time of day or night and conferred with him four times or more weekly. What they conferred about was soon evident from developments inside Egypt.

Prodded by Vinogradov, and armed with information gathered by the Russian intelligence network in Egypt, Nasser cleaned house in his intelligence services and his officer corps.

Late one night, soon after the war, Nasser personally led a

raid on the home of the Mukhaberat's chief, Salah Nasr, seized his personal files and led him off to jail. Elsewhere, in simultaneous raids, dozens of other intelligence agents were roused from bed and hustled away.

Nasser dismissed one thousand officers, sending them home in small batches to avoid an Army uprising. He tried and jailed fifty-six top military and political figures for neglect of duty, among them the minister of war, Shamsuddin Badran.

Most significant for long-range Soviet plans, the Russians took over the reorganization of the officer corps. Only those officers who had completed long tours of training in the Soviet Union and whom the Russians trusted got top posts. The Russians, for instance, dictated the appointment of the new head of the Egyptian Air Force, Madkour Aboul Ezz. For the long haul, the Russians insisted that Nasser recruit officer candidates from "proletarian families," and from those areas of Egyptian life where most sympathy for Communism was likely to be found—from among teachers and from other young professionals.

Under pressure from Vinogradov, Nasser bowed to an old Russian demand, and released Egyptian Communists who had languished in desert jails. Some of these found their way at once into government jobs, others into administrative posts in Nasser's Arab Socialist Union.

At the same time, the Russians moved aggressively to repair their fortunes in southern Arabia.

The regime that succeeded the Egyptian-Soviet puppet in Yemen had declared it meant to govern Yemen for the Yemenis. But Royalist rebels were at the gates of the capital city of Sana, and the new regime turned for help where it could find it. Soviet pilots flew down from Cairo to bomb Royalist troops and villages (while the Russians piously beat their breasts over American bombing in Vietnam). The Russians also mounted an arms airlift from Cairo more massive than the original airlift in 1962, when the USSR and Egypt had deposed the ruling Imam. According to Western intelligence sources, the airlift delivered some $500 million of military equipment—a truly remarkable volume, considering the size of the country and the nature of the Royalist guerilla opposition.

With Russian pilots and weapons, the New Yemen regime prevented the pro-Western Royalists from overwhelming Sana. As the civil war continued, the Russians tapped new proxy sources. First, Syrian pilots flew in from Damascus to take over bombing missions from the Soviet pilots. Then, from the British protectorate of Aden—next door, where the British were preparing to pull out—Russian-equipped and Russian-trained Adeni guerillas arrived to take up, at least in part, where the Egyptian proxy troops had left off.

Within days after the British left Aden and the new regime took power, the Russians had a senior diplomat there. He offered arms, technical assistance, and economic aid. Reports reached Western capitals that the new Republic's leaders had offered the Soviets naval and air facilities in return.

French withdrawal from the giant naval base of Mers el Kebir in Algeria provided the Russians with another opportunity. Mers el Kebir is two hundred and sixty miles from the Straits of Gibraltar. It was once a NATO base, built with NATO funds. Now, the Russians took the first step toward making it a Soviet base with a deal to post Russian technicians who, among other things, would service visiting Soviet naval vessels there. The Soviets already had "de facto" bases at Latakia in Syria and at Port Said and Alexandria in Egypt.

The Russians raced to build a fleet which could, in the words of the Commander-in-Chief of the Soviet Navy, Admiral Gorchkov, "deliver crushing blows against the sea and ground targets of the imperialists, at any point on the seas and coastal states."

By early 1968, the USSR had the world's second most powerful navy, including four hundred submarines, forty of them equipped with Polaris-type nuclear missiles (as against one hundred and fifty-five American submarines, thirty of them with nuclear missiles).

In the Mediterranean, where about twenty Soviet naval vessels cruised before the Six-Day War, some forty to forty-five

Soviet units blossomed. The first Soviet aircraft carrier, the *Moscow*, took its trial runs in the Black Sea and was expected soon in the Mediterranean. Others were under construction, with the plan to erase the advantage of the Sixth Fleet's aircraft carriers. The Soviets were also building a marine corps, an elite fighting force of "black berets," described as "naval infantry." Some were already conducting landing exercises in the Syrian port of Latakia.

With all this, the Soviets had scored some solid successes.

Through its growing Mediterranean power, including access to North African naval bases, the Soviet Union turned the southern flank of NATO. Our European allies took alarm.

"Three-quarters of Italy's territory extends into the Mediterranean," an Italian analyst warned. "Italy receives 75 percent of her raw materials by way of the sea. Should freedom of the seas be quashed, we would die of hunger. But even before this catastrophe occurs, Italy must be concerned with the strategic balance of power in the Mediterranean, a condition which determines its future as a free nation. The Soviet naval presence is altering this balance." [2]

The Soviets were also now in position to deny the vital Near East airspace during war, and to interdict oil shipments to Europe. And the Russians had their sights set on direct control of that oil via penetration of Saudi Arabi and Libya.

A region vital to the world balance of power was going, going. It could soon be gone.

What had the U.S. done, all this while?

This brings us back to President Johnson's well-meaning quest for détente with the Russians.

In pursuit of Soviet friendship, the U.S. had lent the Russians a helping hand.

For instance:

Egyptian soldiers still straggled home from the Sinai when giant Soviet Antonov transports swarmed into Egypt in the biggest military airlift of all time. While the Soviets made this dra-

---

[2] "Livio Pesce," translated from *EPOCA*, MILAN, in *Atlas*, July, 1968.

matic and vigorous show of standing by its friends, the U.S. did exactly the opposite. The Johnson administration clamped an embargo on arms to the area, including Israel—the ally, as James Reston of *The New York Times* put it, "that had the courage of our convictions." In vain the Israelis pleaded for the right to buy arms. The contrast between the resolute Russian action to help its friends and the hesitancy of the American giant was not lost on the Arabs. The Russians' deflated military stock began to rise.

The U.S. helped the Russians recover politically, too. American power in the UN had excluded the Soviets from the political arena. The Soviets were powerless to move the UN toward any action the U.S. opposed. The U.S., not the Soviet Union was in charge. But within five months, the U.S. took the Soviet Union into equal partnership. We permitted the Soviet Union to pose as the dominant power in the UN, and as the political savior of the Arabs.

It happened this way.

When initial Soviet efforts in the UN failed, the Russians tried another tack. The Soviet Foreign Minister, Andrei Gromyko, came over from Russia, and its Ambassador to the United States, Anatoly Fedorovich Dobrynin, came up from Washington to woo Arthur Goldberg, our Ambassador to the UN. They proposed, reasonably, that the two powers sponsor a common resolution. This would require the Israelis to withdraw, but it would also state that Israel had a right to exist within "secure and agreed-on borders."

The Israelis at the UN raised the alarm. They warned this was a trap. If such a resolution passed, the Israelis pleaded with Ambassador Goldberg, the Russians would recognize the first part only, the part that urged Israel to withdraw. They would forget the other part, the part that guaranteed Israel's existence within "agreed-on and secure borders."

Ambassador Goldberg heeded the warning and backed away from the Gromyko-Dobrynin blandishments.

But in November, 1967, the State Department fell headlong into the trap set by the Russian Bear. With the Russians, our UN representatives supported a British resolution that sought a "just and lasting peace in the Near East," by calling for:

1. "The withdrawal of Israeli armed forces from territories of recent conflict.

2. "Termination of Arab claims to a state of belligerency; respect for the sovereignty and independence of every state in the area and their right to live in peace within secure and recognized borders."

As a resolution, this was beyond reproach. It reflected President Johnson's determination not to pressure the Israelis to pull out without a prior settlement.

Trouble was, the Russians seized on the "withdrawal" part of the resolution, just as the Israelis had warned. In total disregard of the UN's demand for an end of Arab belligerency and assertion of Israel's right to exist, the Russians thundered to the world that the UN had ordered the Israelis to withdraw. They accused the Israelis of defying the UN.

More important, the Russians could now claim a great political victory at the UN. They had convinced the UN to move against the Israelis. It was they, not the U.S., who were now piping the tune in the UN.

In President Johnson's eagerness to woo the Russians, we had helped the Russians recoup their lost political prestige in the international political arena. Indeed, we had helped them climb back into that arena.

What can we do to redress the errors of omission and commission which gave the Soviets the upper hand in the Near East?

First, we must realize there is a Cold War on. The Russians know it. And if we are beguiled by consular treaties, air travel arrangements, and cultural exchanges, we should listen to the words of the Russians themselves.

Here is Communist Party boss Brezhnev, on March 29, 1968, before a Moscow City Party Conference:

"Our party has always warned that in the ideological field, *there can be no peaceful co-existence*, just as there can be no class peace between the proletariat and the bourgeoisie."

And Mr. Brezhnev again, on July 3, 1968:

"The United States is the rotten society, the degrading society, the decomposing society.

"Yes," prophesied Brezhnev, "monopolist capitalism is degenerating and will inevitably be replaced by another America, the America of the working class." To the most affluent working class in the world, *his* advice was: Arise, you automobile and steel workers! You have nothing to lose except your freedom, and your own home, and car, and travel abroad!

Once we face up to the fact that the Cold War has not abated, we will realize that the chief protagonists in the Near East conflict are not the Israelis and the Arabs. The chief protagonists are the United States and the Soviet Union. The Israelis and the Arabs are merely pawns in the larger conflict.

We must ask ourselves: what is good for us in the Near East? Peace and stable relations between the Arabs and Israel are good for us. With peace, the Russians would lose their chief instrument of penetration—the arms diplomacy that has flooded the Arab world with weapons. With peace and stability, Arabs won't depend on Russians for arms: they can then turn to the richer West for help in developing their backward economies.

Since the June War, the Russians—knowing that stability in the Near East is bad for them—have done everything in their power to keep the pot boiling. They have told Nasser not to negotiate with the Israelis, and not to agree on anything. The Russians have told the Arabs they will get the Israelis to withdraw without Arab commitments to keep the peace. They have provided the new weapons that encourage the Arabs to dream of a fourth round.

To achieve peace and stability in the Near East, we must convince the Arabs that their preparations and dreams are in vain.

We must convince the Arabs that under no circumstances will we force the Israelis to withdraw without prior agreement on a lasting peace.

We must also convince the Arabs it is futile for them to arm to the teeth. We should do openly what we did in secret during the Six-Day War. Then, we showed the Russians we were willing to risk war to keep the Russians from interceding. Now, we should provide Israel with the arms it needs to defend itself and to deter the Arabs. Sixteen months after the June War, the U.S. still refused to give the Israelis the supersonic jets they needed.

The refusal stemmed from President Johnson's quest for an accommodation with the Russians.

This dogged quest for détente in the face of the Soviet's invasion of Czechoslovakia, and the USSR's drive in the Near East has its ironic side. It may lead to the very proliferation of nuclear weapons President Johnson sought to avoid.

An Atomic Clock Is Ticking in the Holy Land

Six months after the Six-Day War, as the Arabs prepared for the fourth round, Israel's military strategists pondered a decision that would affect the world's future: whether to go for the atomic bomb.

Before the war, Israel's security problem was: how to fashion a conventional striking power that could overwhelm a combination of enemies in the shortest possible time. Now, Israeli military strategists told a Western expert: "As far as defense is concerned, the heart of the matter is whether to go nuclear."

In contrast with the lavishly-armed Arabs, the Israelis were less certain of arms sources than they were before the war. France, Israel's ally in 1956 and chief arms supplier thereafter, refused, under De Gaulle, to honor a contract for the delivery of fifty supersonic Mirages. The United States withheld the sale of Phantom jets.[3] Before the war, the ratio of Israeli to Arab planes was one to three. Six months after the war, it was one to five. And the Russians were riding herd on the Egyptians and Syrians to learn how to use the Migs they gave them.

Equally dismaying was the erosion of Western positions in the Near East: the Russian acquisition of bases in the Mediterranean and their buildup of naval power; the announced British withdrawal of their garrisons on the Persian Gulf by 1970.

[3] American agreement to sell Phantom Jets to Israel came, finally, in December 1968.

Israel's pro-Western foreign policy rests on the proposition that the presence of the Sixth Fleet in the Mediterranean gives it minimum guarantees of security. The Sixth Fleet deterred the Soviets from interceding in the Six-Day War. Should Soviet naval power top that of the U.S., Israel's only shield against the Soviets would be American nuclear power. Here, Israel—and the Soviets —could assume that the United States would not risk the destruction of American cities for the sake of several million Jews. Western complacency in the face of the Hitler holocaust supports this assumption.

Israel had two choices.

One was to re-orient its foreign policy toward the Soviet Union. The Kremlin had asserted repeatedly that it believes in Israel's right to exist—but on Soviet-Arab terms: i.e., within the borders Israel occupied before the war of independence of 1947. It would have to squeeze back into half the territory it held before the June War.

As one Israeli diplomat put it, "Uncle Ivan doesn't want to kill us. He just wants to chop off an arm."

Along with the arm would go Israel's democracy, for accommodation with the Soviet Union would also require a "correct political outlook," i.e., that it become a "progressive (Communist) state."

The other choice is to develop nuclear weapons that will end the threat of a "fourth round" and, with it, the possibility of Soviet intervention.

Several weeks after the Six-Day War, an Israeli told this writer:

"None of us want to produce non-conventional weapons. But if pressed for our survival, we will go for unconventional weapons systems."

Actually, Israel's formidable scientific and military brains have been harnessed for some time not only to the production of nuclear weapons, but to the strategy and political implications of nuclear use. Significantly, one of the classic studies on nuclear strategy, means of delivery, deterrence, and proliferation has been produced by an Israeli, General Y. Harkabi, ex-head of Israeli Army Intelligence. Published in Hebrew and English, under the title, *Nuclear War and Nuclear Peace*, it has become "must" reading in the Defense and Foreign Ministries of many nations.

As this writer learned in Israel after the June War, the Israelis for some time followed the precedent set by Sweden: "Keep abreast of nuclear technology. Prepare everything you need to produce an atomic bomb—but don't produce one."

Israel has two atomic piles: one at Dimona, near Beersheba; the other, a lesser one, is at Nahal Sorek. The Dimona reactor was ostensibly built to produce electricity for large-scale desalinization projects. But it fits the policy of "preparing everything you need to produce an atomic bomb. . . ." Western experts say that the Dimona plant's output of some six kilograms of plutonium a year is sufficient for one bomb. Several years' production would provide enough for a stockpile. (The United States, deeply concerned over the possible introduction of nuclear weapons into the volatile Middle East, has sought and obtained permission to inspect the Dimona plant. But experts say this can't stop the accumulation of fissionable material.)

As for the bomb itself, this—for the Israelis—is the least difficult part of the job. Israel's scientific community includes some of the world's most distinguished physicists, mathematicians, and chemists—so much so that the Chaim Weizmann Institute at Rehovoth has become a world center for international scientific meetings. Israel's scientists have developed a military electronics industry so advanced that it holds a sub-contract for producing the radar equipment for the French Mirage jet.

A study prepared for the United Nations Association of the U.S. named Israel as one of seven countries that could produce an atomic bomb within eight months to two years from the time a decision was made. Some experts believe Israel needs only six months to a year.

In the summer of 1968 Israel wasn't worrying about its ability to go nuclear, but about the political problems involved in doing so.

President Johnson, pushing hard for a nuclear non-proliferation treaty, had achieved agreement with the Russians on a draft.[4] Some eighty nations had signed it. Most of these had no hope of producing an atomic bomb for years—if ever—from Egypt to Ecuador, and from Togo to Zambia. Significantly, virtually all of the nations that could produce a bomb had not signed. India, for instance, would not sign. It wanted to know what certain guarantees of help the nuclear powers would give it if the Communist Chinese—who did not sign the pact—attacked India with nuclear weapons. Brazil and Italy did not sign. And, significantly, neither did Israel.

As a result, experts who before the Six-Day War felt that India would become the next member of the nuclear club (the U.S., USSR, Britain, France, and Red China), now believe that the next member will be Israel.

As far as galloping proliferation is concerned, it is one thing for a big nation such as India to break the self-imposed atomic prohibition; it is another for a small nation like Israel to do so. "Israel, one of the world's smallest nations would wreck the protocol of inhibition far more effectively than a big nation (India) would," a London School of Economics authority has warned.[5]

The Soviet Union's aggressive global war tactics in the Middle East could plunge the world into the atomic proliferation against which the Kremlin has been piously preaching. And the Middle East, which gave birth to three major world religions, could be the burial ground of civilization.

[4] Early in February, 1969, President Nixon, once a foe of such a treaty, pushed for Senate ratification.

[5] Philip Windsor, "The Middle East and the World Balance." *The World Today*, July, 1967.

INDEX

215

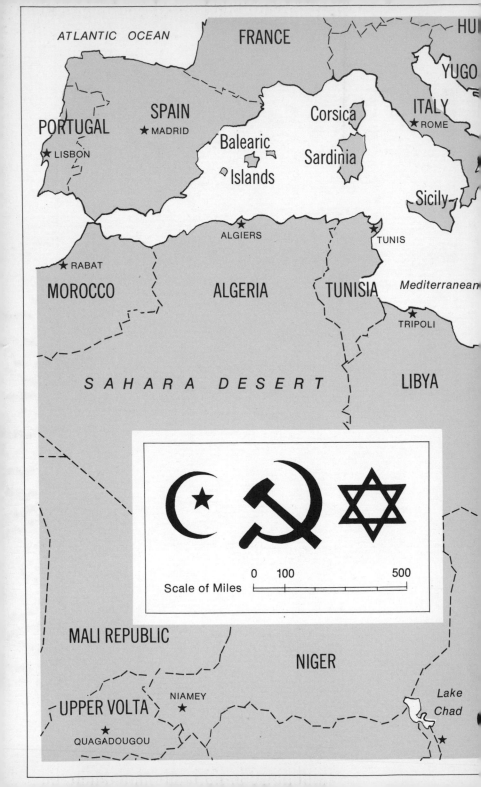